Invoking Hope

Seb. Ricci
Sebastian Ricci.
Entre le Temps et la Mort,
l'Homme invoque l'Espérance.
Horace.
Tibulle

Invoking Hope

Theory and Utopia in Dark Times

Phillip E. Wegner

University of Minnesota Press
Minneapolis
London

FRONTISPIECE. Sebastiano Ricci, *Allegory with Figures of Hope, Time, and Death* (1659–1734), with inscription "Entre le Temps et la Mort, / l'Homme invoque l'Espérance." Metropolitan Museum of Art, New York.

A different version of chapter 3 was published as "The Possibilities of the Novel: A Look Back on the James–Wells Debate," in "Fredric Jameson, Henry James," special issue, *Henry James Review* 36, no. 3 (Fall 2015): 267–79; copyright 2015 Johns Hopkins University Press. A different version of chapter 6 was originally published as "'The Great Sea Voyage Which Marriage Can Be': Repetition, Love, and Concrete Utopia in *50 First Dates*," *The Minnesota Review* 86 (2016): 81–100; copyright 2016 Virginia Tech; all rights reserved; reprinted by permission of the copyright holder and the present publisher, Duke University Press, www.dukeupress.edu. A different version of the Conclusion was published as "Romantic and Dialectical Utopianism in *Cloud Atlas*," in "*Utopia* Anniversary Symposium," *Science Fiction Film and Television* 9, no. 1 (2016): 114–18; copyright Liverpool University Press, doi:10.3828/sfftv.2016.4.

Published by the University of Minnesota Press
111 Third Avenue South, Suite 290
Minneapolis, MN 55401-2520
http://www.upress.umn.edu

ISBN 978-1-5179-0885-0 (hc)
ISBN 978-1-5179-0886-7 (pb)

A Cataloging-in-Publication record for this book is available from the Library of Congress.

Printed in the United States of America on acid-free paper

UMP BmB 2020

For John P. Leavey Jr.

. . . of friendship to come and friendship for the future.

—Jacques Derrida, *Politics of Friendship*

iam mala finissem leto, sed credula vitam
spes fovet et fore cras semper ait melius.

I already would have ended my ills in death; but trusting in life
Hope says to us ever that tomorrow will be better.

—Tibullus, *Elegies,* 2.6

Man, in the end, is alarmed by the idea of time, and unbalanced by incessant wanderings between past and future. The inhabitants of a liquid world have brought past and future together in the maxim: *Après nous le deluge.*

—Isak Dinesen, "The Diver"

Contents

Introduction

Reading in Dark Times

> Given teachers with something to love and something to say and a talent for communicating both, you can afford to forget for a moment about the curriculum. Whatever such teachers say is an education. And there are books the reading of which is also an education.
>
> —Stanley Cavell, *Pursuits of Happiness*

> But say, my brothers, what can the child do that even the lion could not do?
>
> —Friedrich Nietzsche, *Thus Spoke Zarathustra: First Part*

IN THE AFTERMATH of the U.S. presidential election of 2016, I shared with my undergraduate students a translation of Bertolt Brecht's deeply moving wartime poem "An die Nachgeborenen" ("To Those Born After") (1939). The poem begins with the proclamation "Wirklich, ich lebe in finsteren Zeiten!" (Truly, I live in dark times!), and Brecht concludes the first stanza with the observation,

Der Lachende
Hat die furchtbare Nachricht
Nur noch nicht empfangen.

The one who laughs
Has simply not yet received
The terrible news.[1]

In part my response to the terrible news, the essays collected together in this book offer what may be understood as an untimely appeal for the undiminished importance of the practices of theory, utopia, and deep, close, and even critical reading in our current situation of what Brecht refers to as "finsteren Zeiten," dark times. Indeed, my central contention throughout will be that our vocation as students and teachers of reading, theory, and utopia—and especially reading theory and utopia—has taken on a renewed significance in the face of the events of the last few years.

Such an appeal brushes against the grain of certain contemporary trends in literary and cultural studies, especially those toward what has been called "surface reading" and away from theory, historicism, and, as such prominent critics as Rita Felski advocate, critique.[2] These developments take place in a moment of dramatic retrenchment in the university as a whole and within humanities research and teaching in particular. Crystal Bartolovich maintains that such strategies "not only mark a pointed withdrawal from politics and theory but also—while humanities departments are contracting—internalize the economic imperative to scale back."[3] Carolyn Lesjak similarly argues that in such new critical paradigms, "the overarching message seems to be: scale back, pare down, small aims met are better than grand ones unrealized, reclaim our disciplinary territory and hold on to it."[4]

Lesjak further observes that such new-old modes of reading aim to replace "a hermeneutics of suspicion . . . by a suspicion of hermeneutics, a disavowing of interpretation itself, which is part and parcel of the so-called death of theory."[5] A few years prior, Fredric Jameson already pointed out that "the humanist argument is tailor-made for all the contemporary anti-intellectual attacks on interpretation as such (as elitist, manipulative, totalizing, etc.), in the name of the nostalgia for the older defenses of literature."[6] In the domain of film studies, Nico Baumbach names such a disavowing of interpretation as "Grand Anti-theory," which "reenacts the very move it criticizes by lumping a wide range of material into a single rubric that it then dismisses."[7] Hoon Song describes a similar turn in cultural anthropology against "big Theory," especially "the big Theories of the Marxist kind," and toward a "flexible modesty—the 'big enough,' the 'partial.'"[8] While reversing the valences, such disavowals of theory, critique, and deep reading remain locked within the very ethical binary they decry. The concept of good and evil that underlies what Jameson names, in the text that was the initial target of the surface readers, "*ethical* criticism" or moralizing judgment—"the predominant code in terms of which the question

'What does it mean?' tends to be answered"—is "a positional one that coincides with categories of Otherness. Evil thus, as Nietzsche taught us, continues to characterize whatever is radically different from me, whatever by virtue of precisely that difference seems to constitute a real and urgent threat to my own existence."[9] In advancing a claim that it is time to move beyond critiques of literature and culture, these ethical critiques of critique and theory present critique and theory as Others that need to be flushed out and purged from the collective institutional body—relegating them to the status of what George Ciccariello-Maher, following the lead of Frantz Fanon, terms "nonbeing."[10]

This form of moralizing ethical criticism still sadly remains, as Clint Burnham pointed out more than two decades ago, "the dominant mode of literary interpretation in the Anglo-American world."[11] A recent example of such an approach can be found in Joseph North's brief polemic *Literary Criticism: A Concise Political History* (2017). While it may be worth listening to the affirmative things North puts forward in his efforts to infuse new energy into aspects of I. A. Richards's "practical criticism," and indeed his claims resonate with what I will have to say about the New Criticism in my first chapter (although North's reading of the New Critics is far more critical), the larger arc of his narrative is paradigmatic of contemporary moralizing ethical criticism. North begins by positing a binary opposition between a good aesthetic "criticism," represented by Richards in the past and someone like D. A. Miller in the present, and a historicist "scholarship," promoted by such intellectuals as Raymond Williams and Jameson (as is too often the case in this form of ethical criticism, the real enemies are largely on the left). In North's fable, scholarship comes into its own in the 1970s and 1980s and therefore becomes "symptomatic of the wider retreat of the left in the neoliberal period and was thus a small part of the more general victory of the right."[12] In this way, North presents himself as mounting a lonely challenge to what he claims to be "the story of literary studies in the second half [of] the twentieth century as it is usually told: as a continuous democratization or liberalization of literary studies from the 1960s to the present, beginning in the dark days of the new criticism, or else of Leavis-ism, and then breaking outward into glorious heterogeneity of progressive modes. . . . This is a very pleasing story for those on the liberal left of literary studies."[13] Again, as is often the case in these kinds of moralizing criticisms, we are offered neither examples of any specific case study of such a heroic progressive narrative nor the names of those among the "liberal left of literary studies" who believe it.

On the basis of these ungrounded assertions, where all agency and hence all responsibility for later evils lie with a singular "liberal left," North eschews the lessons of close reading—which in his characterization is "a focus on small units of text for the purposes of relating to the text as an aesthetic object."[14] (Such a Cartesianism is antithetical to the deeply dialectical practices developed by the New Critics, for whom, as with Hegel, "the true is the whole. Yet the whole is but the essence which brings itself to fulfillment through its development."[15]) North develops circular "non-readings" (I will return to Pierre Bayard's notion of non-reading, central to my book as a whole, in chapter 2) of those critics who stand accused of the sins of scholarship, citing only those passages from their immense and complex bodies of work that most readily confirm his predetermined conclusions.

Bruce Robbins and Francis Mulhern have already illuminated the misrepresentations of Williams's project that occur in North's book.[16] I would add that similarly no real discussion takes place of any of Jameson's major works, no careful engagement, for example, as the New Criticism at least would demand, of the entirety of *The Political Unconscious* and the concrete relationships of its opening slogan "Always historicize!" to the complex whole of its narrative form—a truly dialectical philological historicism or scholarship, such as that practiced by Erich Auerbach and his students, is always attentive to form—and the specific historical situation to which it forms a response; nor is there any reference in his book to the various prior non-readings that have attempted to do so.[17] Instead, North spends his hasty discussion refuting an "opinion" concerning "the philosophical problem of aesthetic value" Jameson puts forward in a later occasional lecture.[18] North begins his critique with the astonishing claim that this comment represents "perhaps [Jameson's] clearest and most succinct comments on the matter of philosophical aesthetics."[19] North seems to have forgotten the precautionary note Jameson issued nearly a half-century ago: "The peculiar difficulty of dialectical writing lies indeed in its holistic, 'totalizing' character: as though you could not say any one thing until you had first said everything; as though with each new idea you were bound to recapitulate the entire system."[20] North then concludes his discussion by proclaiming, "But surely it is quite wrong to reject the whole project of aesthetic criticism as if it were reducible, in principle, to exercises in establishing the relative rank of various canonical figures."[21]

Assuredly, "the whole project of aesthetic criticism," just like that of historicism or Marxism, is a *problematic,* "not a set of propositions about reality, but a set of categories in terms of which reality is analyzed and interrogated, and a set of 'contested' categories at that."[22] Later, in answer to the question "What is Marxism?" Jameson similarly maintains that "it can best be thought of as a *problematic*: that is to say, it can be identified, not by specific positions (whether of a political, economic or philosophical type), but rather by the allegiance to a specific complex of problems, whose formulations are always in movement and in historic rearrangement and restructuration, along with their object of study (capitalism itself)."[23] Thus, the only way one can reject a problematic, or any social or cultural group for that matter, is to deploy the moralizing ethical strategy of first reducing it to a homogenized and threatening Other (i.e., scholars, the liberal left of literary studies, Marxism, the fake news media, or immigrants).

But this then opens up on to the question, Is this what Jameson is doing at this juncture, let alone in his larger critical project? Jameson begins the passage North cites by explicitly acknowledging that he will be engaging in a form of ethical criticism: he does so by stating that what follows is no more than an "opinion." The very nature of the speech act of "giving an opinion" is not to provide a definitive argument on an issue but to raise certain questions in passing before moving elsewhere. The intent of expressing an opinion can be, and perhaps most often is in our current moment, to shut off discussion; however, opinions can also be read as advancing an invitation "to think about these matters more deeply and to talk them over with him more fully" on another occasion, "If only this were some day possible!"[24] There is no way or reason to determine definitely Jameson's intent here; however, a more charitable, less moralizing non-reading would take as its starting point the latter possibility and respond accordingly. Moreover, as even the most cursory attentive reading would demonstrate, questions of aesthetics, education, and value come up again and again throughout Jameson's project.[25] For example, in his 1983 introduction to the republication of what he terms "perhaps the single most monumental realization of the varied program and promises of a Marxist and a dialectical literary criticism," Georg Lukács's *The Historical Novel* (1962), Jameson already offers what could be taken as a rejoinder to North when he writes, "Lukács's book may stand as a calm refutation of the often repeated misconception that a Marxist historicism (with all the relativism historicisms generally imply) can ultimately have no theory of value in the area of culture."[26] And if his only goal is the moralizing one of "rejecting the whole project of aesthetic criticism," what does one do with the fact that Jameson refers to Sianne Ngai's extraordinary intervention in the problematic of aesthetic criticism, *Our Aesthetic Categories: Zany, Cute, Interesting* (2012), as "one of the most exciting new theoretical books to come along in some time"?[27]

On the basis of his selective non-reading, North concludes that in the present the "project of criticism . . . has largely been forgotten. . . . In its place, we have a broad consensus built around the idea that the proper project of literary studies is the scholarly one."[28] But again, who shares in such an easy consensus, especially in the narrow restrictive form that North defines it? Is it enough to say, I, for one, do not? Surely it is quite wrong to reject the whole project of an extraordinarily diverse range of concrete practices assembled under the sobriquet of historicism as if they were reducible, in principle, to exercises in specialized scholarly antiquarianism. This strategy of creating an ethical straw target and then dismissing it out of hand enables North in his book's conclusion to reinvent in a modest, much diminished, and more constrained (i.e., disciplined) form aspects of Jameson's and other creative readers' actual concrete practices. In the end, moralizing posturing only masks any discussion of the real limitations of the alternative mode of reading being promoted: this is because the value of such practices is largely defined in a negative, "anti-" fashion by the ways in which they are *not* those of an imaginary Other. (I will return to the issue of the ethical "anti-" stance in chapter 3.)

What cannot even begin to be addressed in North's polemic, or that of other kin moralizing criticisms, are the actual "real and urgent threats" to our collective existence as readers and teachers of literature, narrative, and culture texts of all kinds. These threats are not to be found in the best performances of the hermeneutics of suspicion, critique, historicism, theory, cultural studies, scholarship, Marxism, dialectics, psychoanalysis, or whatever other practices these critics find so questionable, but instead in what Christopher Breu refers to as "insistently materialist" political transformations that have taken place in recent decades in higher education and beyond and have resulted in more and more people, especially those from outside elite universities, being excluded from even the possibility of participating in the institutional conversations, the access to which these critics take for granted.[29] These changes would include, among others, the increasing disparities in educational opportunities due to dramatic decreases in funding for public institutions, cutbacks in financial aid, and soaring costs at elite private universities; the replacement of tenure-track faculty in the humanities by contingent, flexible instructors; the redefinition of higher education as exclusively an economic good (another issue to which I will return in chapter 1); the downsizing and even elimination of humanities and other programs; the shift from faculty governance to a euphemistically named "shared" governance among diverse "stakeholders" ("il n'y a pas de rapport administratif"); and the efforts on the part of neoconservative activists and neoliberal administrators to limit intellectual freedoms, including control over syllabus design and course assignments.[30] Bill Readings similarly points out that any discussion of our practices "cannot be understood apart from a reflection on *the institutional context of education.* This reflection refuses both the isolation of education in relation to wider social practices and the subjugation of education to predetermined or externally derived social imperatives."[31] It is not their failures but precisely theory's and a so-called scholarship's successes in making such historical and institutional questions central ones that, alongside their contributions to real positive changes in those institutions, have led to an intensification of such assaults. Indeed, it is no coincidence that those areas where the most diversity has been achieved in the university are also those most heavily under attack—diversity here not in its current dominant liberal or corporate sense but rather in Sara Ahmed's powerful definition of it as including all "those of us who arrive in an academy that was not shaped by or for us" and to which we in turn "bring knowledges, as well as worlds, that otherwise would not be here."[32]

Thus, if we entertain North's scholarly historicist claim that "scholarship" is "symptomatic of the wider retreat of the left in the neoliberal period," then the resurgence of a moralizing ethical criticism equally should be understood as a symptom of the emerging post-truth Trump era: a giving in to what North terms an "irresistible" shift further to the "right," to a place wherein self-identified authorities of all kinds, proclaiming themselves the defenders of noble past traditions, can assert, without any real demonstration or argument, their judgments of who and what are good and evil and where grand global ambitions give way to narrowly parochial, disciplinary, professional, and even nationalist agendas.[33] Or, to put this in the terms of the reimagining of Hegel's dialectic, and hence of all theory, advanced in Andrew Cole's *The Birth of Theory* (2014), if dialectical critique or theory finds its origins in Hegel's return to medieval philosophy and the dialectic of identity/difference, then postcritique antitheory can be read as an effort to "modernize" in a way appropriate to the emerging twenty-first-century university the practices of reading literature and culture.[34] This is not to suggest that these ethical critics overtly endorse the anti-intellectualism and viciously divisive politics promoted by Trump and his supporters (although, and to deploy the ethical critics' own mythologizing tactic of guilt by association, there are a few who continue to be more than willing to do so).[35] Rather, and to draw upon Raymond Williams's terms, these humanities intellectuals eschew an explicitly "oppositional" stance to the "dominant and effective" values and practices of our culture—the hard and risky political work of speaking truth to the actual local powers that constrain our existences and, far more importantly, organizing across various interests and practices collective resistances to these transformations on the levels of the university and the state and creating working alternatives to them. One of the preeminent scholars of the contemporary university, Christopher Newfield, argues that successfully realizing any truly new practices of reading and education will require a change in how we do things:

> This means that advancing the new education can't rest mainly on appeals to the better angels of society's top brass. Its advancement will depend on intellectual and social movements, on political, ethical, and sociocultural justifications that address a wide range of society's conflicted publics and seek to build political majorities, often in opposition to business elites and their politicians. One last twist: tenured faculty members will need to join this opposition even though, as descendants of the postwar professional-managerial class, they are traditionally allied with business elites and have used professional rights, like self-

> governance, quite sparingly. As any of our students might say to us—good luck with that.[36]

Instead, these ethical criticisms promote practices that would be simply "alternative," where teachers define a "therapeutic role of poetry," using it "as a means of ordering our minds"—a therapy that will be available increasingly only to a select few who have the training and free time necessary to create or experience poetry ("One cannot think well, love well, sleep well, if one has not dined well").[37] What vanishes utterly in such a vision of the world is "the sheer guilt of Art itself in a class society, art as luxury and class privilege"—and the same holds true for reading—as well as any projects aimed at changing this fact.[38] (This last issue will again be on center stage in chapter 5.)

If theory represents a call to read more widely and expansively, moralizing ethical criticism is a practice of *anti*reading, a prophylactic review of a text—and the genre of the review has long been especially amenable to moralizing criticism[39]—aimed either at dissuading engagements on the part of later readers or, at least, narrowing and directing the avenues down which any future non-reading might travel. An example of the latter practice of prereading is in play at the dawn of European modernity in Martin Luther's sixteenth-century penning of his first catechisms. Richard Gawthrop and Gerald Strauss maintain that a careful and full reading of Luther's writings indicates that he only stands behind "the principle of 'every man his own Bible reader' until about 1525, then falling mostly silent on the subject and, at the same time, taking actions that effectively discouraged, or at least failed effectively to encourage, an unmediated encounter between Scripture and the untrained lay mind."[40] The shift was the consequence of an outbreak across Germany in 1525 of popular peasant rebellions, movements that founded themselves in an unprecedented manner on a close reading of the Christian Bible: "it is our conclusion and final resolution that if any one or more of the articles here set forth should not be in agreement with the word of God, as we think they are, such article we will willingly retract if it is proved really to be against the word of God by a clear explanation of the Scripture."[41] In the aftermath of these upheavals, Luther concludes "chaos and confusion as the results of uncontrollable personal relations with Scripture, and he could point to enough recent events to give substance to his fears. Expert guidance was needed now, above all preaching by authoritative interpreters."[42] The solution was to be found in the disciplining pedagogical technology of the popular catechism:

> Once public education had been firmly set in the track of catechization, with the catechism established as the single source of religious knowledge, authorities no longer feared the spread of false ideas. In an approved Lutheran catechism one could not find a false idea. This was certainly not true of the Bible, and it was always from the Bible that deluded spirits in recent experience had drawn their destructive notions. Given the central position—virtually the monopoly—of the catechism in school and parish education, therefore, no further need existed for anxiety about the consequences of common reading.[43]

A not unrelated strategy of moralizing antireading is on display in John R. Searle's 1977 "Reply" to Jacques Derrida's essay "Signature Event Context," the latter originally published in French in 1972. Anointing himself the heir to the speech act theorist J. L. Austin, with whose work Derrida engages in his essay, Searle in his brief eleven-page catechism engages in a twofold agenda. First, Searle draws upon his disciplinary authority as a philosopher to establish a "proper" reading of Austin's text, asserting, for example, with very little in the way of supporting evidence, that Derrida "has misunderstood and misstated Austin's position at several points" and that "Derrida's Austin is unrecognizable."[44] Second, Searle works throughout his essay proactively to dissuade a careful and sustained engagement with Derrida's project, which, in this historical moment, was then just beginning to be made widely available to an English-language reading public (Gayatri Chakravorty Spivak's translation of Derrida's *De la Grammatologie* was published only a year prior to Searle's reply). Searle does so through such unsubstantiated moralizing judgments as "Derrida has a distressing penchant for saying things that are obviously false" and claiming that Derrida engages in "what is more than simply a misreading of Austin."[45] While Searle's catechism will prove to be foundational for later "Against Theory" polemics, it more immediately provides Derrida with the occasion, beginning with his extended essay "Limited Inc a b c . . ." (1977), for a careful performance of what a postethical non-reading might look like—an example that influences in a profound way my practice in the book that follows.[46]

Four centuries after Luther's efforts and a little more than two decades before Searle's catechism, Aldous Huxley offers in his 1953 essay "Ozymandias, the Utopia that Failed" another illustration of the practice of preemptive ethical readings. First published near the nadir of his own wildly vacillating utopian hopes (his darkest novel, *Ape and Essence* (1948), being published only five years earlier), Huxley's essay meditates on the fate of the short-lived intentional community of Llano del Rio, established in 1914 in Southern California's high desert (my home as well as a high school student in the late 1970s and early 1980s) and led by Job Harriman, who, two years prior, had suffered a narrow defeat as a socialist mayoral candidate in Los Angeles.[47] Harriman's Llano experiment failed, Huxley determines based on his scanty secondary reading, because of its founder's lack of "realism": "The acceptance of facts as they present themselves, the facts of nature and of human nature, and the primordial fact of that spirit which transcends them both and yet is in all things. The original Ozymandias was no realist; nor was poor Mr. Harriman."[48] A good illustration of Harriman's moral shortcomings, according to Huxley, can be found in his refusal to take into account the concrete challenge of procuring water for his community in a place "where it rains eight or nine inches during the winter and not at all from May to November. To the brute facts of meteorology in arid country Job Harriman was resolutely indifferent. When he thought of human affairs, he thought of them only as a Socialist, never as a naturalist."[49]

Huxley's ethical non-reading of the community's history remained for many years, and even for some today, the final word on the topic. However, later, more careful non-readers show that far from hubris or lack of foresight, it was precisely the community's early successes that led to the increased assaults on them, including legal actions undertaken to cut off their water rights, despite "engineering studies" and "prepared charts to outline its proposed irrigation plans": "When the prosecuting attorney gave his summation, he spoke of 'socialistic plunderers' [who would] 'cover the face of the earth' [and] 'soon become a mischief in fact.'"[50] Thus, Mike Davis observes in the late 1980s, "Huxley grossly underestimated the negative impact of wartime xenophobia and the spleen of the Los Angeles *Times* upon Llano's viability. There but for fortune (and [*Times* publisher and real estate speculator] Harry Chandler), perhaps, would stand a brave red *kibbutz* in the Mojave today, canvassing votes for Jesse Jackson and protecting Joshuas from bulldozers."[51] As Davis's hopeful alternate history hints, the real roots of the community's vulnerability to these attacks may have been located in Harriman's decision, as with his great predecessor, the nineteenth-century French Utopian socialist Étienne Cabet, to vacate, even if only for a time, the field of political struggle in the "now here": "work and struggle here, because it is only in [Los Angeles] where there already exists all the elements for the establishment of a community of wealth, and this community will be established here or it will be nowhere ('nulle part')."[52]

In contradistinction to the facile characterizations offered by contemporary moralizing critics, engaged younger critical readers such as Robert S. Lehman and Ciccariello-Maher, the latter one of the first academics to fall victim to our current political nightmare, remind us that at its best—and one of my absolute presuppositions in what follows is that we should always begin from the best and most successful examples of any practice[53]—critique was never simply "assessment," "attack, disapproving analysis, or attempt to replace" but rather always already "an interrogation of the conditions of possible experience" and a delineation of "both the usefulness and limitations" of the texts under examination.[54] This is akin to the double work of what Jameson refers to as *analysis*—"the peculiar and rigorous conjuncture of formal and historical analysis . . . the investigation of the historical conditions of possibility of specific forms," which involves "a very different set of operations from a cultural journalism oriented around taste and opinion"—and *evaluation*—"assessments of a sociopolitical kind that interrogates the quality of social life itself by way of the text or individual work of art, or hazard an assessment of the political effects of cultural currents or movements."[55] Critique understood in this expanded sense—aiming for not the uncovering of error, sin, and evil but rather the dialectical grasp at once of limitations and possibilities—offers a way beyond the deadlock of dominant moralizing ethical criticism.

In a discussion of earlier antireading and antitheory polemics, Jameson observes that its founding gesture is one of prohibition, an inaugural *No*: "We feel very strongly that we are being told to *stop* doing something, that new taboos whose motivation we cannot grasp are being erected with passionate energy and conviction."[56] Gilles Deleuze and Félix Guattari similarly maintain that in the domain of philosophy, "those who criticize without creating, those who are content to defend the vanished concept without being able to give it the forces it needs to return to life, are the plague of philosophy. All these debaters and communicators [and polemicists] are inspired by *ressentiment*."[57] However, Nietzsche's Zarathustra proclaims that for "the game of creation . . . a sacred 'Yes' is needed: the spirit now wills his own will, and he who had been lost to the world now conquers his own world."[58]

In the pages that follow, I take up Nietzsche's challenge and thereby express my preference to *not*-engage in a moralizing ethical critique that would be satisfied with an uncovering of the failures of reading or listening that are part and parcel of such polemics.[59] As necessary as I believe such engagements remain (and to be clear, I am fully aware of the fact that the preceding paragraphs in part engage in an ethical critique, an antiethical critique), I prefer instead to listen deeply to the reminders of such earlier postmoralizing thinkers as William Blake, who writes in *The Marriage of Heaven and Hell* (1790) in one of the "Proverbs of Hell"—also cited by Xebeche, "Nobody" (Gary Farmer), in Jim Jarmusch's great film *Dead Man* (1995)—"The eagle never lost so much time, as when he submitted to learn of the crow" and Martin Luther King Jr., who opens his "Letter from Birmingham Jail" (1963) noting, "Seldom, if ever, do I pause to answer criticism of my work and ideas. If I sought to answer all of the criticisms that cross my desk, my secretaries would be engaged in little else in the course of a day, and I would have no time for constructive work."[60]

Thus, I aim in this book to persuade the attentive reader of the undiminished value of reading, theory, and utopia through such constructive work—that is, by way of practicing reading theory and utopia. Another of the underlying absolute presuppositions of this book, which I will elaborate in more detail in chapter 2, is that all reading is writing, and all writing a creative act. One of the great lessons of the revolution in the humanities that is theory is that it is our first duty as teachers not to order students' minds, or inculcate certain beliefs "by way of the systematic cultivation of capacities for value"—"'Who is the greatest Italian painter?' 'Leonardo da Vinci, Miss Brodie.' 'That is incorrect. The answer is Giotto, he is my favorite.'"—or even to enlighten them to the pleasures to be obtained from art and literature—"Good

Lord, we would be happy precisely if we had no books, and the kinds of books that make us happy are the kinds we could write ourselves if we had to. But we need the books that affect us like a disaster, that grieve us deeply, like the death of someone we loved more than ourselves, like being banished into the forests far from everyone, like a suicide."[61] Literature understood in this last sense functions as part of the more general project of critique that Ahmed defines as that of the feminist *killjoy*: "She kills joy because of what she claims to exist. She has to keep making the same claim because she keeps countering the claim that what she says exists does not exist."[62] Our task is both to expose our students to as many and diverse cultural practices as possible, which, of course, will only ever represent a minuscule fraction of what Pierre Bayard, in a book I take up in some detail in chapter 2, terms our global "collective library," and to empower them thereafter to engage—"Can you work the second for yourself?"—in the practice of what I refer to as *creative reading*.[63] By maintaining a deep fidelity to these values and practices, I hope I might contribute in some small way to what Slavoj Žižek refers to as a "repeating" of the grandly ambitious, interdisciplinary, and even utopian project of humanistic scholarship, interpretation, and teaching that flourished not so very long ago in a galaxy not very far away.[64]

Earlier versions of all but one of the chapters in this book were first presented or appeared in print in 2016 and thus should also be understood as responses to events unfolding in what turned out to be an extraordinarily consequential year. To the extent that this book engages in an act of periodization, it stands as a sequel of sorts to my earlier periodizing studies *Life between Two Deaths, 1989–2001: U.S. Culture in the Long Nineties* (2009), *Shockwaves of Possibility: Essays on Science Fiction, Globalization, and Utopia* (2014), and *Periodizing Jameson: Dialectics, the University, and the Desire for Narrative* (2014). First of all, 2016 was the five-hundredth anniversary of the publication of one of the most influential works of European modernity, Thomas More's *Utopia* (1516). A number of symposia, conferences, and special issues of journals were put together to mark the occasion, and as someone who, beginning with my first book, *Imaginary Communities: Utopia, the Nation, and the Spatial Histories of Modernity* (2002), has read creatively on the topic of utopia in its many manifestations, I had the great privilege of being invited to participate in a number of these forums.[65] The essays in this volume represent the fruits of these collective labors, and I would like to thank again those in Huntsville, Alabama; Athens and Delphi, Greece; Urbana-Champaign, Illinois; Columbus, Ohio; Oneonta, New York; Evanston, Illinois; Winston-Salem, North Carolina; Gainesville, Florida; and many other places for giving me the opportunity to engage in conversation, to speak with and, more importantly, to listen to you.

Jameson notes that one of the significant consequences of the theory turn was the replacement of "a tradition-oriented canon (whether this tradition is in the service of a conventional Right, as is most frequent, or of a Left or radical movement-building inspiration, as with Raymond Williams, or Lukács, or even the left-modernists such as Kristeva and *Tel Quel* or the surrealists themselves)" by what he terms a *disposable canon*: "a set of relativistically privileged references in which contingency is inscribed from the outset" and "a kind of curatorial practice, selecting named bits from our various theoretical or philosophical sources and putting them all together in a kind of conceptual installation, in which we marvel at the new intellectual space thereby momentarily produced."[66] The labor of composing any disposable canon thus involves the countermimetic practices Walter Benjamin identifies as central to the repertoire of children and collectors alike, which he in turn deploys in the production of his own monumental disposable canon in *The Arcades Project.* Nicola Gess characterizes such labor as "not simply a break, but rather a simultaneous involvement with and destruction of the past, a recovery and new configuration through which the past maintains its relevance for the present or even receives it for the first time."[67] Another implication of Jameson's claims concerning the productive labor of constructing disposable canons is that perhaps one of the most underappreciated creative acts in which we as teachers can engage is the design of new course syllabi. Indeed, a syllabus should be considered along the lines of an architectural plan, which, while perhaps too often doing no more than replicating the banalities of a standardized business office complex, may, on occasion and with a bit of active imagination, result in Frank Gehry's Santa Monica house or his Museo Guggenheim Bilbao. (I will suggest in chapter 2 why I think the necessary dialogic practices of architecture might be a better model for us as readers and teachers than other pictorial or plastic arts.) Of course, the real art lies in the plan's realization: "In the ruins of great buildings the idea of the plan speaks more impressively than in lesser buildings, however well preserved they are."[68]

I undertake in this book the construction of such a disposable canon, and thus while some of the texts I examine are at the center, for both the right and the left, of any tradition-oriented canon—Plato's *Republic* and More's *Utopia,* to take the two most prominent examples—my choice of others may be unexpected and even puzzling for some readers. While I am convinced that the close and careful creative reading of all of the texts I engage with in these pages is a valuable education in its own right (and whose lessons might be otherwise than expected)—and throughout I also touch on more briefly or allude to a host of others, with the explicit aim of inspiring at least a few readers, the wedding-guests, to take them up and create further[69]—I hope that the discovery of the motivation for these choices becomes another occasion for intellectual delight as well as teaching.

What More a half millennium ago gave a name—and the power of naming is another significant concern in my book—is not only a literary genre but also, as the twentieth century's greatest advocate of utopia, Ernst Bloch, tirelessly taught, both one of the deepest and most fundamental of human impulses and an innovative hermeneutic or practice of creative reading.[70] In the middle of the 1970s and following Bloch's lead, Jameson characterized such a reading practice in this way: "To maintain that everything is a figure of Hope is to offer an analytical tool for detecting the presence of some utopian content even within the most degraded and degrading type of commercial product."[71] More recently, in what could also be understood as a rejoinder to surface and postcritique readers, Jameson maintains:

> The interpretation of the Utopian impulse, however, necessarily deals with fragments: it is not symbolic but allegorical: it does not correspond to a plan or to Utopian praxis, it expresses Utopian desire and invests it in a variety of unexpected and disguised, concealed, distorted ways. The Utopian impulse therefore calls for a hermeneutic: for the detective work of a decipherment and a reading of Utopian clues and traces in the landscape of the real; a theorization and interpretation of unconscious Utopian investments in realities large or small, which may in themselves be far from Utopian in their actuality.[72]

Finally, early in his latest book, Jameson writes, "The Marxist practice of ideological analysis is in other words also Utopian and draws up into the light not only all those features of class consciousness we wish to avoid thinking about, but also the thoughts and visions (wish fulfillments) that are designed to replace or displace them; it is a practice of allegorical enlargement rather than one of reduction, as its less consequential critics have always liked to maintain."[73] Similarly, Ruth Levitas, in her groundbreaking study *The Concept of Utopia* (1990), affirms that our "task" as readers is "to reveal and recover the anticipatory essence from the dross of contingent and compensatory elements in which utopia is dressed up in particular circumstances."[74] Thus, to read for Utopia involves developing both a more attentive practice of reading, what I will characterize in chapter 2 as *deep listening,* and an openness to a wider array of narratives and cultural practices.

A similar expansion of what we could and did read was a direct consequence of another development that is of central concern in this book. The year 2016 also witnessed a less acknowledged but no less significant anniversary: the centenary of Ferdinand de Saussure's posthumously published lectures, assembled under the title *Cours de linguistique générale* (1916). Among its numerous contributions, Saussure's volume helped make possible—via its influence in the development in mid-century France of a structuralism through which "dialectical thought was able to reinvent itself in our time"[75]—one of the most significant intellectual events of the century: the emergence of the interdisciplinary discursive practice named *theory.* Through its shift of attention from the literary "work" to diverse "texts" and, even more significantly, through its valorization of the fundamental world-making practice of narrative ("mythical thought is as rigorous as that of modern science, and . . . the difference lies, not in the quality of the intellectual process, but in the nature of things to which it is applied"), theory opened up an expansive new field of materials for deep and sustained creative reading.[76] Indeed, it is this expansion, and the concomitant erosion of "the radical disjuncture and separation of literature and art from culture," that is the real threat in structuralism and theory against which rail the ethical critics referred to above.[77] Moreover, as Louis Althusser maintains, theory also transforms "the meaning of the 'simplest' acts of existence: seeing, listening, speaking, reading—the acts which relate men to their works, and to those works thrown in their faces, their 'absences of works.'"[78] Such a new reading practice, which for Althusser finds its roots in the work of Marx, "might well be called '*symptomatic*' (*symptomale*), in so far as it divulges an undivulged event in the text it reads, and in the same movement relates it to *a different text,* present as a necessary absence in the first."[79]

My previous book *Periodizing Jameson* told a history of the event of theory through an immanent reading of the work of one of its most accomplished U.S. practitioners.[80] In that book, I propose that theory's impact was felt in three waves (although, of course, there are no easy divisions between them): first, transforming the practice of how we read, then expanding what we read, and finally, intervening in the very spaces in which such reading takes place.[81] If theory thus addresses the how, what, and where and when of our practices of reading, utopia, understood as the fundamental human principle of hope (*Prinzip Hoffnung*), offers an effective answer to the why: beyond any liberal individualist notions of pleasure or self-cultivation, we read in order to immerse ourselves in the shared story of the past and to hope for the future—and, in hoping, begin to move toward realizing more fulfilling and just ways of collective being and doing in the world.

As I suggested in the first part of this Introduction, recent years have seen a proliferation of claims that theory's revolution and the innovative interdisciplinary modes of creative reading it encouraged have come to an end, and hence the time is ripe for a return to traditional disciplinary endeavors and more "modest" forms of intellectual engagement. However, another fundamental axiom underlying my endeavors in this book is that such a "return" to innocence, to a moment before the box was opened and a reflexive "thinking about thinking" had been let loose into the world, is impossible.[82] To paraphrase another of the most influential of the theorists and creative readers, Derrida, "il n'y a pas de hors-théorie," there is no outside-theory, no unmediated access to the real.[83] Theodor Adorno similarly maintains, "in regard to philosophy—and I am almost tempted to say with regard to anything whatsoever—there is actually no such thing as presuppositionless knowledge."[84] Jameson observes that such an "argument was renewed in the 1960s by all the varied partisans of theory, who delighted in demonstrating with gusto that all these Anglo American empirical statements which formed our then hegemonic discourse were deeply if secretly theoretical at their heart and that plain homespun realistic thinking was rotten to the core with theoretical presuppositions."[85]

Learning any theory is akin to learning a new language, and hence theory is the very possibility of reading, writing, and thinking the world. To put this in another way, theory is not the new things Brecht's Galileo sees through his telescope—"But it is. They're mountains."—but rather the telescope itself.[86] Thus, as Roland Barthes maintains in that most Brechtian of books, *Mythologies* (1957), we need always to "challenge anyone's ever exercising an *innocent* criticism [akin to Brecht's *Das arglose Wort,* the "innocent word"], pure of all systematic determination: [these] critics are indeed committed to a system, which is not necessarily the one to which they proclaim allegiance."[87] Those who advocate a return to mere, surface, or anticritical reading, no matter its external trappings, are like the officials who dispute Galileo, doing no more than asserting that good old optical systems, old theories, remain more than adequate and that all the bad new ones should be set aside once again. ("A Brechtian maxim: 'Don't start from the good old things but the bad new ones.'"[88])

The significant questions are thus not what would still be the ethical ones of which side are you on, are you "for" or "against" theory, but rather: What does any particular and concrete theory and practice allow us to do, what is the value of so doing, and who benefits? Modesty and the averted gaze from uncomfortable truths can only ever be virtues for those occupying offices of sinecure—an Odysseus chained to her or his mast. Those who look away, who disavow theory, interpretation, and critique, are among those Bruce Robbins has recently theorized as the *beneficiaries*: those, including in our current moment all tenured and tenure-track faculty, whose "fate is *causally linked,* however obscurely, with the fates of distant and sometimes suffering others" (including such not-so-distant but still suffering others as adjuncts, graduate students, peer teachers, support staff, and all other forms of underemployed, flexible, and contingent labor in the university).[89] Robbins further maintains that the value of his "graceless" concept-term is that it "help us see ourselves, as we deserve, in an estranged and uncomfortable way."[90] But not only for seeing ourselves but seeing these others subject to, as Ciccariello-Maher points out, "the utterly nonreciprocal oppression of those deemed not even worthy of recognition." Thus, Ciccariello-Maher concludes, "Until such deaths—and lives—count . . . a dialectics grounded in the illegibility of exteriority and nonbeing will be an indispensable weapon."[91] In this fashion, as Robbins's and Ciccariello-Maher's examples bear out, theory inevitably brings us back to questions of institutions and the people who occupy them and hence remains of great importance in a moment when those institutions are changing in significant ways. In the end, then, I hope to remind readers that both utopia and theory not only enable us to read new things and read familiar things in new ways but also enable us to read altogether anew.

Any full history of theory needs to take into account the post–World War II context from which it emerges and to which it, as any symbolic action must, responds: a moment when anxieties over anti-intellectualism, right-wing populism, and fascism were very much still pressing concerns. All of the pioneers of what we would come to think of as theory worked to forge intellectual tools, frameworks, and communities that might help ward off the return of these scourges. Even as late as the beginning of the 1970s, Michel Foucault could advocate reading Deleuze and Guattari's monumental *L'Anti-Oedipe* (1972) as "an *Introduction to the Non-Fascist Life*."[92] This was the case not only among those intellectuals and educators in Germany and France who are sometimes identified as the practitioners of high theory but also, as I show in my opening chapter, among those in the United States in perhaps that most unexpected of places, the New Criticism, where again, and perhaps unbeknownst to the New Critics themselves, dialectical thought was able to reinvent itself. It will be my claim in that chapter that the experiences of the Second World War mark a fundamental divide between earlier developments such as Richards's practical criticism, linked as it is to the then still existent realities of British imperialism or what Giovanni Arrighi refers to as the "long nineteenth century," and later ones like the New Criticism. In this way, I hope to brush against the grain of another commonplace assumption, which posits a discontinuity, whether for good or ill, between the New Criticism and the belated arrival on our shores of other practices of theoretical discourse.

Part of the reason that such a significant aspect of the theory revolution has been overlooked, at least in the United States, has to do with the reception and translation of key texts, sometimes decades after their original publications. For example, when Max Horkheimer and Theodor W. Adorno's *Dialektik der Aufklärung: Philosophische Fragmente* (1944) was first translated as *Dialectic of Enlightenment* (1972), a great deal of excitement rightly arose concerning the book's first two major sections and their rigorous critiques of, respectively, instrumental reason and the culture industry. Furthermore, redacted versions of the culture industry section were reprinted in a number of anthologies and catechisms of theory and cultural studies. At the same time, the book's third major section, "Elements of Anti-Semitism: Limits of Enlightenment," was for many readers relegated to the back burner, focused as it is on issues and concerns that no longer seemed relevant for an emerging postindustrial, communication, and consumer society. This was the case even though, as Jameson later demonstrates, the section is fundamental to the larger intervention undertaken in the formal unity of the book as a whole.[93] Lost in such a reception then is the crucial role Horkheimer and Adorno assign to Nietzschean populist ressentiment in the rise of both past and future fascisms:

> The thought of happiness without power is unbearable because it would then be true happiness. The illusory conspiracy of corrupt Jewish bankers financing Bolshevism is a sin of innate impotence, just as the good life is a sign of happiness. The image of the intellectual is in the same category: he appears to think—a luxury which the others cannot afford—and he does not manifest the sweat of toil and physical effort. Bankers and intellectuals, money and mind, the exponents of circulation, form the impossible ideal of those who have been maimed by domination [*durch Herrschaft Verstümmelten*] an image used by domination to perpetuate itself.[94]

Such a maiming leaves a "scar" (*Wundmal*), which Horkheimer and Adorno term "*stupidity*" (*Dummheit*) in their book's final paragraph: "Every partial stupidity of a man denotes a spot where the play of stirring muscles was thwarted instead of encouraged. . . . Such scars lead to deformities. . . . They can breed stupidity—as a symptom of pathological deficiency, of blindness and impotency if they are quiescent, in the form of malice, spite, and fanaticism, if they produce a cancer within." These two readers then conclude with the observation, "the mental stages within the human species, and the blind-spots in the individual, are stages at which hope petered out [or in their original Benjaminian formulation, "die Hoffnung zum Stillstand kam"] and whose petrifaction demonstrates that all things that live are subject to constraint."[95]

Appearing in the same year as both *L'Anti-Oedipe* and the translation of *Dialectic of Enlightenment* was the first English-language version of Barthes's *Mythologies.* For the next four decades, this edition would remain a key text for the introduction not only of Barthes's work but of theory in general to generations of students, myself included. (I recently discovered a receipt dated January 6, 1986, tucked in my first copy, bought for an undergraduate reading group whose previous selection had been the then recently published American jeremiad by Christopher Lasch, *The Culture of Narcissism: American Life in an Age of Diminishing Expectations* [1979].) On the title page of this edition appears the attribution "Selected and translated from the French by Annette Lavers."[96] In 2012, a new complete edition of Barthes's book appeared, and Richard Howard points out in his translator's introduction that the earlier version left out twenty-five of the book's original fifty-three opening "reflections on certain myths of everyday French life."[97] Howard further confesses that he "had always assumed that Lavers or her publisher regarded the excluded Mythologies to be insufficiently tempting to British tastes at the time."[98]

Barthes himself offers the grounds for such a culling by pointing out the specific historical and spatial boundaries of any particular myth: "Some objects become the prey of mythical speech for a while, then they disappear, others take their place and attain the status of myth. . . . One can conceive of very ancient myths, but there are no eternal ones."[99] This acknowledged, however, when one compares the two editions what quickly becomes apparent is how many of the excluded mythologies deal with the challenges posed in postwar France by the twinned forces of anti-intellectualism and right-wing populism. Indeed, in the complete edition, restored to a place of privilege as the final entry, entitled "Poujade and the Intellectuals," is one of a number of mythologies concerned with the French populist politician, Pierre Poujade, whose Union de défense des commerçants et artisans was a powerful political force from 1953 to its dissolution in 1962.[100] Kristen Ross notes, "During its brief but significant heyday, Poujadism dug in its heels and announced itself incapable of crossing the historical threshold of modernity; it sought not to found a world but to restore one" (Make France Great Again!).[101] In a way that recalls Horkheimer and Adorno, Barthes thus concludes the collection with the observation, "Poujade needs intellectuals, for if he condemns them it is on account of a magical evil: in the Poujadist society the intellectual has the accursed and necessary role of a lapsed witch doctor."[102]

All of which brings us back at last to a third crucial development that occurred in 2016 and with which I opened this Introduction. Chapter 1 of this book was the last to be drafted and was presented in its earliest form only a week after the last U.S. presidential election. As I am confident no reader of this book needs to be reminded, 2016 witnessed a global tsunami of right populism, culminating in the election as U.S. president of an unqualified, unprepared, and deeply unstable real estate mogul and reality television personality, "a man with no experience in public office, little observable commitment to constitutional rights, and clear authoritarian tendencies."[103] Only a year following Trump's inauguration, the V-Dem Annual Democracy Report observed that "autocratization is now manifesting in a number of large countries including Brazil, India, Russia, Turkey, and the United States" and that the United States in particular "is now significantly less democratic in 2017 than it was in 2007. . . . The backsliding is mainly found in the liberal components of democracy. Measures of effective oversight and use of the legislature's power to investigate the executive, opposition party oversight, compliance with the judiciary, and executive respect for the constitution have all declined."[104] Needless to say, these trends have only intensified more recently.

These shifts were made possible by longer-term transformations that began in earnest in the late 1970s and swelled to a high-tide mark in the last decade: again not the rise of the academic practices of theory or historicism (although even a brief search on the internet will discover a depressing number of unsubstantiated moralizing claims that the "postmodern," whatever that term is supposed to mean in this context, reading practices of Derrida and others contributed to Trump's ascendancy[105]) but rather the systematic assault on the university and public education I described above, the attacks on and defunding of scientific research, the rise of fundamentalisms and neoauthoritarianisms, the slow erosion of democratic institutions, the dismantling of unions and other instruments of collective political activism, the ongoing global war on terror and ballooning of military budgets, the increasing reach of far-right "post-truth" media and information outlets, and the opening in the aftermath of the 2008 economic crisis of a new phase in global political economic history that William Davies terms "punitive neoliberalism."[106] In many ways, Donald Trump is an exemplary post-postmodern Poujade—if not an Arturo Ui ("Our distant past or even very recent, / History's violent, bloody and indecent. / But as political scientists observe, / We only get the leaders we deserve")[107]—and hence the original interventions made by Deleuze and Guattari, Horkheimer and Adorno, Barthes, and a host of other later theorists take on renewed significance in our ongoing state of emergency. In *Anti-Oedipus,* Deleuze and Guattari describe the more general situation of capitalist modernity in a way that has special applicability to our current moment:

> The social axiomatic of modern societies is caught between two poles, and is constantly oscillating from one pole to the other. Born of decoding and deterritorialization, on the ruins of the despotic machine, these societies are caught between the Urstaat that they would like to resuscitate as an overcoding and reterritorializing unity, and the unfettered flows that carry them toward an absolute threshold. They recode with all their might, with world-wide dictatorship, local dictators, and an all-powerful police, while decoding—or allowing the decoding of—the fluent qualities of their capital and their populations.[108]

They subsequently note, "How things turn fascist or revolutionary is the problem of the universal delirium about which everyone is silent."[109] The time for such silence has again passed. One of my further absolute presuppositions throughout this book is that utopia and theory are akin in that both aim to reeducate collective desire for other ways of being and doing in the world. Hence our efforts to creatively read theory and utopia, to develop creative theories of utopia and reading, and to think the creative utopias of reading and theory will contribute significantly to the chances that we "shall emerge from the flood" ("auftauchen werdet aus der Flut") this time.[110]

As I suggested above, a consideration of the form of any theoretical or literary critical narrative is as important as of its contents, and the book that follows offers a number of possible decodings of its form. I leave it to my non-readers to move down the paths they find most productive. The first three chapters make appeals for continued efforts to foster more effective and creative practices of reading and of creatively reading theory and utopia. Chapter 1 continues to build upon my recent work with A. J. Greimas's semiotic square in order to develop a strategy of reading for the concrete utopian horizons illuminated in an unlikely collection of texts: a conversation overheard on Athens's Acropolis in the midst of Greece's ongoing austerity crisis, the Brexit vote, and the U.S. presidential campaign; early essays in the New Criticism; Alain Badiou's daring 2012 hypertranslation of Plato's *Republic*; and Kojin Karatani's *Isonomia and the Origins of Philosophy*, also from 2012. These interventions remind us, I maintain, of the tremendous danger of allowing education to be transformed, as is currently the agenda in the United States, exclusively into an economic good. My next chapter takes up Pierre Bayard's notion of *non-reading* and compares responses to Bayard's book *How to Talk about Books You Haven't Read* (2007)—one prominent critic dismissing it as advocating for a "non-reading utopia"—to those in the long history of non-reading Thomas More's *Utopia*. I argue that More locates his concrete utopia in the form of his book, an open-ended dialogue that requires both a speaker and, even more significantly, one who listens deeply. I conclude the chapter by touching on other versions of the utopian practice of deep listening offered in a surprisingly diverse range of texts, including the film *Fight Club* (1999), Theodor Reik's *Listening with the Third Ear* (1948), and Thich Nhat Hanh's *Silence: The Power of Quiet in a World Full of Noise* (2015). Concluding this first section, chapter 3 returns to the issue of a moralizing ethical criticism in revisiting a debate in the early twentieth century between Henry James and one of the century's great utopian thinkers, H. G. Wells, concerning the future of the novel. In this chapter, I elaborate further on Jameson's strategy of a "post-ethical" creative reading and set it to work in assessing the very different practices made available by each writer and their undiminished value in our increasingly global world.

The next four chapters build on a project of reading first broached in my book *Shockwaves of Possibility* on what I theorize—drawing deeply upon Jacques Lacan's mapping of the knot of the four discourses (master, hysteric, analyst, and university) and Badiou's articulation of the conditions of truth (politics, art, love, and science)—as four interrelated evental genres. In *The Political Unconscious: Narrative as a Socially Symbolic Act* (1981), Jameson theorizes all genres as "literary *institutions* or social contracts between a writer and a specific public, whose function is to specify the proper use of a particular cultural artifact."[111] Similarly, the notion of the "heuristic genre" I deploy in these chapters—heuristic as opposed to historical or institutional genres—is as a device produced by the theorist aimed at encouraging the creative, and from a certain perspective deeply improper, reading of not only unknown texts but familiar ones in new ways.[112]

These four chapters unfold in chronological order in terms of the specific events upon which each chapter's central text focuses and build upon each other in fleshing out a theorization of the evental genres. Chapter 4 takes up Susan Buck-Morss's heuristic genre of the universal history in order to read W. E. B. Du Bois's masterful biography, *John Brown* (1909). Du Bois's book offers a pointed challenge to the assumptions about Brown and his actions then being set into place by liberal and even progressive white historians and writers who would locate Brown's efforts as those of an isolated individual and an evil extreme along a continuum of white abolitionist activities. Instead, Du Bois reframes them within the context of multiracial, collective, and transnational actions to overturn the monstrous global structure of repression, violence, and exploitation known as slavery—a system that in Du Bois's view continues into his, and our own, present. The following chapter similarly reads the Danish writer Isak Dinesen's brilliant and underappreciated short story "Babette's Feast" (1950) through the lens of Ernst Bloch's landmark essay on the utopian practice of the *Künstlerroman* or artist narrative. I do so in order to recover a double fidelity in the story, one effaced in the more well-known 1987 film adaptation, both to the work of the artist and to the radical possibilities of what Kristen Ross calls "communal luxury," which come into being in one of the most significant political events of the late nineteenth century, the Paris Commune of 1871. I conclude with reflections on the story's intervention in a postwar context, which, as I also suggest in chapter 1, has significant parallels with our own. Chapter 6 uses Stanley Cavell's influential notion of the popular comedy of remarriage to read in the contemporary Hollywood film *50 First Dates* (2004), an unexpectedly rich and profound meditation on the day-by-day labors, the unending processes of remaking, renewal, and reinvention, that are required in any authentic condition of love, and hence in all of the conditions of truth.

Concluding this section, chapter 7 explores the underappreciated role of the romance plot in two of the most significant science fiction utopias of the twenty-first century, Kim Stanley Robinson's *2312* (2012) and Karen Lord's *The Best of All Possible Worlds* (2013). I do so to underscore the claim that what is distinctive about the modern utopia as a genre lies in the figures of events it develops in all four of Badiou's conditions. In this way, utopia contributes to an education in hope, of a collective desire for a world very different from the one we currently inhabit. The strategy of creative reading I develop here promises to transform how we understand utopian narratives, ranging from the obvious cases, like Edward Bellamy's *Looking Backward* (1888), to those that may be less expected, such as James Joyce's *Ulysses* (1922).

The concluding chapter reads the very different dialectics of optimism and pessimism found in David Mitchell's monumental novel *Cloud Atlas* (2004) and its 2012 film adaptation, directed by the great left popular auteurs Lana and Lilly Wachowski and Tom Tykwer. An important aspect lost in the film adaptation is the way Mitchell's formal structure echoes the plot of one of the founding works of modern science fiction, Wells's *The Time Machine* (1895). However, Mitchell's narrative borrows more than its formal structure from Wells's work, and in order to tease out these connections I recall the still vitally important lessons Antonio Gramsci has to teach us, especially in light of the proliferating intellectual pessimisms that mark our dark times. To paraphrase Mitchell's narrator, Daniel Ewing, and invoking Brecht one final time, all the works examined in this book teach us that a life spent shaping a world we want "those born after" to inherit, and not the one we fear they shall inherit, is truly a "life worth the living."

PART I

Reading Theory

[1]

Reading the Event of the New Criticism and the Fate of the *Republic*

It has become difficult to challenge opinion, even though this would seem the duty of any philosopher since Plato.

—Alain Badiou, *Second Manifesto for Philosophy*

This is not a genuine argument: it is a sophistical excuse for refusing to read the book.

—R. G. Collingwood, *An Essay on Metaphysics*

Truth is the child of time, not of authority.

—Bertolt Brecht, *Life of Galileo*

LIKE MANY SCHOLARS in the United States, the first provocative rumors I heard of the immense and ongoing theoretical project of Alain Badiou arrived in the 1990s by the way of the writings of Slavoj Žižek; and my first direct encounter likely came in 2001 with the publication of Peter Hallward's translation of and superb introduction to Badiou's *L'éthique: Essai sur la conscience du mal* (1998). On my first reading, this extraordinary short book struck me with all the force of an event, a profound encounter with truth on what turned out to be a personal and intellectual road to Damascus, and Badiou's writings, as the following pages will make evident, have continued to shape in profound ways all my subsequent work.

In his author's preface to the anthology of essays and excerpts published under the title *Theoretical Writings*, Badiou asks, "In what sense can this present book really be said to be one of my books? Specifically, one of my books of philosophy? Is it not rather a book by my friends Ray Brassier and Alberto Toscano [the volume's compilers and editors]?" Badiou then proceeds to thank these friends for providing him, "along with other readers, with the opportunity of reading a new, previously unpublished book, apparently authored by someone called 'Alain Badiou'—who is reputed to be none other than myself."[1] I have long been struck by the intellectual generosity of this statement, as I understand it as an invitation to take up a relationship to the profound corpus of his work as not that of the disciple, one who inhabits what Jacques Lacan names the "discourse of the university"—a position Fredric Jameson further characterizes as pedantic in orientation, concerned as it is first and foremost with "the authority of the letter, texts, doctrine: the scholastic weighing and comparing of juridical formulas; the concern with coherency and system; and the punctilious textual distinction between what is orthodox and what is not."[2] Rather, Badiou invites us to occupy a position more akin to that of Lacan's late figure of the analyst, which Jameson further characterizes as "a position of articulated receptivity, of deep listening *(l'écoute)*, of some attention beyond the self or the ego, but one that may need to use those bracketed personal functions as instruments for hearing the Other's desire"; or what Clint Burnham calls the rare figure of the "dialogic theorist," one who listens deeply to the profound things Badiou's work has to teach us and then puts these lessons into play in productive, creative, and even heterodox ways—to use them, in other words, to force truths.[3] (The issue of deep listening will be taken up again in the next chapter.) This is not unlike, as I shall discuss below, what Badiou himself does in his "hypertranslation" of a work that he too holds in the highest regard. It is in this spirit then that I offer this chapter, as well as the larger project in which it participates.

To begin, I would like to share with you a little anecdote from my recent travels. In May 2016, I was invited by the Onassis Cultural Center along with the brilliant Greek political theorist Yannis Stavrakakis and others to participate in a workshop and symposium held in Athens and Delphi in honor of the five hundredth anniversary of the publication of Thomas More's *Utopia*. While our conversations over the course of the event were rich and productive ones, sparking a number of new avenues of investigation—some of which I will also take up in my next chapter—my story today concerns another unexpected encounter that took place on the margins of our gathering. As this was my first visit to Greece, at the top of my itinerary was a trip to one of the singular accomplishments of

Periclean Athens and among the highest universal triumphs, or artistic truths, produced by human intellect—the Parthenon temple towering over the city on the pinnacle of the rock of the Acropolis.[4]

Now on the warm and bright afternoon of my visit, as I was passing through the propylaea, I happened to overhear a Greek tour guide addressing his British, Irish, and American audience. He told his group that one of the greatest accomplishments of classical Greece was its formulation of the basis for our modern understanding of the possible forms of governance. First, he informed them, we have anarchy, where everyone is free to do as they please; however the price they pay for such an arrangement is that things are, more often than not, deeply unstable, and hence they are unhappy. On the opposite extreme, he maintained, there are dictatorships, where although there is a great deal of social order and stability, the only one who is free to do as he will—grabbing whomever he will, wherever he will—is the dictator. A balance between these two extremes, where a modicum of both freedom and happiness or social stability is achieved, occurs in the practice of democracy. Finally, there is the form of governance where no one is free and where chaos, instability, and unhappiness are at their greatest—that, he concluded, is what they have today in Greece under the austerity regime imposed by the European Union.[5]

The deep bitterness in the tour guide's tone and his willingness to share such a charged set of ideas with his particular audience highlighted for me in a new way the depth of resentment directed at the European Union by so many different people, which would culminate not long after in the Brexit vote, the summer's perilous precursor, as Donald Trump predicted it would be, to our own presidential election and its populist revolt against the global elites. At the same time, I realized that the model the tour guide was offering them was quite appropriate for this context, as it was a creative appropriation for contemporary conditions of the foundational discussion of governance developed in the book that I also happened to be rereading at the time—Plato's *Republic,* and in particular, Badiou's extraordinary translation, whose English-language version, accomplished by Susan Spitzer, Badiou himself describes as "truly a tour de force."[6] As I reflected further, I realized that there are two very different possible ways of understanding the Greek tour guide's words and took out my notebook and sketched the schemas in Figures 1 and 2.

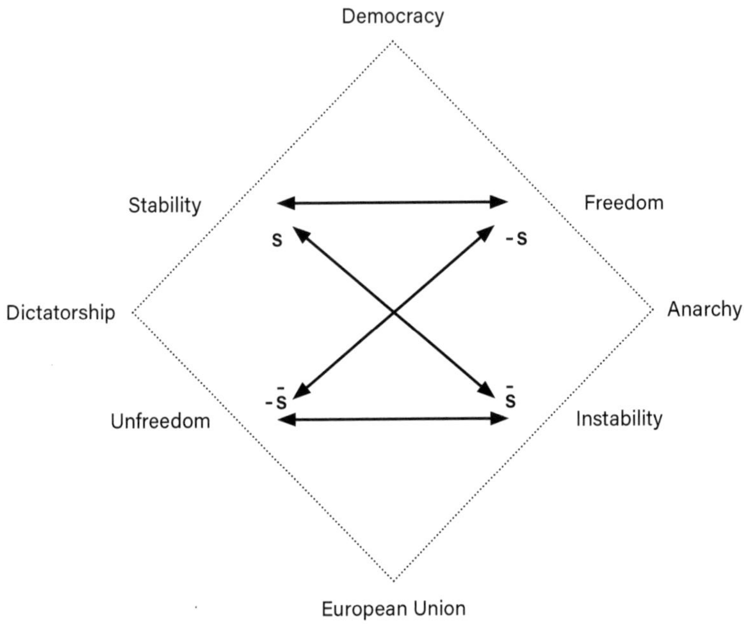

FIGURE 1

Alas, as I was finishing my notes, and before I could confirm my hypotheses, the oracular guide and his group moved on, dissolving into the crowds thronging the Acropolis.

Some readers will recognize the first of these two formalizations as a version of the classical semiotic square developed by A. J. Greimas and whose most well-known proponent, in the U.S. context at least, has long been Jameson. I investigate in some detail in the central chapter of my book *Periodizing Jameson: Dialectics, the University, and the Desire for Narrative* (2014) the square and the shifting uses to which Jameson puts it.[7] Greimas first explicitly theorizes the workings of the square in an essay coauthored with François Rastier, "The Interaction of Semiotic Constraints" (1968), although, as Ronald Schleifer demonstrates, it already implicitly underlies Greimas's earlier major intervention, *Sémantique structurale: Recherche de méthode* (1966).[8] Greimas based his particular formalization on the square of opposition developed by Aristotle in *De Interpretatione* in order to present formally

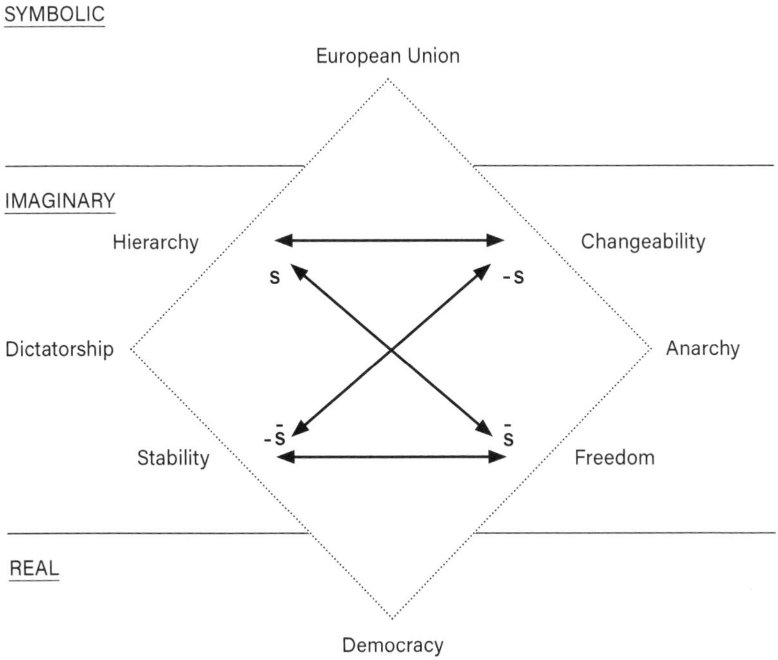

FIGURE 2

the set of logical relationships that develop around a concept.[9] If, as Gilles Deleuze and Félix Guattari maintain, "philosophy is the discipline that involves *creating* concepts," then the practice of semiotics—and, we might say, of interdisciplinary or postdisciplinary theory in general—is to read creatively the narratives where such concepts are set into motion.[10] (It may be for this very reason that theory first and most effectively took hold, in the United States at least, in comparative literary studies programs.) According to Greimas, any particular concept—let us use "law" as our example, which is placed in the slot in the square labeled "S"—presupposes two primary relationships: that of logical contradiction or simple negation (in this case, not-law, or crime, in the place of "S-barred") and that of contrariety or dialectical contradiction, which in our example would be expressed in the notion of "order" (the "-S")—hence the popular expression, again made prominent during the 2016 campaign, of "law and order." Greimas further maintains that the latter term of the contrariety produces its own contradiction (not-order, or disorder/chaos, "-S-barred"), and the four terms together suggest a pair of deixical relationships, those of simple implication. Figure 3 illustrates these relationships.

Greimas, however, then goes beyond Aristotle in a way that both highlights the imperatives of Greimas's structuralist agenda and, in Jameson's hands, makes the square such an extraordinarily productive tool for literary and cultural scholars in our labor of reading narratives of all kinds. Greimas builds upon the insights of one of structuralism's founders, Claude Lévi-Strauss, in order to claim that all narratives think in profound and complex ways, offering deep meditations upon a concept or concepts, as well as a staging of its varied relationships—this occurs in narratives as diverse as the Oedipus myth, Caduveo face painting, Bororo village design, the story told by our tour guide, and, as we shall see shortly, some of the founding essays of the New Criticism and Plato's *Republic*.[11] Thus, Greimas concludes, we can always uncover in any narrative not only a presentation of the four internal

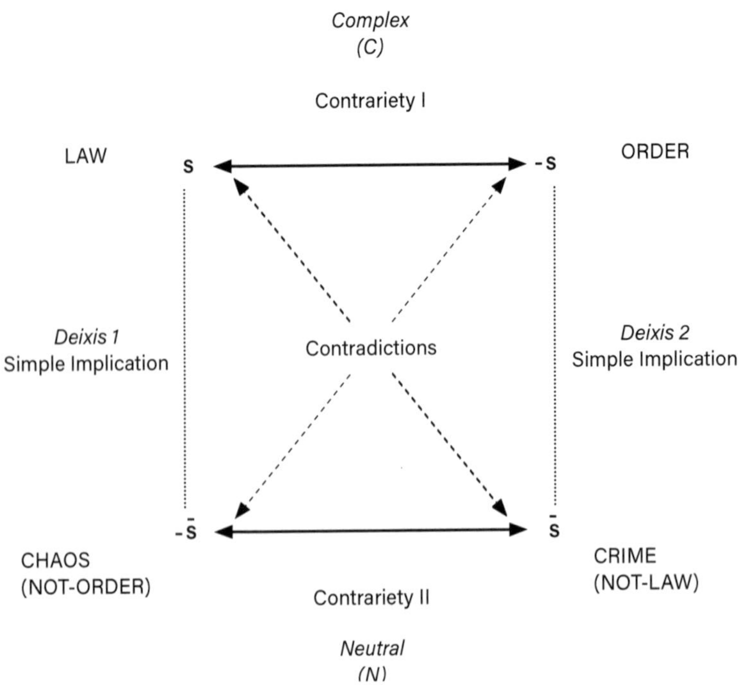

FIGURE 3

terms of a square but also concrete manifestations of the resolutions of the two contrarieties and the two simple implications. (The two logical contradictions resist anything more than formal presentation for the simple fact that they are self-consuming artifacts, a collision of matter and antimatter, or concept and not-concept.) The result is the full semiotic square, an example of which I demonstrated in *Life between Two Deaths, 1989–2001: U.S. Culture in the Long Nineties* (2009) as at work in a classic midcentury American narrative meditation on the contradiction of law and order, John D. MacDonald's *The Executioners* (1957) (the inspiration for J. Lee Thompson's 1961 anti–civil rights noir thriller, *Cape Fear,* and its very different 1991 remake by Martin Scorsese).[12]

One of the things that I find most "interesting" about the semiotic square is the way it illustrates the rigorous axiomatic structure at work in not only Jameson's thinking but that of any of the great theorists of the past century.[13] Burhanuddin Baki characterizes the specific axioms of Zermelo-Fraenkel set theory along with the axiom of choice (ZFC), so foundational for Badiou's work, in a way that applies to all similar axiomatic structures. Baki maintains that the axioms together constitute "a deductive, demonstrative, formal, symbolic, technical, inventive, rigorous and systematic discourse, a science that can be communicated and whose statements can be positively predicated within the regime of knowledge."[14] These axioms take the form, either explicitly or implicitly, of the "all" statements that appear throughout the most important theoretical projects. For example, Jameson famously argues in his major programmatic essay "Reification and Utopia in Mass Culture" (1979) that "all contemporary works of art—whether those of high culture and modernism or of mass culture and commercial culture—have as their underlying impulse—albeit in what is often distorted and repressed unconscious form—our deepest fantasies about the nature of social life, both as we live it now, and as we feel in our bones it ought rather to be lived."[15] Similarly, Deleuze and Guattari posit, "All concepts are connected to problems without which they would have no meaning and which can themselves only be isolated or understood as their solution emerges."[16] Or finally, to take another axiom that is fundamental not only for both Jameson and Deleuze and Guattari but for many of the great theoretical projects of the preceding century, "Die Geschichte aller bisherigen Gesellschaft ist die Geschichte von Klassenkämpfen" (The history of all previous societies is the history of class struggle).[17]

Badiou's "late lamented colleague," Jacques Derrida, maintains, in what we could take as a formulation of the axiom of such axioms:[18]

> Every concept that lays claim to any rigor whatsoever implies the alternative of "all or nothing." Even if in "reality" or in "experience" everyone believes he knows that there is never "all or nothing," a concept determines itself only according to "all or nothing." Even the concept of "difference of degree," the concept of relativity is, qua concept, determined according to the logic of all or nothing, of yes or no: differences of degree or nondifference of degree. It is impossible or illegitimate to form a *philosophical concept* outside this logic of all or nothing.[19]

The alternative to this rigorous "all or nothing" thinking is, as we saw in the Introduction, moralizing ethical judgment: the tallying up of distinctions between "normal" and "abnormal" or "good" and "evil" cases, be they speech and writing, procreative sex and masturbation, or, in the case of the Derrida essay just cited, "standard" and "parasitic" speech acts. Any such judgment, be it ethical or aesthetic, is, as Sianne Ngai points out, a performative utterance "that performs best when disguised as a constative."[20] Ngai subsequently presents her insight in the form of an axiom: "All aesthetic judgments, however cloaked as constative statements, are really performative utterances and, more specifically, demands."[21] It is precisely such moralizing judgments that Derrida carefully and thoroughly demonstrates his interlocutor, the philosopher John Searle, repeatedly falls back upon in the declarative "virile candor" of his essay "Reiterating the Differences: A Reply to Derrida."[22] (Indeed, Derrida's entire intervention could also be read as a stinging rebuke of the narrowly ethical protocols of judgment demanded by such journalistic genres as the "reply" and "review."[23])

The differences between these two ways of proceeding are nicely illustrated in a scene late in the *Stars Wars* film *Revenge of the Sith* (2005). In their climactic battle, the young Jedi knight Anakin Skywalker (Hayden Christensen), soon to be transformed into the dreaded Sith Lord Darth Vader, declares to his mentor, Obi-Wan Kenobi (Ewan McGregor), "If you're not with me, then you're my enemy." To this Obi-Wan replies, "Only a Sith deals in absolutes." The former is an ethical judgment: all cases are divided up into this side or the other—the former, of course, asserted to be the only proper one. Obi-Wan's statement, conversely, and based on years of experience, offers an axiom—all X are Y (all Jedi who deal in absolutes are Sith)—which thereby produces a concept, the Sith, that has tremendous value in reading, and acting, in his present context.

The heuristic value of axioms—or what R. G. Collingwood calls "absolute presuppositions," to which "the distinction between truth and falsehood does not apply"[24]—of which the semiotic square offers us an especially useful example, thus lies in the ways their inclusivity, inescapability, and universality force us to read in new ways, "generating new knowledge," as Kenneth Reinhard argues, "from within a current situation by, in a sense, wagering on the future perfect completion of a currently fragmentary truth."[25] For example, if one makes the decision to accept Greimas's axioms—and, as such diverse thinkers as Jameson and Louis O. Mink maintain, axioms can only be inhabited or rejected, never empirically "'proven' or disproven" (which is not, as Ian Stewart also points out, the same thing as saying any axiom is not accountable to the narrative demonstration of a proof)[26]—and, in particular, the axiom that all narratives are the thinking of a concept and its relationships—its contradictions, contrarieties, and implications—then one will be forced to return to any particular narrative as many times as necessary until all these manifestations or their concrete and specific absences become fully evident. To do so, Jameson suggests, will require that you "blacken many pages before you get it right."[27]

In his landmark manual on reading more effectively, *The Political Unconscious: Narrative as a Socially Symbolic Act* (1981), Jameson characterizes the semiotic square as "the privileged instrument of analysis of ideological closure," and on this basis he proceeds throughout the rest of his book to produce original creative readings of fiction by Honoré de Balzac and Joseph Conrad.[28] However, as I continued to investigate Jameson's deployment of the Greimasian square, I began to notice a significant shift in his usage, beginning in fact four years before the publication of *The Political Unconscious* with his 1977 review of his former colleague Louis Marin's *Utopiques: jeux d'espaces* (1973).[29] Such a shift entails a move from an emphasis on the narrative manifestation of the topmost contrariety, which Greimas labels the Complex term, to the lower, or Neutral. The effect, I maintained, is to transform the square from a device for thinking ideological closure to a way of formally presenting the processes involved in the emergence in any concrete situation, narrative or historical, of the unexpected or uncounted new. The thinking that takes place in this reconfigured square is what Jameson later describes as an *absolute formalism,* "in which the new content emerges itself from the form and is a projection of it."[30] In effecting this change of usage, Jameson completes a process, begun by Greimas, of breaking with what had heretofore remained primarily an Aristotelian deployment of the square—a practice that Badiou describes in *Theory of the Subject* (1982) as a finite structural dialectic ("The structural dialectic immobilizes the position of the terms into a symmetry, or into an invariant symmetry")—and replacing it with a Platonic formalization that illuminates in a lightning flash an infinite historical dialectic ("seizing the becoming-principle of the secondary, the rupture of any splace by the explosion of its rule and the loss of principle of the initial position").[31]

I further demonstrate in *Periodizing Jameson* that the most effective way to grasp what occurs in such a redeployment of the square is to overlay it with (*avec*) the three orders—the symbolic, imaginary, and real—at the heart of the project of Greimas's contemporary, the psychoanalyst Jacques Lacan.

The plane of the Greimasian schema occupied by the complex term is that of the symbolic order, the Big Other (A), or "the parasitic symbolic machine (language as a dead entity which 'behaves as if it possesses a life of its own')," that operates as both a third to and ground of any of the concrete exchanges and encounters that take place on the plane of the imaginary.[32] The complex term thus serves to name the totality encompassed by the square, including both the lived experience of the imaginary and the void of its real. The middle plane of the square presents Lacan's imaginary, primarily a matter of dualities and oppositions—"most notably all those which accumulate around the self and the other (or the subject and object)"—the irresolvable antinomies that constitute the lived experience of a particular situation.[33]

Finally, and most importantly, the neutral term becomes a placeholder for the real, which Lacan describes in his first seminar as "ce qui résiste absolument à la symbolization" (what resists symbolization absolutely), and which in Jameson's earliest characterization becomes another name for "History itself."[34] Lorenzo Chiesa summarizes Lacan's insight in this way: "there is something real in it which escapes

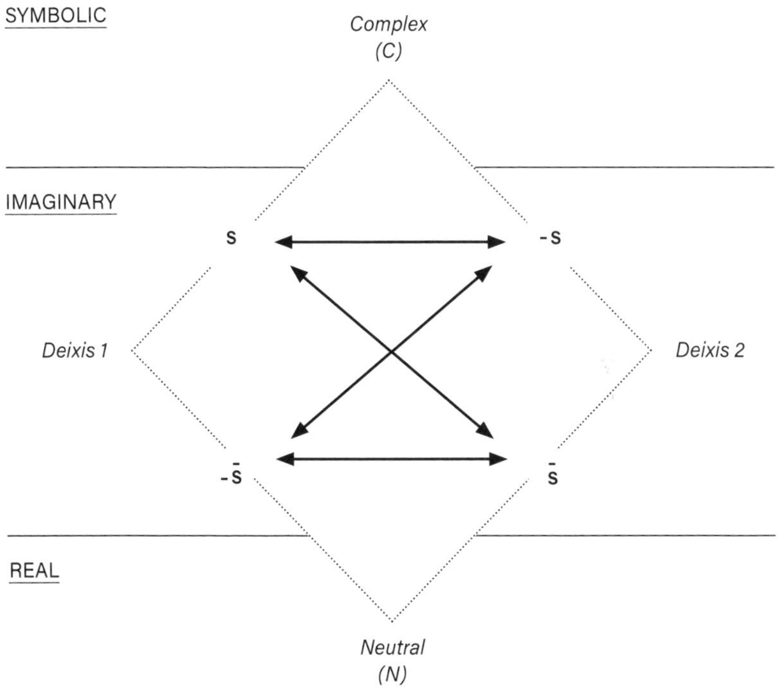

FIGURE 4

the Symbolic, something which renders the symbolic Other 'not-all' and, for the same reason, makes it possible precisely as a differential symbolic structure."[35] Crucially, such a resistance to symbolization—to incorporation into the reigning order or a named set—both accounts for the traumatic experience of any encounter with such a real—the "impossible-real" of freedom in Žižek's recent work[36]—and, equally significantly, assures the nonclosure or suturability of any reality or set, the latter presented by the other two planes of the square.

I have already indicated the tremendous value of further advancing with (*avec*) Badiou such a rethinking of the semiotic square, drawing upon, in particular, his central notions of forcing and the couple of the structural and historical dialectic. Indeed, the very Lacanian notion of "with," the coupling of one thinker or system of axioms with another in order to make evident unexpected potentialities, can now be better understood as a naïve version of the rigorous operation of forcing central to Badiou's project. Moreover, what I identify as the place of the real in the Greimasian square is the locus of what Badiou theorizes as the *event.* An event, according to Badiou, is something that happens "that cannot be reduced to its ordinary inscription in 'what there is.'"[37] Badiou further maintains, "the event is both *situated*—it is the event of this or that situation—and *supplementary*; thus absolutely detached from, or unrelated to, all the rules of situation."[38] Peter Hallward similarly argues that the event "takes place in a situation but is not 'of' that situation," and hence it presents the "void of the situation, that aspect of the situation that has absolutely no interest in preserving the status quo as such."[39] In short, the event is the very possibility, though by no means the guarantee, of a radical new beginning, the inauguration of that which was heretofore uncounted, unexpected, and unknown, "forced" by conditions that have become unfavorable for continuing in the same ways as in the past. Moreover, as we shall see in the chapters making up the second section of this book, the Badiouian subject differs from the mere individual through their sustained fidelity to the truth emerging on the horizon of any evental void.

More speculatively, I would propose that the square also offers a productive way of thinking, at least for nonmathematicians, Badiou's radical deployment of set theory. In such a presentation, the complex term or the symbolic identifies the set, the "count-as-one" of a situation. The imaginary expressed in the two deixes, however, figures its elements by way of the demarcation of the limits of its multiples. Finally, the real of the neutral term, in another important Badiouian notion, *names* for the first time the void of the situation formalized by the square; or in set theoretical terms, the last identifies the indiscernible or generic set, what Baki describes as the point of excess, the element every set "fails to contain" as a subset, such that "a set is never equivalent to its power set, by virtue of the Axiom of Extensionality."[40] (Moreover, when the elements of the power set are ordered by inclusion, the resulting distribution of subsets corresponds to the planes of the Greimasian square.) In fact, the terms on all three planes function to name: the first, the symbolic or complex term, names, to borrow Deleuze and Guattari's distinction, an *axiomatic* language, which "deals directly with purely functional elements and relations whose nature is not specified, and which are immediately realized in highly varied domains simultaneously"; the second, the imaginary or two deixes, *codes,* which "are relative to those domains and express specific relations between qualified elements"; and finally, the real or neutral, the aspect of a situation that as of yet can be neither axiomatized nor coded, what Christopher Breu refers to as an "uncoded materiality."[41] It is this last deep materiality that forces new possibilities to emerge, transforming the original set of which it is and is not a part.

In order to demonstrate the real value of the kind of thinking of Greimas with Lacan, and now with Badiou, that I am proposing here, I would like first to turn to one of the most profound events to occur in American intellectual life in the middle part of the twentieth century—the founding of the rigorous theory and practice of creative reading named the New Criticism—before concluding with an examination of Badiou's hypertranslation of Plato's *Republic.* I am confident that most readers will be familiar with two of the New Criticism's most influential early essays, "The Intentional Fallacy" and "The Affective Fallacy," coauthored by the literary scholar W. K. Wimsatt Jr. and the aesthetic philosopher Monroe C. Beardsley. These essays originally appeared in 1946 and 1949, respectively, in the journal *Sewanee Review* and were reprinted in Wimsatt's 1954 collection, *The Verbal Icon: Studies in the Meaning of Poetry.*

In these essays, Wimsatt and Beardsley help clear the intellectual space for the New Criticism through a thoroughgoing dismantling of what they posit as the two dominant reading practices at work in their moment: "two roads which have seemed to offer convenient detours around the acknowledged and usually feared obstacles to objective criticism, both of which, however, have actually led away from criticism and from poetry."[42] In the opening of "The Affective Fallacy," Wimsatt and Beardsley characterize these two approaches in the following manner:

> The Intentional Fallacy is a confusion between the poem and its origins, a special case of what is known to philosophers as the Genetic Fallacy. It begins by trying to derive the standard of criticism from the psychological *causes* of the poem and ends in biography and relativism. The Affective Fallacy is a confusion between the poem and its *results* (what it is and what it does), a special case of epistemological skepticism, though usually advanced as if it had far stronger claims than the overall forms of skepticism. It begins by trying to derive the

> standard of criticism from the psychological effects of the poem and ends in impressionism and relativism. The outcome of either Fallacy, the Intentional or the Affective, is that the poem itself, as an object of specifically critical judgment, tends to disappear. (*VI*, 21)

The real problem for Wimsatt and Beardsley lies where each of these theories locate the ultimate source for an artwork's meaning: either in statements of the author's intents—recoverable by testimony, biography, or the inherent authority of the authorized scholar-reader—or, conversely, in its impact on multiple individual readers. Crucially, Wimsatt and Beardsley here do not, as too many later critics will wrongly claim, deny the existence of some ultimately determining instance of authorial intention (and later theories will expand tremendously our sense of what constitutes an "author" of any particular text) or readerly affect; rather, they maintain that neither should be taken as the starting point for reading. To do so in either case would be to leave readers in an impossible bind when attempting to ground and prove their reading. In the first case, the reader has no way to question the oracular truth issued by the voice of the author or his representative;[43] in the latter, there is no way to prove the legitimacy of one reading over any other, because each reading ultimately is no more than a personal and individual claim. Truth in the first case takes the form of declarations of authority from one who remains absolutely confident that *he* is the master of his domain; and in the latter, the assertion of opinion. In the first case, one possible meaning reigns over all others by the force of its origin; while in the second, all expressions of meaning, wherever they arise, are at least formally equal and hence equally meaningless (unless, of course, a particular affective response is proclaimed—again, what Ngai reminds us is a performative utterance disguised as a constative—to be the "normal," "proper," or otherwise privileged one; but in such a case we are thrown right back into the first fallacy, authority now located in a singular reader).

Wimsatt and Beardsley therefore propose what at the time was understood as a radical break with established practices in their theorization of what became known as close reading.[44] The theory of close reading begins with what today might be understood by many as a common sense axiom (but common sense is, of course, only the indication of the success of any theory): to wit, the starting point and ultimate ground for the meaning of all poems is "the poem itself." (Also keep in mind in what follows that for the New Critics the poem stands in as a privileged minimal figure for all true works of art, of whatever length or genre—drama also occupies a special place in their readings, as they claim, in another foundational axiom, that "even a short lyric poem is dramatic, the response of a speaker [no matter how abstractly conceived] to a situation [no matter how universalized]" [*VI*, 5].) In the opening paragraphs of "The Intentional Fallacy," at the conclusion of a "series of propositions," which the authors claim have been "summarized and abstracted to a degree where they seem to us axiomatic," Wimsatt and Beardsley maintain:

> The poem is not the critic's own and not the author's (it is detached from the author at birth and goes about the world beyond his power to intend about it or control it). The poem belongs to the public. It is embodied in language, the peculiar possession of the public, and it is about the human being, an object of public knowledge. What is said about the poem is subject to the same scrutiny as any statement in linguistics or in the general science of psychology. (*VI*, 4–5)

On the basis of this axiom, the New Critics formulate a whole series of protocols for rigorous reading. These would include the refusal of appeals in the determination of meaning to anything "outside the poem"—again, such evidence may be used to guide, shape, and direct the reading but should never ground it. Wimsatt and Beardsley maintain:

> There is a difference between internal and external evidence for the meaning of a poem. . . . What is (1) internal is also public: it is discovered through the semantics and syntax of a poem, through our habitual knowledge of the language, through grammars, dictionaries, and all the literature which is the source of dictionaries, in general through all that makes a language and culture; while what is (2) external is private or idiosyncratic; not

> a part of the work as a linguistic fact: it consists of revelations (in journals, for example, or letters or reported conversations) about how or why the poet wrote the poem. (*VI*, 10)

Indeed, for the New Critics such "revelations" would constitute no more than one additional reading of the poem, subject to the same criteria of evaluation and demonstration as any other reading. The great consequence of this is to level the field between all readers, offering every reader the tools to challenge critically and rigorously the authority of any other. The differences between readers will ultimately become largely quantitative, a measure of their experience and practice in reading in such a fashion, rather than qualitative (only in the impossible ideal situation of absolute equality of such experience and practice might one truly be able to measure the qualitative differences—intelligence, talent, and so forth).

There is a scene in Woody Allen's *Annie Hall* (1977) when Allen's character becomes annoyed by the pompous declarations concerning the work of Marshall McLuhan spouted by a professor of media at Columbia University (played by the character actor Russell Horton, otherwise most well-known as the voice of the Trix Rabbit in the breakfast cereal commercials). When the professor further asserts that his qualitative position of authority is enough to mean that his "insights" into McLuhan's work "have a great deal of validity," Allen pulls in from off-camera McLuhan himself. McLuhan pointedly informs the man, "You know nothing of my work. You mean my whole fallacy is wrong. How you got to teach a course in anything is totally amazing." The scene concludes with Allen expressing the wish, "Boy, if life were only like this." While I am confident at least some readers will, as I confess I do, take delight in this fantasy of comeuppance, we should keep in mind that this is, in fact, exactly what happens far too often in real life, as one structure of authority confronts and upends another (and perhaps it is this intentional fallacy to which McLuhan refers).[45] At the conclusion of "The Intentional Fallacy," Wimsatt and Beardsley state in no uncertain terms, "Critical inquiries are not settled by consulting the oracle" (*VI*, 18). On this basis, I have long imagined a possible New Critical coda to the scene, where, in response, the Columbia professor would take out his copy of McLuhan's book and then explain precisely how he arrived at his reading, offering specific contextual evidence from the text to ground his claims. McLuhan then in turn would respond by producing his own copy and showing the man the things he had to overlook in developing such a reading and perhaps offering some minimal contextualizing information to clarify his specific use of words and terms. In this case, both would occupy the same plane as readers, refusing appeals to authority and referring only to the text itself, and the possibility might ensue of the "minimal communism" of a real and productive dialogue—truly listening to one another rather than each just waiting for their turn to talk.

This also underscores the fact that New Critical reading demands close attention to all aspects of any text in relationship to what the New Critics formulate as "context," the totality of the text itself. Perhaps the greatest of the New Critical creative readers, Cleanth Brooks, whose work I will return to momentarily, states in the conclusion of *The Well Wrought Urn: Studies in the Structure of Poetry* (1947):

> The characteristic unity of a poem (even of those poems which may accidentally possess a logical unity as well as this poetic unity) lies in the unification of attitudes into a hierarchy subordinated to a total and governing attitude. . . . Thus, it is easy to see why the relation of each item to the whole is crucial, and why the effective and essential structure of the poem has to do with the complex of attitudes achieved. A scientific proposition can stand alone. If it is true, it is true. But the expression of an attitude, apart from the occasion which generates it and the situation which it encompasses, is meaningless.[46]

In short, as Brooks makes fully explicit, close reading is dialectical—that is, relational and *totalizing* reading (Hegel's *Vernunft*). It is here precisely where close reading most fully—in the present as much in its own moment—brushes against the grain of established common sense concerning reading practices (*Verstand*): the suspension of appeals at once to external authority and readers' opinions means that every moment in a text becomes potentially significant and, equally significantly, must be taken into account when discussing the meaning of the whole. As Rebecca Comay and Frank Ruda put in terms of the practice of dialectical reading established by Hegel, "to read speculatively—to read at all—one needs to suspend every advance decision about what is major and what is minor, what is essential and what is inessential. There is no preexisting standard by which to assess what may be significant; you must proceed as if anything and everything is important, as if there is a necessity at work in the most ordinary contingencies of existence."[47] Difficulties arise later, when, in the moments of structuralism and historicism (theory and scholarship), that text begins to expand exponentially; however, to the degree that they remain dialectical, the same totalizing and relational principle established here also holds in these cases.

The title of the chapter in which Brooks's observation occurs is "The Heresy of Paraphrase," a title that also identifies a third of the foundations of New Critical reading practice: the activity of paraphrase, while finally inescapable, must be kept to a minimum, and all claims made about the work's meaning grounded in concrete evidence in the form of citations from the text itself. This is exactly what the close reader Derrida does in "Limited Inc a, b, c . . ." (1977), pushing this logic to its furthest extension by citing almost the entirety of the text in question; and in so doing, Derrida demonstrates in practice his original point concerning the impossibility of any final closed reading of the text, anything beyond an open-ended activity of citing and reciting the text, grafting it into a potential infinity of different contexts. Such a conclusion is what another close reader, Paul de Man, celebrates five years later as the "resistance to theory" inherent in the practice of theory itself.[48] Brooks himself maintains, in what I think of as the asymptote of New Critical reading, "We may, it is true, be able to adumbrate what the poem says if we allow ourselves enough words and if we make enough reservations and qualifications, thus attempting to come nearer to the meaning of the poem by successive approximations and refinements, gradually encompassing the meaning and pointing to the area in which it lies rather than realizing it."[49] This is because of the simple fact that the meaning or truth of the work of art, like that of any other event or utopia, is a singular experience ("My task which I am trying to achieve is, by the power of the written word to make you hear, to make you feel—it is, before all, to make you *see*"[50]) and hence not subject to abstraction, summary, or representation. Badiou similarly argues, "What arises from a truth-process . . . cannot be communicated [*ne se communiqué pas*]. Communication is suited only to opinions (and again, we are unable to manage without them). In all that concerns truths, there must be an *encounter*."[51]

Finally, for the New Critics this act of reading must be able to be reproduced by any other reader adhering to the same learned set of protocols—true reading must be collective, dialogical, critical, and transmittable—that is, teachable. Wimsatt and Beardsley conclude their paired essays by claiming:

> A structure of emotive objects so complex and so reliable as to have been taken for great poetry by any past age will never, it seems safe to say, so wane with the waning of human culture as not to be recoverable by a willing student. And on the same grounds a confidence seems indicated for the objective discrimination of all future poetic phenomena, though the premises or materials of which such poems will be constructed cannot be prescribed or foreseen. (*VI*, 39)

(This last sentence offers an important caveat to which I will return.) Such a "willing student" is one who has been carefully trained and becomes practiced in the rigorous activity of creative reading outlined above and who then decides to express their fidelity by putting it into play in their own engagement with texts.

What all this suggests is that the New Criticism represents an event in Badiou's full sense, the emergence of an unexpected and radically new way of operating in the specific condition of the science of reading. It will be the New Critics' fidelity to these practices, especially in the face of resistance to their theory on the part of an entrenched literary faculty, that will ultimately transform in a profound, far-reaching, and unexpected manner the practices of both reading and teaching to read, as well as the institutions in which these activities take place. The repercussions of this event are still felt today—indeed, I would maintain that all of the later developments in U.S. literary theory unfold in terms of a deep fidelity to this event, regardless of their specific and extraordinarily productive divergences and disagreements with and resistances to the particular claims of a New Criticism that had by then become orthodoxy or even dogma.

I mentioned earlier that the value of axiomatic readings such as that enabled by the semiotic square or the New Criticism lies in the ways they force new knowledge, making us take account of aspects of a narrative text we may have earlier overlooked, and this is very much the case with *The Verbal Icon*. Less well remembered today is the fact that in the context of the book, the essays on the intentional and affective fallacies are accompanied by a third, authored by Wimsatt alone, and bearing the title "The Chicago Critics: The Fallacy of the Neoclassic Species" (originally published in 1953).[52] The "critics" Wimsatt refers to in his title are the group of scholarly readers then assembled at the University of Chicago—R. S. Crane, Richard McKeon, Norman Maclean, Elder Olson, and others—who represented in this moment the most significant institutional challenge to the ascendancy of the New Criticism. Wimsatt's essay emerges in part as a response to critiques leveled by Crane and others to the reading strategies advocated by the New Critics and especially the charge that the New Critic's axiomatic formulations make them "'dogmatic' and restrictive"—a charge often leveled at any consistent, rigorous, and noncontradictory theory (*VI*, 46). Wimsatt argues in reply that the professed openness and pluralism of the Chicago critics serve as blinds for a deeper and more rigid, closed systemization, based largely on Aristotle's *Poetics*. In part citing Crane, Wimsatt claims, "it turns out . . . that they look on the Aristotelian 'hypotheses about poetry and poetics' as 'capable of being developed into a comprehensive critical method, at once valid in itself and peculiarly adapted to the study of [certain] problems'" (46). Wimsatt further points out, "One of the central Chicago doctrines says that every poem ought to be seen as belonging to a specific kind, species, or genre of poems (tragic, comic, lyric, didactic) and ought to be treated according to the 'causes' which determine this specific kind. A poem should be treated not as an instance of poetry in general but as a specific kind of poetry" (52–53).

The dilemmas for Wimsatt in such an approach—and I am less interested here in the accuracy of Wimsatt's reading of the Chicago Aristotelians than in what he imagines them to be arguing[53]—are twofold. First, they once again move the locus of meaning and value from the particular and concrete verbal performance of the "poem itself" into a set of abstract institutional criteria, which, whatever their historical origins, have now ascended into a transcendental realm of fixed truth (the neoclassicism of his title). As a result, Wimsatt concludes, the reading process becomes "strictly self-contained—that is to say, circular" (*VI*, 64). This is the form of evil Badiou names *disaster*: "Rigid and dogmatic (or 'blinded'), the subject-language would claim the power, based on its own axioms, to name the whole of the real, and thus to change the world. . . . A disaster of the truth induced by the absolutization of its power."[54] The failure of any such axiomatic structure to achieve such final closure is precisely what is demonstrated by the deployment of the semiotic square I outline above. Moreover, as access to true meaning is limited to those who possess knowledge of these reified institutions, the real power to read is located not in individual authority or in all readers as individuals but rather in an oligarchy of trained professionals whose duty is to transmit this reified and naturalized knowledge to their audience. What this institutionalization of reading in the university really masks, however, is the fact that in actual practice the Chicago critics occupy "mutually inconsistent positions as, on the one hand, relativism and 'aesthetic atomism' and, on the other 'pseudo-Aristotelian formalism'"—that is, the imaginaries of both the affective and intentional fallacies, intention here relocated from the individual author into institutional norms, which delimit not only how we read but also "prescribe" how all future literature will be "constructed" (*VI*, 64). The structural dialectic of the Chicago critics' neoclassical formalism thus becomes the name for the entire order of reading within but not of which the unexpected event of the New Criticism erupts.[55] With this last term now accounted for, I can complete my Greimasian presentation of the institutional situation from which emerges the New Criticism (see Figure 5).

In the final paragraph of his foreword to *On Meaning,* the 1987 English-language collection of Greimas's writings, Jameson maintains, "That Greimassian semiotics should be 'true' in some sense . . . and at the same time stand as a profound historical symptom of the nature of the age [in which it appears] I find no difficulty in reconciling."[56] A similar claim of universal truth and particular historical situatedness can be made for the New Criticism. A great deal has been written about the specific institutional context in which the New Criticism comes into being, in the midst of the unprecedented post–World War II expansion of the U.S. public university, a transformation that in turn demanded the elaboration of compact and readily transmittable reading practices, as well as a new kind of professional institutional status for the literary critic.[57] Much too has been made in recent decades concerning the ideological and political limits of the original New Critics: their roots in the conservative Southern Agrarian movement; their racial, class,

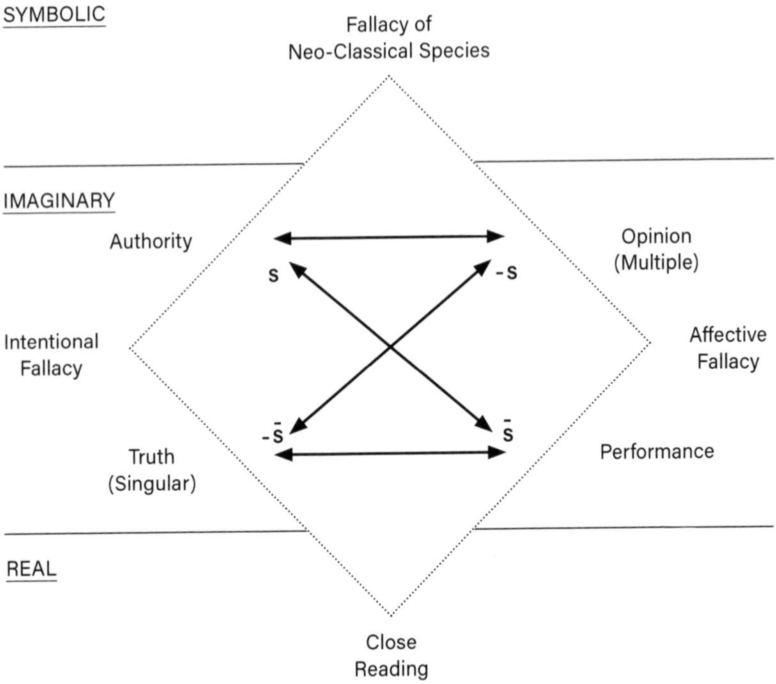

FIGURE 5

and gender ideologies; and their narrow "late modernist" assertion of the divide between art (what in the culture wars of the 1980s and 1990s will come to be referred to as the "canon") and culture, effectively circumscribing for a generation—that is, until the full effects of the structuralist and so-called poststructuralist revolutions were felt in this country—what might be understood to constitute complex and effective narrative and verbal performances.[58] Vincent Leitch summarizes these conclusions when he notes, "What we find is that New Critical formalist criticism was invariably linked with a conservative social, moral, religious, and political assessment of the past, present, and possible future. . . . The practice and theory of these American formalists was typically tied to a traditional conservative—a Tory—ideology and value system."[59] Terry Eagleton, in his influential *Literary Theory: An Introduction* (1983), even more damningly maintains, in a way that is also readily applicable to the more recent new ethical critics

I discussed in my Introduction, that "New Criticism was the ideology of an uprooted, defensive intelligentsia who reinvented in literature what they could not find in reality."[60] (It is worth noting here that Eagleton violates one of the key New Critical axioms, confusing the meaning of the text with one of its causes.) While such ideological unmaskings remain essential and at the foundation of any measured assessment of the achievements and limits of New Critical theory, they too often end up throwing out the baby with the bathwater, and thereby lose the truth given expression in the New Criticism's fidelity to the creative activity of close reading. It is the duality of the New Criticism, at once a historical symptom and truth, that my Greimasian formalization helps us more effectively grasp.

Near the conclusion of his well-known essay "Irony as a Principle of Structure" (1949), Brooks identifies a special task for the modern verbal artist: the challenge of "rehabilitating a tired and drained language so that it can convey meanings once more with force and exactitude" to a "a public corrupted by Hollywood and the Book of the Month Club."[61] With this statement, Brooks underscores the nearness of New Criticism to the contemporaneous late modernist critique of the "cultural industry" developed by Max Horkheimer and Theodor Adorno in *Dialektik der Aufklärung* (*Dialectic of Enlightenment*) (1944). Brooks then proceeds to identify an additional and vitally significant consequence of learning not only to write but to *read* literary art (and, as everyone from Stanley Fish to Pierre Bayard teaches us, and as I shall discuss in my next chapter, all readings are writings). Brooks maintains, "What we ask is that the poem dramatizes the situation so accurately, so honestly, with such fidelity to the total situation that it is no longer a question of our beliefs, but of our participation in the poetic *experience*. . . . Participating in that insight, we doubtless become better citizens. (One of the 'uses' of modern poetry, I should agree, is to make us better citizens.")[62]

In this claim, Brooks takes up directly one of the fundamental challenges brought to bear on a modern university education: to prepare citizens for the responsibilities of democratic self-governance. The intellectual habits fostered by learning to read closely—those of rigor, attention to context, proof, and the necessity of citing concrete evidence to support one's claims—are also among those required by anyone who will participate in the body politic. That is to say, the New Critics hold that education must have a political as well as an economic value. In this way, as Geoffrey Galt Harpham also notes in a recent assessment of the movement and its achievements, "the New Critics managed to create a discipline that could be deployed on behalf of many of the broader objectives of the general education program that was at the time being designed to meet the needs of the American democracy."[63]

In the months before the 2016 U.S. election, or the beginning of the nightmare from which we have not yet awoke, Alan Taylor, the noted historian of the American Revolutionary War period, published an essay entitled "The Virtue of an Educated Voter." Taylor maintains that the "founders who led the American Revolution" believed that "republics depended on a broad electorate of common men, who, to keep their new rights, had to protect them with attentive care." The best way to enable them to do so was by providing them with an education that promoted the good of the polis as well as the economic self-interests of the individual: "More than a mere boon for individuals, education was a collective, social benefit essential for free governments to endure."[64] Conversely, "poorly educated voters might also elect reckless demagogues who would appeal to class resentments and promote the violent redistribution of wealth."[65] Taylor further shows that this Jeffersonian ideal of the university was at its highest point of influence in the post–World War context from which emerged the New Criticism, a period when the number of college graduates increased "from four percent of young adults in 1900 to nearly 50 percent by 1980."[66] Wendy Brown similarly points out that the postwar university's, and especially the public university's, extension of "liberal arts education from the elite to the many was nothing short of a radical democratic event, one in which all became potentially eligible for the life of freedom long reserved for the few."[67] Brown further observes, "While the remarkable postwar extension of liberal arts education to the many did not generate true educational equality let alone social equality, this extension *articulated* equality as an ideal. It also articulated the value of a public educated for the individual and collective capacity for self-governance."[68]

However, Taylor goes on to point out that one of the aims of the neoconservative and neoliberal revolution of the early 1980s was to redefine education exclusively "as an economic good, rather than a political one. The proponents of higher education promised economic growth, not political virtue, as the prime goal. It became quaint at best to raise an alarm about demagogues and aristocrats as the dangerous consequence of an ignorant electorate."[69] Beginning from a very different political starting point, Patrick J. Deneen similarly concludes, "Advanced liberalism is eliminating liberal education with keen intent and ferocity, finding it impractical both ideologically and economically. . . . Universities scramble to provide practical 'learning outcomes,' either by introducing a raft of new programs aimed to make students immediately employable or by rebranding and reorienting existing studies to tout their economic relevance."[70]

The New Critics held to the fundamental truth that without an educated electorate—in a situation of a downsized and marginalized humanities and other noncommodifiable areas of university teaching and research, a reorientation, as Jean-François Lyotard already warns in the early 1980s, toward efficiency, assessable and quantifiable outcomes, and a shift from an interdisciplinary general education to increasingly narrow vocational training—our democratic institutions would be fundamentally compromised, creating the opportunity for the emergence of a new tyranny.[71] Robert H. Brinkmeyer Jr. further underscores the New Critical fidelity to the democratizing vocation of culture and education when he notes that the New Critics "confronted head-on the increasingly strident demands for openly patriotic art that colored cultural debate in the late 1930s and then into World War II. [They] believed that such demands smacked of the totalitarianism to which democracy stood opposed. Rather than through simplistic patriotic subject matter, they argued, art best manifested—and thus defended—democratic principles through its complicated interior dynamics."[72] The New Critics' most well-known pair of fallacies—the intentional and affective—should be understood similarly as analogues to the political positions—acquiescence to authority and the tyranny of the mob—that found their fullest expression in fascism.

While the New Critics, like the founders of the American Revolution, may have held to the affective or ideological opinion that only a "'natural aristocracy' of virtue and talents," all privileged white men, would be capable of learning the skills necessary for self-rule, the truth of the very practices they formulate made them available universally.[73] This was born out in subsequent decades as student bodies became increasingly diversified in terms of their class, racial, and gender compositions. Thus, we should not underestimate the degree to which the practices of New Criticism, once they unexpectedly came into the hands of these new student readers and the next generation of literary theorists, contributed to the intellectual, institutional, and political transformations of the 1960s and 1970s. Crucially, this is not a standpoint epistemology that privileges the perspective of any reader or group of readers as unassailable but rather one that enables confrontation and communication, Mikhail Bakhtin's much-abused notion of the dialogic, across these different divides. What these new readers were able to show was precisely the failures to read closely in some earlier readers. This is why, as Christopher Newfield so carefully demonstrates in his landmark study *Unmaking the Public University: The Forty-Year Assault on the Middle Class* (2008)—a book that should be required reading for all of us—that one of the earliest neoconservative strategies for reversing the expansion of the democratic participation that began to take hold in the 1960s was a full frontal assault on the monumental, if by far from perfect, achievement of the postwar public university—an achievement to which I, as a first-generation public university graduate, remain deeply indebted.[74]

All of this brings us back at last to Badiou's hypertranslation of *The Republic* and in particular Badiou's re-presentation in the book's twelfth chapter of the forms of education that would be foundational for the ideal state. The system of education advocated by Socrates, like that of the New Critical practice of close reading, is one very much oriented more toward collective political than individual economic goods:

> The guardians of our communist political community—the militants, the workers, the soldiers, the leaders, everyone—are both men of action and philosophers. So I think that you practically have to say that the study of higher, or even transcendental arithmetic must be compulsory. Everyone who really wants to take part in our community and be able to hold their own when their turn comes to exercise a position of leadership will have to commit to studying it and work at it, not superficially, merely to take away a few practical formulas from it, but until they achieve a synthetic understanding of the nature of numbers through pure thought.[75]

However, such a mathematical or scientific education is only a step in a grander process:

> The whole problem is that, however great they may be, mathematicians and scientists are not yet true dialecticians. Although the sciences are necessary—just like the arts, political action, and transference love—they're not sufficient. Singular truths are merely the prelude to philosophy. Sure, without them our musical score wouldn't contain a single note. But the philosophical song, properly speaking, can only be sung by those who are able to carry a dialectical discussion through to its conclusion. (*PR*, 235)

This then requires a new practice of education, one with deep kinship to that advocated by the New Critics:

> It's the teachers' responsibility to kindle in our human young the creative spark they all have within them. Only in an atmosphere of active freedom like this will everyone find the path to the dialectic that's most natural to him. A dialectician is someone whose thinking is able to see the big picture. But, for any given state of the world, there's an infinite number of paths to constructing the big picture of that state. Education is worthless if it doesn't give everyone the means of choosing the best path for himself so that, with the help of circumstances and as a Subject, he can become the dialectician as an individual he was capable of becoming. (242)

The result will be a polis capable of true self-governance and hence the highest form of freedom. In the rousing climax to the chapter, Badiou's version of Plato's Socrates declares:

> They'll have completed what it takes for an individual to have the greatest chance of becoming incorporated into one or several different truth processes and thereby becoming a Subject. They'll be able to lift their eyes upon everything that exists, toward that which, revealing as it does the being underlying this existence, is like its hidden light. When their turn comes, guided by that light, they'll tackle the difficulties imposed by positions of leadership in politics. They'll have nothing but the public welfare in mind and will regard such an activity not an honor but as

> a necessary duty. They'll use their position, which is temporary anyway, only to further reinforce by their example the education of their successors, the people who, when their turn comes, will be responsible for the supreme guardianship of the communist system of government, in any and all circumstances. (244)

As in the case of the New Criticism, the development of such a utopian figure rests on its careful differentiation from already existing practices. However, Plato's *Republic* reverses the New Critical presentation by developing a two-chapter long "Critique of the Four Pre-Communist Systems of Government" only after first modeling the Republic's ideal educational practices. The text reverses the New Critical narrative in another way, by beginning its critique with the two linked forms of governance, timocracy and oligarchy, that bear the most resemblance to Wimsatt's third and last to be described fallacy, that of neoclassical species. This underscores the fact that for Plato, at least in Badiou's presentation, as much as for Wimsatt, these forms bear the nearest kinship to the ideal: "This timocracy mimics the communism it comes from and the oligarchy that follows it. After the fall of the Soviet Union, the apparatchiks of the Communist state, like their so-called enemies, became the super-rich 'oligarchs' of post-Communist capitalism. 'Oligarchs'—let me stress the word: that's the name they're given. That speaks volumes" (252).

The next form of governance to be discussed is that of democracy, and its kinship to the affective fallacy is indicated in the opening of chapter 14: "The shift from oligarchy to democracy occurs when the imperative to enjoy, along the lines of a nineteenth-century French minister's dictum 'Get rich!,' becomes an unlimited general imperative" (PR, 263). Of this third system, Badiou's Socrates proclaims, "You've got a government with an anarchic, many-splendoured appearance. In addition to this freedom, so dizzying that it boggles the mind, there's a sort of purely formal equality that actually lumps equality and inequality together" (269). As in the case of the New Critical affective fallacy, the abstract equivalence between all opinions, voices, or readings masks the absence of effective collective norms, or what we could term a theory, to mediate between them. Badiou writes that "the essence of such normless personal freedom is, quite simply . . . private interest . . . the competitive fury of private interest, the indifference to anything else, including any principle, or even any truth—that's what destroys our third system of government, democracy, from within and replaces it with one version or another of the fourth: a fascist-like tyranny" (274). Such an absolutization of private interest is what Deneen forcefully terms an "unsustainable liberalism," and in such a world, "gratitude to the past and obligations to the future are replaced by a nearly universal pursuit of immediate gratification. . . . As a result, superficially self-maximizing, socially destructive behaviors begin to dominate society."[76] Derrida similarly warns in the case of any act of reading, "without recognizing and respecting all its classical exigencies, which is not easy and requires all the instruments of traditional criticism, critical production would risk developing in any direction at all and would authorize itself to say almost anything. . . . Although it is not a commentary, our reading must be intrinsic and remain within the text."[77]

A Greimasian mapping of the five possible systems narrated in Badiou's text would thus appear as in Figure 6. My decision to combine Plato's timocracy and oligarchy into a single term follows the precedent of Plato's Hellenistic successor, Polybius, who, in the sixth book of *The Histories,* similarly articulates three historical forms of governance (monarchy, aristocracy, and democracy), along with their three "*parekbaseis,* or deviant forms" (tyranny, oligarchy, and mob rule).[78] However, Polybius's model—which, as we shall see shortly, is modeled in part on Plato's *Statesman*—is even more a closed cyclical one, each form invariably giving rise to the next, and thus the only potential way to arrest this cycle lies in a form of constitution that would be a mixture of these three historical types (hence, Polybius's deep influence on the development of the U.S. constitutional system).[79] This Greimasian representation makes evident the fact that Badiou's hypertranslation offers a double reading of Plato's text homologous to my reading of the New Criticism, both accounting for the narrative's particular historical situatedness and its universal truth content.

The historical situation of Plato's *Republic* is of such deep interest here precisely because of its parallels with our own. Such a link is suggested by another book contemporaneous with Badiou's hypertranslation, Bettany Hughes's *The Hemlock Cup: Socrates, Athens, and the Search for the Good Life* (2010). Hughes underscores the fact that Socrates's trial and execution correspond with a deep and ultimately fatal crisis in the Athenian polis: "Yet many Athenians were, in fact,

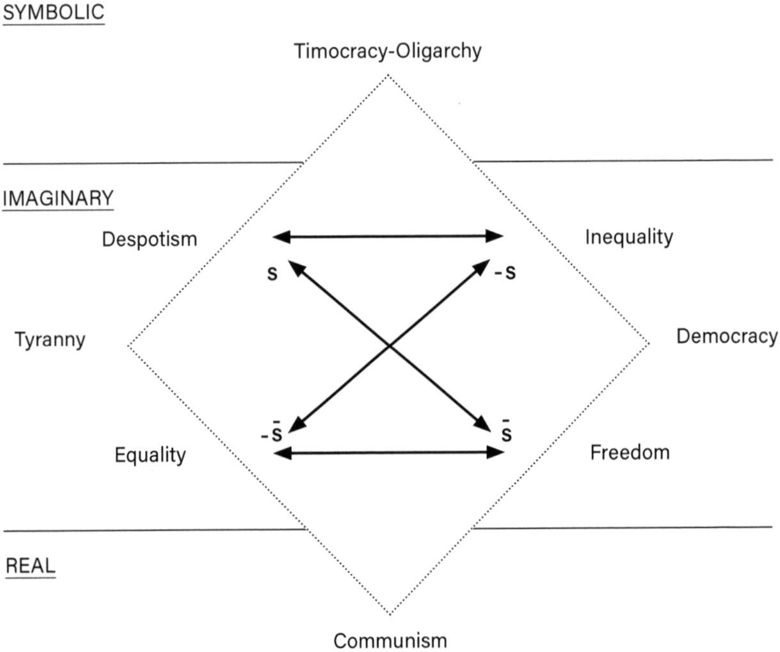

FIGURE 6

troubled by articulate people-power. In a full democracy, citizen status and influence are not dependent upon social or economic standing or education or talent or virtue; the bigoted, the mildly crazed, the vindictive also have their say. A direct democracy is ideologically perfect and in practice, flawed. Why believe that the outcome of a political process will be communal order and justice?"[80] Later in her book, Hughes further points out:

> When the democracy was developing and expanding, it was bullish, confident it could cope with Socrates' eternal questions. . . . But now, after two decades of battle, after plague, after five years of civil strife, this high-handed, apparently self-indulgent questioning must have seemed intolerable. . . . All of civilization's darkest hours have been bayed on by men who want scapegoats, who want the finger of blame to turn in any

> direction, as long as it is away from their own face. Loose, jealous tongues are the bane of history.[81]

In a similar vein, Joan Breton Connelly notes:

> Under a common autochthonous origin, even the lowliest citizen was of noble birth and, therefore, superior to any noncitizen. This was especially important in a cosmopolitan city like Athens where the population of outsiders was ever growing. . . . Athenians believed themselves superior to everyone else, in the Greek world and beyond, and looked upon outsiders—fish eaters and abstainers alike—with a measure of contempt. The irony, perhaps, from our perspective at least, is that such chauvinism was the lifeblood of their notion of democracy.[82]

In these passages, the parallels become apparent between the situations of Plato's Athens, the World War context that gave rise to the New Criticism along with the continental movements of critical theory and structuralism, and our own global reality, with its neonationalist chauvinism and belligerent conservative populism. The final connection between Socrates's moment and our own is made explicit in the introductions to two 2009 translations of plays by one of Socrates's great contemporaries, Euripides. Anne Carson writes, "Another serious way to read a play like *Orestes* is as an indictment of the age and society in which the playwright lived. His was a time of constant warfare, imperialist greed and astonishing political corruption, rather like our own."[83] And Peter Burian observes, "*Trojan Women* gains special relevance, of course, in times of war. Today, we seem to need this play more than ever."[84]

At the same time, however, Reinhard points out that the hypertranslation expresses Badiou's "fidelity to Plato. . . . Badiou's translation of the *Republic* is faithful to the event that 'Plato' names—the origin of philosophy itself in its antagonism to sophistry and rivalry with poetry—more than it is to Plato's text as a historical document."[85] Reinhard continues, "Badiou's hypertranslation lifts the *Republic* out of the cave of 'Platonism' precisely through its fidelity to the Platonic idea, to that which, we might say, to continue our Lacanian terminology, is 'in Plato more than Plato.'"[86] Badiou's hypertranslation thus needs to be understood as a deeply interested, creative reading of Plato's text, one aimed at conveying to the reader an experience of its truth, rather than an effort simply to communicate what the text has to say. This creative reading strategy requires Badiou to write Plato's text anew, something I have also undertaken here in my exposition of the work of the New Critics.

Such a creative rewriting strategy is most dramatically on display in Badiou's replacement of the conventional names given to Plato's ideal form of the republic—the aristocratic regime of the politically educated and cultivated philosopher-kings or state guardians—with that of *communism*. Reinhard further maintains that this is a manifestation of the key operation of universalization unfolding in the hypertranslation:

> Whereas philosophy is apparently reserved for a select group of "guardians" of the state in the *Republic*, for Badiou this restriction is not essential to Plato's thinking, but merely a function of his historical situation and of his tendency to suture philosophical ideas to their political conditions. Indeed, the philosophical temperament is aristocratic, "exceptional," but Badiou insists that there is nothing to prevent it from being a *universal* exception, open in principle to all.[87]

A similar universalization of Plato's text takes place in Jo Walton's marvelous Thessaly trilogy (*The Just City* [2015], *The Philosopher Kings* [2015], and *Necessity* [2016]), when, we are told, Plato "'could imagine humans who grew up in a Just City, but he could not imagine what it would be like for either Workers or gods,' I said. 'But we all have souls that yearn for excellence and justice.'"[88] What I find most striking about Reinhard's formulation is the resonances it suggests between Badiou's and Walton's operation of universalizing the truth of Plato's text, opening it to all exceptional temperaments or souls (that is, all souls), and the reading forced by my Greimasian formalization of the New Critical narrative: all three creative readings, or rewritings, of these texts are hypertranslations, a recovery of truth enmeshed within local, historical particularities.

This presentation also helps clarify Badiou's too often misunderstood observations concerning neoliberal parliamentary democracies, or what he names the practices of democratic materialism, whose fundamental axiom is "There are only bodies and languages."[89] What is at stake in Badiou's critique becomes more evident when we return to the double reading I offered in the beginning of this chapter of the Acropolis tour guide's adaptation of Plato's schema, which I presented through two radically different writings, or Greimasian formalizations. (As the New Critics would have it, the guide's "intention" becomes irrelevant, as both readings are immanent in his text itself, thereby making any singular reading, to use de Man's term, "undecidable."[90]) If democracy occupies the fullness of the complex term, then it is decidedly an ideological notion, an imaginary resolution to a real contradiction, a mythology, in Roland Barthes's sense, or what Badiou calls an emblem, "the 'untouchable' in a symbolic system."[91] If, however, it occupies the "absolute formalist" place of Greimas's neutral or Lacan's real, then it becomes the name of the void of our current situation, as well as an expression of a fidelity to a truth, call it radical democracy or communism—"if veracity touches on language (in the most general sense of the term), truth only exists insofar as it is indifferent to the latter"—that is still to come.[92] Thus, Badiou elsewhere can write, "we can go right back to the literal meaning of democracy if we like: the power of peoples over their own existence. Politics immanent in the people and the withering away, in open process, of the State. From that perspective, we will only ever be true democrats, integral to the historical life of peoples, when we become communists again."[93] Moreover, the radical democracy theorized by the tour guide and the communism of Badiou's hypertranslation occupy the same place in the square as the truth condition of love; and thus, it should come as no surprise that Badiou also characterizes love as *minimal communism*: "love is communist in that sense, if one accepts, as I do, that the real subject of love is the becoming of the couple and not the mere satisfaction of the individuals that are its component parts."[94] Finally, in both Plato's text as rewritten by Badiou's hypertranslation and in my re-presentation of the New Criticism, the road to the ideal state, decidedly not a royal one, occurs through a rigorous education motivated first and foremost by the interests of collective political rather than individual economic goods.

A similar radical rethinking of the notion of democracy in the context of early Greek philosophy is at work in Kojin Karatani's brilliant *Isonomia and the Origins of Philosophy,* originally published in Japan in the same year as Badiou's hypertranslation. Karatani recovers in

Socrates's words a radical strain of political *isonomia* (equal-rule or, in Karatani's terms, no-rule) derived from the thought and political realities of the Ionian cities. This tendency is then covered over when Plato puts into Socrates's mouth the notion of the philosopher-king. (The character of Socrates in Walton's Thessaly trilogy is also quite critical of the ideas his former student attributes to him: "Nothing in the *Republic* is anything I ever said, or thought, or dreamed. The *Apology* is fairly accurate, as is the account of the drinking party after Agathon's first victory at the Dionysia. But even there Plato was inclined to let his imagination get the better of him."[95]) The latter, Karatani argues, "comes from Pythagoras and has little to do with Socrates," especially the mind-body dualism characteristic of the thought of the former.[96] Karatani maintains:

> Pythagoras had come to reject democracy because of his bitter experience witnessing democracy transform into tyranny. Yet he did not abandon the principle of isonomia itself. He did, however, come to the conclusion that the path lay not in democracy but in the rule of the philosopher. As a result, his pursuit of isonomia ended in the political form in a sense most antithetical to isonomia, and in a philosophy most antithetical to natural philosophy.[97]

Karatani's creative reading has the advantage of underscoring the closed structural dialectic at work in Plato's political notions as developed in both the *Republic* and *Statesman*: "In the *Statesman,* Plato divides government into six possible forms. First is the division into three forms: rule by one, rule by few, and rule by the many. Within each of these forms then is distinguished a favorable form in which the rule of law is upheld, and a corrupted form in which law is scorned." The "rule by the philosopher-king" is then conceived as "a seventh possibility beyond these six," but one that, in fact, recapitulates the implicit or explicit despotisms of the historical forms.[98] Karatani further maintains that both Socrates and Plato were equally "critical of democracy" as it was practiced in the Athenian polis. However, Socrates's "reasoning differs from Plato. Subsequent to the reforms of Solon, the Athenian people came into the contact with the Ionian spirit of isonomia (no-rule), but in reality settled on the degraded form of isonomia called democracy (rule of the many), a form constrained by the distinctions of public and private, and spiritual and manual labor. Socrates's aim was to dismantle the dual world of public and private existence that served as the premise of Athenian democracy. This meant nothing other than the restoration of isonomia."[99] Karatani produces a fourfold schema of forms of governance—two historical forms, in tyranny and democracy, and two as of yet "non-existent," in the rule of philosopher-kings and isonomia—that, with some adjustment, corresponds to the Greimasian presentations we have been developing throughout this chapter. (See Figure 7.) Finally, in a subsequent footnote critiquing Karl Popper's Cold War and anti-Utopian ideological notion of the "open society," Karatani defines isonomia in a way that immediately resonates with Badiou's renewed figure of communism:

> However, what Popper presents as isonomia is not worthy of the name. It is similar to Athenian democracy, or more to American liberal democracy. Here people are equal under the law but unequal economically. Consequently, democracy (rule by the many) consists in the majority taking power and dissipating inequality by redistribution. By contrast, isonomia indicates a system in which all are not merely equal under the law, but conditions are such that economic divisions also do not arise.[100]

Badiou's Plato, Karatani's Socrates, and my New Critics are understood to draw upon the hard experience of the catastrophes of their recent pasts and come to recognize tyranny and historical democracy, or the intentional and affective fallacies, or the reigns of authority and opinion (or our tour guide's dictatorship and anarchy, or Deneen's classical and progressive liberalisms), as two faces of the same coin. The symbolic order in all three cases remains one dominated by an elite—in our global present, this takes the form of the financial, bureaucratic, and technocratic oligarchies of the neoliberal states, what Bertram Gross perspicaciously termed more than three decades ago "friendly fascism."[101] Finally, and perhaps most chillingly of all, Badiou's narrative gives expression to what invariably occurs when in a reputedly

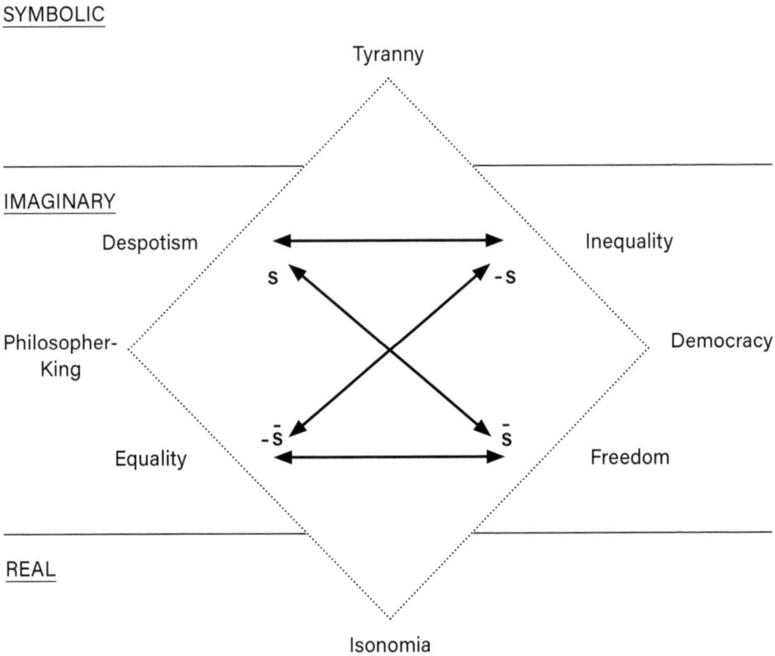

FIGURE 7

democratic state education is allowed to be refunctioned from a dual good, at once political and economic, to an exclusively economic one:

> The first symptom of decline will be the emergence of a broad current of public opinion favoring spectacular games, the idolization of sports, the sexual misadventures of celebrities, and TV shows for ignorant viewers, to the detriment of everything that belongs to thought: deductive and experimental sciences, intense loves, egalitarian political organization, the shifting of the dividing line between the formal and the formless in art, and so forth. Future generations will acquire a taste for instant gratification, superficial trivialities and the listless cult of non-being. On this subjective breeding ground will bloom the showy, artificial flowers of proudly proclaiming dissimilarity, of minor self-centered differences, of discord at once furtive and passion-

> ate, and ultimately of the desire for the most abject inequality to take root. (*PR*, 251)

> —And it's then, I think, that a charismatic leader will make his appearance, right?
>
> —He's the man of the hour. The motley conglomeration of the corrupt middle classes and the deluded people will install as its leader some guy who was created out of nothing and whose power only comes from this alliance, against a backdrop of social unrest and fears. This creature of circumstance will declare himself to be "the nation's savior" and will combat conservative moderation, of course, but he will especially combat any independent popular organization whose aim is to unleash the people's political power and bring its scattered masses back together.
>
> —So is it this "savior," *asked Amantha,* who'll become a tyrant or a fascist leader?
>
> —Every time. (*PR*, 279)

> The fascist dictator is the opposite of the doctor. The doctor removes the worst from the individual body in order to save the best. The fascist works the other way around as far as the collective body is concerned: he eradicates the best to save the worst, which he rules over. (*PR*, 281)

> Tyranny is the solitude of the person who has lost the power to love and thus can only wield the sterile power to doom both himself and others to death. (*PR*, 290)

A bit later in the text, Badiou's original character of Amantha—she who, Reinhard observes, is "always pushing Socrates to extend his arguments to 'all people without exception'"[102]—queries the philosopher, "But what about the communist?" He replies, "I'd say he's the one whose glorious political energy is in the service of the passion for the True" (*PR*, 299). The challenge before us as teachers is to reconfirm our commitment to educational practices aimed at cultivating political goods and the passion for the True in those who will come after, lest the current "flood in which we have gone under" continues unabated.

[2]

Toward Non-reading *Utopia*

> Of course one thing above all is necessary in order to practice reading as an *art* to this extent, a skill that today has been unlearned best of all—which is why more time must pass for my writings to be "readable"—something for which it is almost necessary to be a cow and in any case not a "modern man": *rumination . . .*
>
> —Friedrich Nietzsche, *On the Genealogy of Morality*

> *J'avais (très) sincèrement promis d'être sérieux. Ai-je tenu ma promesse?*
>
> I promised (very) sincerely to be serious. Have I kept my promise?
>
> —Jacques Derrida, "Limited Inc a b c . . ."

> I knew what death meant now. It was conversations cut off.
>
> —Jo Walton, *The Philosopher Kings*

MY TITLE FOR THIS CHAPTER is taken from the influential postmodern American novelist Jay McInerney's conclusion to his *New York Times* review of the French psychoanalyst and literary scholar Pierre Bayard's beneficial and entertaining book *How to Talk about Books You Haven't Read* (2007). While McInerney confesses to being amused and even intrigued by what he describes as Bayard's "tongue-in-cheek example of reader-response criticism," he closes his review with the following note of caution:

> Bayard finally reveals his diabolical intent: he claims that talking about books you haven't read is "an authentic creative activity."

> As a teacher of literature, he seems to believe that his ultimate goal is to encourage creativity. "All education," he writes, "should strive to help those receiving it to gain enough freedom in relation to works of art to themselves become writers and artists."
>
> It's a charming but ultimately terrifying prospect—a world full of writers and artists. In Bayard's non-reading utopia the printing press would never have been invented, let alone penicillin or the MacBook.
>
> I seriously doubt that pretending to have read this book will boost your creativity. On the other hand, reading it may remind you why you love reading.[1]

While there is a good deal of mischievousness in McInerney's review as well, in the end, it tells us—indeed, as we shall see shortly, as Bayard claims it must—less about Bayard's book than it does about the review's author, in terms of both his personal and professional desires and anxieties and the collective myths in which he, perhaps, un-self-consciously participates.

At the center of McInerney's review is the claim that Bayard advocates "pretending" to have read books we have not. Indeed, McInerney further cautions his reader, "And make no mistake about it, this prof is far more literate and widely read than he pretends to be." However, in order to be able to pretend to do or not do something, we assume we have a clear notion of exactly what it means to do, or not do, that thing: in this case, to read or not-to-read a book. It is precisely to such unspoken presuppositions concerning reading that Bayard mounts throughout his study a careful and pointed challenge.

Bayard begins by dispensing with the common sense binary of reading and not-reading—and like all such binaries, as readers from Nietzsche to Derrida and Jameson remind us, the two terms stand in an implicit hierarchical relationship, reading understood as the good, as virtue, and not-reading as evil, an indicator of our squalid, torpid, and perhaps truer natures. (I will return again to the question of the ethical binary in our reading practices in the next chapter.) In the place vacated by the deconstructed binary of reading and not-reading, Bayard then introduces what Derrida would call his *arche* notion—that which "cannot, as the condition of all linguistic systems, form a part of the linguistic system itself, be situated as an object in its field"—that of *non-reading*.[2] In his opening chapter, Bayard advances the absolute presupposition or axiom underlying his project: all "reading is first and foremost non-reading" ("La lecture est d'abord la non-lecture").[3] Non-reading thus very quickly comes to encompasses a more wide-ranging and varied set of relationships to those books we have already encountered, or even those of which we remain only dimly aware.

Early on, Bayard suggests that these relationships can be characterized in one of three ways: "books we've skimmed, books we've heard about, and books we've forgotten" (*HT,* xix). Reading unfolds in time—and as artistic practices such as Cubism and early cinema remind us, even the act of looking at an image is a reading practice. (The radical alterity of a truly spatial reading is one of the central themes of Ted Chiang's remarkable narrative "Story of Your Life" [1998].) For this reason, each of Bayard's categories of books also occupies a different place in time. The second category, books we have heard about, are those for which our actual encounter still stands before us, in the future:

> Besides actually reading a book, there is, after all, another way to develop quite a clear sense of its contents: we can read or listen to what others write or say about it. . . . This is, in fact, the extent to which we have access to most books, most of the time. Many of the books we are led to talk about, and which have, in certain cases, played important roles in our lives, have never actually passed through our hands (although we may sometimes be convinced of the contrary). (*HT,* 32–33)

Forgetting, however, is what begins the instant our encounter with a book—or even a page of a book, or a sentence, phrase, or word on it—begins to recede into the past. Bayard later maintains, "We do not retain in memory complete books identical to the books remembered by everyone else, but rather fragments surviving from partial readings, frequently fused together and further recast by our private fantasies" (56).

Thus, skimming—the halting, distracted, and inevitably partial focus on a book that even the most attentive reading will involve—is Bayard's term for the ineffable present moment of our encounter with a book, or any part of it:

> When we have a book in our hands, it is rare that we read it from cover to cover, assuming such a feat is possible at all. Most of the time, we do with books what Valéry recommends doing with Proust: we skim them. . . . But the fertility of this mode of discovery markedly unsettles the difference between reading and non-reading, or even the idea of reading at all. . . . It appears that most often, at least for the books that are central to our particular culture, our behavior inhabits some intermediate territory, to the point that it becomes difficult to judge whether we have read them or not. (*HT,* 29–30)

A corollary to Bayard's initial axiom thus would read, "All non-reading is skimming." In the end, Bayard points out, all non-readings are "reconstructions of originals that lie so deeply buried beneath our words and the words of others that, even were we prepared to risk our lives, we stand little chance of ever finding them within reach" (46). In this regard, Bayard recalls one of the opening axioms or absolute presuppositions of Jameson's *The Political Unconscious: Narrative as a Socially Symbolic Act* (1981): "We never really confront a text immediately, in all its freshness as a thing-in-itself. Rather, [all] texts come before us as the always-already-read: we apprehend them through sedimented layers of previous interpretations, or—if the text is brand-new—through the sedimented reading habits and categories developed by those inherited interpretive traditions."[4] This then leads Jameson to further posit an alternative method of non-reading he terms "metacommentary . . . according to which our object of study is less the text itself than the interpretations through which we attempt to confront and to appropriate it."[5]

Finally, only those books—and for everyone there remains a well-nigh infinity of these as well—we have neither heard of nor encountered should be placed in the final category of the *not*-read: "Even in the case of the most passionate lifelong readers, the act of picking up and opening a book masks the countergesture that occurs at the same time: the involuntary act of *not* picking up and *not* opening all the other books in the universe" (*HT,* 6). It is these books that guarantee the nonclosure of the set of all "books." However, even these not-read books can be talked about if they are understood to be part of a larger *collective library*: "It is our mastery of this collective library that is at stake in all discussions about books. But this mastery is a command of relations, not of any book in isolation, and it easily accommodates ignorance of a large part of the whole" (12). The relationships between the four terms in Bayard's schema—heard about and forgotten, skimmed and not-read—can be re-presented through a Greimasian semiotic square, which would appear as in Figure 8.

In his subsequent chapters, Bayard draws deeply upon a wide-ranging non-reading of world literature—including fiction and essays by, among others, Michel de Montaigne, Honoré de Balzac, Oscar Wilde, Marcel Proust, Natsume Sōseki, Paul Valéry, Graham Greene, Umberto Eco, David Lodge, and Pierre Siniac. Bayard does so to illustrate and expand upon his initial thesis and to remind us that non-reading and talking about are activities we perform with all kinds of texts, including films—as we shall see shortly, Harold Ramis's *Groundhog Day* (1993)

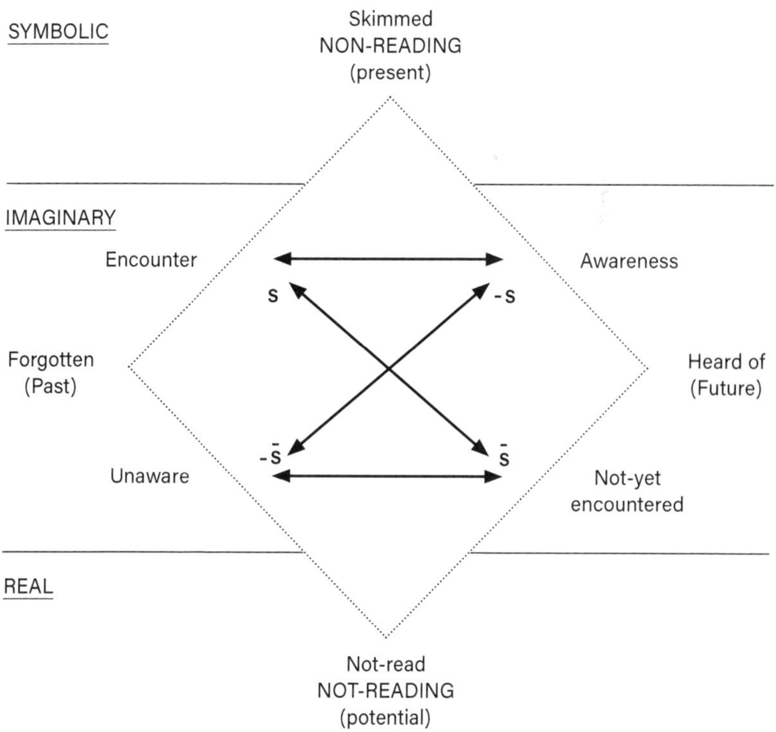

FIGURE 8

occupies a place of privilege in his overall argument—and even with those people we encounter every day, especially those with whom we are most intimately acquainted.

Throughout, Bayard indicates his own relationship to books with a simple code system: "The four abbreviations used will be explained in the first four chapters. UB designates books unknown to me; SB, books I have skimmed; HB, books I have heard of; FB, books I have forgotten. . . . These abbreviations are not mutually exclusive. An indication is given for every book title, and only at its first mention" (*HT,* xxn1). One of the great pleasures of Bayard's book lies in its encouragement to both non-read books we have now heard of but have not yet encountered—in my case, for example, Pierre Siniac's mystery *Ferdinaud Céline* (1997), translated in 2010 under the title *The Collaborators*—and to return anew to those we skimmed in the past and have subsequently forgotten—Lodge's *Small World,* a book published the same year, 1984, as McInerney's deeply influential *Bright Lights, Big City* and that together can be understood as forming part of the collective library of that monumentally significant year.

If all one ever does is non-read—I no less than McInerney am a non-reader of *How to Talk about Books You Haven't Read*—then any communication we offer of a book, verbal, written, or otherwise, is a local and deeply contingent act of creatively *writing* that book; this is the case even if such a writing takes place in our head and only for the audience of our future selves. Such a collapsing together of reading and writing is literalized in Charles Yu's brilliant metafictional novel *How to Live Safely in a Science Fictional Universe* (2010) (SB, FB):

> And so I'm reading this book and somehow in act of reading it, I am, with the help of TOAD and TAMMY, creating a copy of it, in a very real sense I'm generating a new version, actually, that is being simultaneously written into and stored in TAMMY's memory banks. In doing this, I am making the book my own, in retyping a book that already exists in the future, producing the very book I will eventually write. I am transcribing a book that I have, in a sense, not yet written, and in another sense, have always written, and in another sense, am currently writing, and in another sense, am always writing, and in another sense, will never write.[6]

Bayard notes in his final pages that his goal has been to show his readers "that a book is reinvented with every reading"; arriving at this knowledge, he hopes, will aid them "in overcoming their fear of culture, and in daring to leave it behind to begin to write" (*HT,* 184, 185).

Bayard maintains, in a way that recalls the New Critics' ban I discussed in the previous chapter on the intentional fallacy, that among a book's readers is the author, and "an author is in no position to explain his own work" (*HT,* 16). Thus, Bayard concludes, following Flaubert's lead, that a book is to any of these readers as the "real world" is to the fiction writer, an excuse for the exercise of the craft of writing:

> Though Flaubert's work is often called "realist," literature for him was autonomous in relation to the world and obeyed its own rules. Art had no need to concern itself with reality, even if it remained in the background, and was to find its own coherence in itself. . . . The critical text is no more *about* the work than the novel, according to Flaubert, is about reality. (175)

Non-reading stresses the deep, active creativity involved in all reading of, as well all talking and writing about, books. This notion thus shifts our attention away from the impossible goal of giving an accurate account of the singular truth of a book—that is, the fantasy of an objective, disinterested reading—and toward a heightened awareness of the specific and local aims and interests we always have in mind, consciously or not, when we engage in any particular activity of non-reading. Bayard writes, "In truth, readers and non-readers alike [and again, for Bayard, they are not only alike but identical] are caught up in an endless process of inventing books, whether they like it or not, and the real question is not how to escape that process, but how to increase its dynamism and range" (157).

This is by no means to suggest that all non-readings are equal: people make their own readings, but they do not make them in circumstances of their own choosing. This recognition shifts the criteria for evaluating any particular non-reading from its truthfulness in re-presenting the book in question to the success, or limitations, encountered in enacting the specific aims of its reading in its particular situation. The effect, as throughout the deconstructive project of Derrida, is not to destroy or even contest "the value of truth" but rather to reinscribe it "in more powerful, larger, more stratified contexts. . . . Within interpretive contexts (that is, within relations of force that are always differential—for example, socio-political-institutional—but even beyond these determinations) that are relatively stable, sometimes apparently almost unshakeable, it should be possible to invoke rules of competence, criteria of discussion and of consensus, good faith, lucidity, rigor, criticism, and pedagogy."[7] This is precisely the situation I articulated in the previous chapter in terms of the event of the New Criticism: what occurs is a making explicit and calling into question of the dominant and even naturalized rules of competence for reading, followed by the articulation of a new set, a not insignificant consequence of which, they believed, is to foster an environment hospitable to democratic engagement. Subsequent theories then "resist," in Paul de Man's specific sense, the conclusions of the New Criticism: not rejecting them out of hand, as would a moralizing ethical criticism, but rather forcing them in turn into new, more powerful, larger, more stratified contexts.

McInerney also observes a kinship of Bayard's claims with those of both Derrida and Stanley Fish, especially in terms of the latter's groundbreaking formulation of the notion of "interpretive communities." Fish maintains, "interpretive strategies are not put into execution after reading (the pure act of perception in which I do not believe); they are the shape of reading, and because they are the shape of reading, they give texts their shape, making them rather than, as it is usually assumed, arising from them. . . . either decision would give rise to a set of interpretive strategies, which, when put into action, would *write* the text I write when reading."[8] A little further on, Fish explicitly states, "Interpretive communities are made up of those who share interpretive strategies not for reading (in the conventional sense), but for writing texts, for constituting their properties and assigning their intentions."[9] More recently, Derrida's former student Catherine Malabou makes similar claims in developing her Hegelian concept of *plastic reading*: "Plastic reading accords a determinative and decisive role to the subjectivity of the reader, the reader having become the author of the enunciation. The reader rewrites what he or she reads. . . . The speculative proposition checks our confidence in 'knowing how to read,' thus training the reader in an illiteracy of the second power which will make the reader write what he or she reads."[10]

All of these non-readers would thus reject Roland Barthes's distinction between what he defines as writerly (*scriptible*) and readerly (*lisible*) texts:

> Why is the writerly our value? Because the goal of literary work (of literature as work) is to make the reader no longer a consumer, but a producer of the text. . . . Opposite the writerly text, then, is its countervalue, its negative, reactive value: what can be read, but not written: the *readerly*. We call any readerly text a classic text.[11]

This is because for these other readers all texts are writerly: the difference Barthes articulates here lies in the fact that some texts, particularly the modernist ones of such interest to him, foreground, in an estranging manner, rather than mask, as is usually the case, exactly this fact.[12] Equally significantly, Barthes's concept of the writerly text shares with Bayard's, Fish's, and Malabou's notions of non-reading-as-writing a challenge to the myth of reading as a private, isolated, individual act: that is, if all non-reading (all reading) is the writing of texts, then all non-reading is collective, an interaction between the self and others—even if that other is our own self at another moment to come.

Bayard's central goal is thus to abolish the long-standing, internalized, and naturalized ethical hierarchy between writing and reading—a hierarchy again at work in the mythic notion of "creative writing," presupposing as it does the inferior "not-creativity" or not-productivity of other acts of writing/reading. Barthes's earlier comments in his *Mythologies* entry, "Neither/Nor Criticism," still has a great deal to teach us in this regard: "But, with all respect to our *Neither/Nor* critics, ever the adepts of a bipartite universe of which they would constitute the divine transcendence, the opposite of *good writing* is not necessarily *bad writing*: nowadays it is perhaps just *writing*."[13] It is this challenge thrown down to an entrenched status quo that someone like McInerney—a student of the short fiction writer Raymond Carver and a product of a specific institutional context Mark McGurl defines as the "program era" in American literature—finds threatening.[14] Early on in his review, McInerney expresses his discomfort with the fact that a book like Bayard's "would hit the best-seller lists in France, where books are still regarded as sacred objects and the writer [meaning of course, people like McInerney himself] occupies a social position somewhere between the priest and the rock star." This sense of menace represented by Bayard's study to McInerney's understanding of how the world should work accounts for the particular way the latter non-reads—that is, writes creatively about—the particular book *How to Talk about Books You Haven't Read.*

Bayard makes explicit in his manifesto-like epilogue the deep utopian impulse at the heart of his project and to which McInerney refers. Bayard proclaims, "We must profoundly transform our relationship to books," and then continues:

> To begin with, such an evolution implies extricating ourselves from a whole series of mostly unconscious taboos that burden our notion of books. Encouraged from our school years onward to think of books as untouchable objects, we feel guilty at the very thought of subjecting them to transformation.
>
> It is necessary to lift these taboos to begin to truly listen to the infinitely mobile object that is a literary text. The text's mobility is enhanced whenever it participates in a conversation or a written exchange, where it is animated by the subjectivity of each reader and his dialogue with others, and to genuinely listen to it implies developing a particular sensitivity to all the possibilities that the book takes on in such circumstances. (*HT,* 181)

McInerney's lack of a willingness to "listen" to the possibilities that Bayard's book makes available is by no means unique and has even been expressed by some teachers of literature. Indeed, in a review contemporary with McInerney's, one member of the latter tribe declares, "As a dyed-in-the-wool, first-page-to-last reader, I could not disagree more with Bayard's theses." However, this non-reader adds, "I have been amused, bemused, and invigorated by this book, despite the sense that the joke, inevitably, is on me. It is smart, funny, insightful, and harrowing, by turn."[15] Other non-readers share McInerney's assumption that Bayard really cannot be serious: for example, in *The Guardian,* Toby Lichtig opines, "Bayard's tone is relentlessly tongue in cheek; it rests on the supposition that what he is saying is very naughty."[16] Even one of the readers of the manuscript of my book described Bayard's theory as "bizarre."

One of the things I find most interesting about these non-readings of *How to Talk about Books You Haven't Read* is their uncanny resemblance to the long history of non-reading that has taken place in the case of the very first utopia: Thomas More's 1516 *De Optimo Reipublicae Statu Deque noua insula Utopia libellus uere aureus, nec minus salutaris quam festiuus,* translated in the standard Yale edition as *The Best State of a Commonwealth and the New Island of Utopia, A Truly Golden Handbook, No Less Beneficial than Entertaining.* Based on my own now nearly three-decade-long history of non-reading—hearing about, skimming, and forgetting—I would claim that these responses can be divided into two broad camps. On the one hand, we have those non-readers who begin with the assumption that More is fully serious in his intent in the book (but how do we know someone is being serious: Am I being serious? "You can take my word for it").[17] It is on this presupposition that they proceed to non-read and either celebrate or, perhaps more commonly, especially in the last century or so, critically condemn the book. On the other hand, we have those who assume that More is far too intelligent to have been serious ("All this remains forever in doubt"[18]), and hence the work should be understood as a satire, making the narrator, Raphael Hythlodaeus, into what the commonly accepted translation of his surname holds to be a speaker of "cunning or skilled nonsense." (I am more partial, for reasons that will become clear shortly, to an alternate translation I recently encountered in the pages of *Moreana,* "Hostile to, destructive of nonsense.")[19]

Some of the most effective or creative non-readings of *Utopia*—that is, those I still find the most useful for what I would prefer to do—straddle both camps. For example, Louis Marin, in his brilliant structuralist and semiological study *Utopiques: jeux d'espaces* (1973), non-reads More's "speaking picture" as a figure of a reality then only beginning to emerge in England and Europe and thus "not yet having found its concept."[20] Similarly, Robert C. Elliott, in his golden little book *The Shape of Utopia* (1970)—a work that influenced Elliott's colleagues at UC, San Diego, Marin and Jameson, along with Elliott's and Jameson's student, Kim Stanley Robinson—maintains that the genre of utopia finds its origins in ancient Saturnalian festivals and thus brings together both the powers of imagining a redeemed other world and of satire. Crucially, according to Elliott, the satire in these texts is directed not at the utopian world, as is too often assumed, but rather at the conditions reigning in contemporary society: "Here are the two sides of [More's] *Utopia*: the negative, which exposes in a humorous way the evils affecting the social body; the positive, which provides a normative model to be imitated."[21] (I will take up Elliott's book again in chapter 7.) Non-readings of More's *Utopia,* especially as they move from a description of what the text formally does—Elliott issuing among the earliest calls for "an interpretation that will tell us what *Utopia* is, that will place it with respect to the literary conventions which give it form and control its meaning"[22]—to judgment of its contents, become examples of moralizing ethical non-reading or criticism that I discussed in my Introduction and in chapter 1, and will return to again in chapter 3.

Whatever judgments at which they arrive, however, all these non-readings share an absolute presupposition that they know what More's book is about, and this is because they have already located the utopia, the Optimo Reipublicae, presented in the text. This, they presume, is to be found in *Utopia*'s second book, where the loquacious and indefatigable traveler and storyteller, Raphael Hythlodaeus—not unlike Joseph Conrad's later Charles Marlow—elaborates in great detail to his audience—and especially the "privileged man" ("there was only one man of all these listeners who was ever to hear the last words of the story"),[23] Thomas More (Morus)—the modes of living in the distant island community in which he, again like Marlow, resided for an extended period. However, I want to suggest here that in this regard, as in so much else in More's golden handbook, the matter is not so clear cut, and we should entertain the possibility that the actual utopia of *Utopia* is to be found elsewhere.

The question of "the location of the island" of Utopia described in Book Two is raised early on in the text by one of More's very first non-readers, the Antwerp resident and fellow Renaissance humanist, Peter Giles:

> As to More's difficulty about the geographical position of the island, Raphael did not fail to mention even that, but in very few words and as it were in passing, as if reserving the topic for another place. But, somehow or other, an unlucky accident caused us both to fail to catch what he said. . . . I shall not rest, however, till I have full information on this point, so that I shall be able to tell you exactly not only the location of the island but even the longitude and latitude—provided that our friend Hythlodaeus be alive and safe.[24]

Later non-readers have taken up Giles's quest, resulting in some having "discovered" that Utopia is a real place, located either in the past—in, say, the Catholic monastery, which More had visited—or in the New World, of which More has heard and about which he then non-reads, or writes, in the imaginative fashion in which he does.[25] The link between non-reading, writing, and non-traveling is also explored in Bayard's sequel, *How to Talk about Places You've Never Been: On the Importance of Armchair Travel* (2016), where he offers the advice, "If you want to be able to talk about a place, the best thing to do is stay home."[26] Not unexpectedly, Bayard's more recent book contains its own four-part *combinatoire* of such practices of non-journeying: places you do not know, places others have talked about, places you have been through, and places you have forgotten. (See Figure 9.)

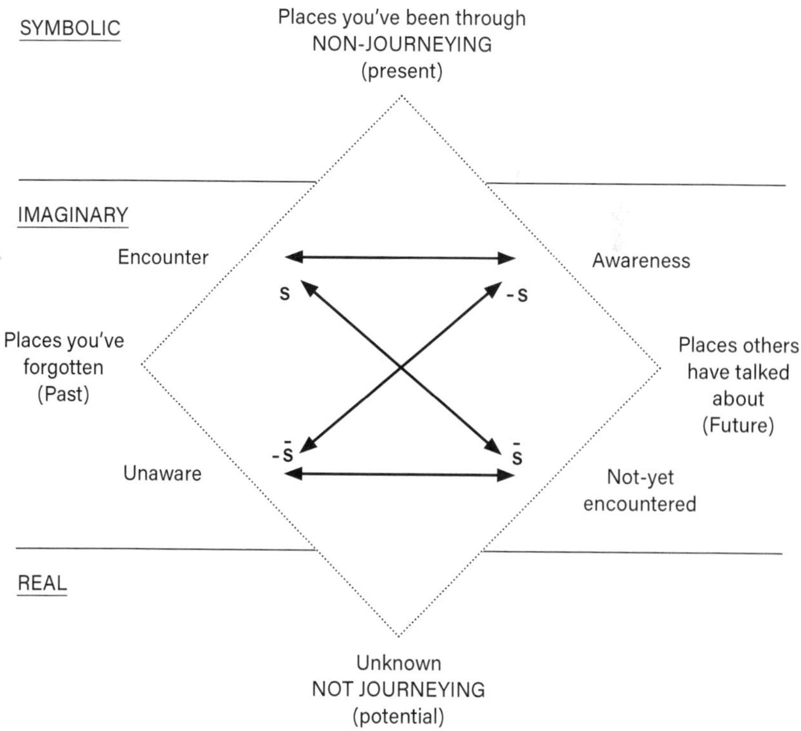

FIGURE 9

Numerous non-readers point out that More follows Plato's lead in presenting *Utopia* in the form of a dialogue. This is most clearly evident in *Utopia*'s first book, which includes, among other matters, a deeply contentious discussion of the responsibility of intellectuals in regard to the monarch and the state, and a devastating exchange, which also influenced Karl Marx in his stirring non-reading of *Utopia,* on the disruptive and violent processes of transformation then underway in England.[27] In his own influential non-reading of More's work, Stephen Greenblatt points out that this dialogue is "a literary set-piece," one of the mixture of genres (*genera mixta*) out of which More's original invention is composed. However, Greenblatt further notes:

> This debate . . . also represents a real and pressing problem, both in More's personal life and in his culture. There are periods in which the relation between intellectuals and power is redefined, in which the old forms have decayed and new forms have yet to be developed. The Renaissance was such a period: as intellectuals emerged from the Church into an independent lay status, they had to reconceive their relationship to power and particularly to the increasing power of the royal courts. For most, not surprisingly, this simply meant an eager, blind rush into the service of the prince; as Hamlet says of Rosencranz and Guildenstern, they did not make love to this employment.[28]

Of course, to take up a theme raised in my previous chapter, the late 1970s in which Greenblatt is writing is another such moment when "the relation between intellectuals and power is redefined," as we move from the radical experimentation of the 1960s into the new institutional situation of the 1980s—and once again, not surprisingly, many would eagerly embrace service to new princes; as Hamlet further notes of Rosencranz and Guildenstern, their defeat does by their own insinuation grow.

More ends Book One in this fashion: "Peter Giles and I urged Raphael to fulfill his promise. As for him, when he saw us intent and eager to listen, after sitting in silent thought for a time, he began his tale as follows" (*U,* 109). The give and take of the dialogue fades throughout much of *Utopia*'s second book, the other voices growing silent as his interlocutors apparently listen deeply to how Hythlodaeus describes the history, appearance, customs, practices, and so forth he encountered on the island. It is only near the book's conclusion that these other voices reemerge. At this point, the character Thomas More addresses the book's non-reader directly: "When Raphael had finished his story, many things came to my mind which seemed very absurdly established in the customs and laws of the people described" (*U*, 245). In this assertion, he appears at first glance poised to set the stage for so many of the later non-readings of More's book and other subsequent utopias ("I could not disagree more with Bayard's theses"). However, shortly after this statement, More reconsiders his next act: "I knew, however, that he was wearied with his tale, and I was not quite certain that he could brook any opposition to his views, particularly when I recalled his censure of others on account of their fear that they might not appear to be wise enough, unless they found some fault to criticize in other men's discoveries" (*U*, 245).

More here recalls Hythlodaeus's observation in Book One:

> Among royal councilors everyone is actually so wise as to have no need of profiting by another's counsel, or everyone seems so wise in his own eyes as not to condescend to profit by it. . . . If anyone, when in the company of people who are jealous of others' discoveries or prefer their own, should propose something which he either has read of as done in other times or has seen done in other places, the listeners behave as if their whole reputation for wisdom were jeopardized and as if afterwards they would be though plain blockheads unless they could lay hold of something to find fault with in the discoveries of others. (*U*, 59)

Such a figure appears in the dialogue itself: "Even while I was saying these things, the lawyer had been busily preparing himself to reply and had determined to adopt the usual method of disputants who are more careful to repeat what has been said than to answer it" (*U*, 71). Not desiring to take up a place among such a company, More concludes: "I therefore praised their way of life and his speech and, taking him by the hand, led him in to supper. I first said, nevertheless, that there would be another chance to think about these matters more deeply and to talk them over with him more fully. If only this were some day possible!" (*U*, 245). (Bayard offers similar advice for when we encounter a book's first writer: "Praise it without going into detail. An author does not expect a rational analysis of his book and would even prefer you not attempt such a thing. He expects only that, while maintaining the greatest possible degree of ambiguity, you will tell him that you like what he wrote" [*HT,* 100].) The deep ambiguity and even wistfulness of what is being expressed by the character of More is made even more evident in the final clause of the original Latin: "quod utinam aliquando contingeret" (*U,* 244). This literally means "which would sometimes happen" and can also be translated as "wish that would happen" or "that will never happen." A world that might someday be possible, which one wishes for but fears will never come about: here More gives voice to the complex of desires and fears that will come to cluster in the coming five centuries around any vision of utopia.[29]

Based on my non-reading of these passages, I would like to suggest that the utopia in *Utopia* is to be found not in Utopia, the island figure presented in Book Two and through which More contributes, as I demonstrate in *Imaginary Communities,* to the development of the "imagined community" of the modern nation-state (a non-reading, I should add, to which I still very much hold).[30] Rather, utopia is to be located in *Utopia,* More's book itself, and most particularly in the figure of a dialogue it offers us. Christopher Kendrick suggests as much when he notes that at the end of Book Two, "What is clear is that the debate goes on, it is not over, at least as far as Morus is concerned, hoping as he does that the parties will have a chance to return to it on a later occasion. . . . In other words, from this angle Book II is but an episode in the debate begun and turned over in Book I."[31] The very form of the book itself is presented as a dialogue: prefacing and appended to More's two books are statements from some of the book's first non-readers, among which are included Thomas More himself. It is also significant to keep in mind that More composed Book Two and its description of Utopian life before he began to work on Book One, and hence all of Book One might be considered another non-reading of, or a dialogue with, Book Two. More thus departs from his teacher Plato, who expresses the deep anxiety that the written text by its very nature makes any such dialogue impossible:

> You know, Phaedrus, that's the strange thing about writing, which makes it truly analogous to painting. The painter's products stand before us as though they were alive: but if you ques-

> tion them, they maintain a most majestic silence. It's the same with written words: they seem to talk to you as though they were intelligent, but if you ask them anything about what they say, from a desire to be instructed, they go on telling you just the same thing for ever.[32]

Rather, for More, as much as for Bayard, every non-reading of a book or any part of it leads it to respond in a different way—if only we have ears trained to hear it. In presenting, in both form and content, a speaking picture of the utopia of dialogue, More takes up in his text the task of educating his non-reader's desire, in a way very similar to what occurs in Bayard's book, to develop such a practice: "If only this were some day possible!"

The notion of the pedagogical labors of utopia to "educate desire" was first formulated by the French political theorist Miguel Abensour in his 1973 doctoral thesis on the political writings of William Morris. However, the concept's wider circulation would begin three years later, by way of E. P. Thompson's 1976 postscript to the revised edition of his landmark study, originally published in 1955, *William Morris: Romantic to Revolutionary.* Citing positively Abensour's work, Thompson notes that the education of desire "is not the same as 'a moral education' towards a given end; it is, rather, to open a way to aspiration, to 'teach desire to desire, to desire better, to desire more, and above all to desire in a different way.' Morris's Utopianism, when it succeeds, liberates desire to an uninterrupted interrogation of our values and also to its own self-interrogation."[33] More recently, Jameson similarly maintains, "every utopia today must be a psychotherapy of anti-utopian fears and draw them out into the light of day, where the sad passions like blinded snakes writhe and twist in the open air. More than that, they must be indulged, for nothing cures a sad passion as fully as its passionate embrace, its wholehearted endorsement."[34]

Ruth Levitas axiomatizes Thompson's claim, underscoring the education of desire as a crucial function of all utopias:

> Utopia entails not just the fictional depiction of a better society, but the assertion of a radically different set of values; these values are communicated indirectly through their implications for a whole way of life in order for utopia to operate at the level of

> experience, not merely cognition, encouraging the sense that it does not have to be like this, it could be otherwise. . . . However, there is plainly no point in the education of desire for its own sake, and if the function of utopia is the education of desire, the function of the education of desire is the realization of utopia.[35]

If in all cases of desire, "we have an object, which is originally lost, which coincides with its own loss, which emerges as lost," then the education that takes place in all utopias is toward the recognition that the object that we have lost is, in fact, one we have not yet possessed—indeed, the fantasy that we did once possess it is at the root of contemporary right-wing populism: make America great *again*—and that it is in our power to bring into being.[36] Crucially, such an education of desire is an unending process: there will be no final realization of utopia, no end of history, no perfection to be realized, but rather a continuous reformulation of the object cause of desire pulling us forward.

The tremendous heuristic value of this axiom thus lies in the way it turns our non-readerly attention away from what Levitas calls the "blueprint" or representational aspects of utopian texts.[37] Abensour himself more recently notes that More "did not so much want to present his readers with 'the best form of government' as to invite them to look into the topic themselves—and hence the importance of dialogue—that is, to invite them to explore the question of what humanity would be like situated within wisely ordered cities, and the question of what a just and good political order would look like."[38] The concrete lived reality of such a transformed situation, as with the Badiouian event I discussed in the previous chapter—in short, utopia—cannot be represented, it can only be experienced. Of course, such an experience is impossible outside of this dramatically other reality. Thus, the utopian text attempts to bridge this gulf by presenting or figuring such a lived experience in order to encourage the reader to desire that it might some day be possible in their own lives. This is precisely what More accomplishes in his presentation of the utopian situation of authentic dialogue in both the form and content of *Utopia*. As we shall see in chapter 7, later utopias will undertake the education of desire through their presentation of the experiences in other aspects of the human condition.

Bayard also underscores the utopian labor of educating desire taking place in the unlikeliest of places, the popular adventure stories written by the nineteenth-century German author Karl May. Bayard argues that the image of the Western United States found in May's works "does not correspond to the real country he would have encountered had he traveled there in person. It corresponds to what this country potentially could be and effectively became, at least in part, a century later when the crimes the Indians were subjected to were recognized."[39] Bayard then concludes in a way that echoes Abensour: "The improvement Karl May subjected America's Wild West to does not occur exclusively in literature. The new stereotypes he helped create through the considerable success of his works imposed themselves little by little on the collective unconscious, notably through that extraordinary vehicle for transforming stereotypes, the western."[40] Jo Walton similarly already locates such a utopian process underway in Plato's dialogues: "I think he invited us all into the inquiry. Nobody reads Plato and agrees with everything. But nobody reads any of the dialogues without wanting to be there joining in. Everybody reads it and is drawn into the argument and the search for truth."[41]

To claim, as I am doing here, that More's *Utopia* presents a utopia of dialogue—and further, encourages the book's non-readers to work to create the conditions for such an experience in their own lives—leaves open the question of what constitutes such experience, especially if we accept Bayard's conclusions that all non-readings, all dialogues, are at best skimmings, forgotten soon on the heels of the ineffable moment of contact. To begin to answer this question, I would like to recall another unlikely utopian figure momentarily called into being in what many would take to be an otherwise deeply dystopian text: David Fincher's 1999 film adaptation of Chuck Palahniuk's novel *Fight Club* (1996).[42] In the scene in question, the film's unnamed protagonist, sometimes referred to as Jack (Edward Norton), an insurance adjuster for automobile manufacturers—his job is to determine whether it is cheaper to do a recall or simply pay the victims of mechanical-failure-caused crashes—has developed a severe case of depression and insomnia. Later, Jack discovers that by attending therapy sessions for those with terminal illnesses he learns to relax enough finally to sleep again. Jack actively participates with a wide variety of these groups, listening to their harrowing tales of pain, isolation, and loss and inventing some of his own to share with them; he goes along happily until weeks later when he discovers another person, Marla Singer (Helena Bonham Carter), who similarly engages in such exercises of apparent therapeutic deception. Her actions anger Jack tremendously, and he decides to confront Marla at the first opportunity that arises. It is during their initial encounter, as they embrace one another as part of their therapy, that the following exchange occurs:

> JACK: When people think you're dying, they really, really listen to you, instead of just . . .
>
> MARLA: . . . Instead of just waiting for their turn to speak.

The brilliance of this scene is that it figures for us utopia reduced to its most basic form. There can be no individual utopias; keep in mind, even alone—think of Thoreau at Walden Pond—you are in dialogue with others. *Fight Club*'s utopia thus takes the form of a dialogue that is about dialogue, and in it we encounter another attempt to educate our desire into a desire for such an experience. Another name for this minimal utopia, enacted, as we shall see in chapter 6, in the great utopian subgenre of the comedy of remarriage, is *love,* or what Alain Badiou characterizes in his dialogue *In Praise of Love* as *minimal communism.*[43]

All three of our utopias thus teach us that real dialogue, real love, involves two sides and a continuous changing of positions, between speaking—or, more broadly, communicating, including writing (books) and other practices in what Derrida refers to as "the general graphematic structure of every 'communication'"[44]—and the far more challenging and rarer practice of *listening.* Derrida further points out that it is precisely "those who claim ceaselessly to reinstate the classical ethics of proof, discussion, and exchange, [who] are most often those who excuse themselves from attentively reading and listening to the other . . . confounding science and chatter as though they had not the slightest taste for communication or rather as though they were afraid of it."[45] Derrida's observation underscores the ironic fact that it is his moralizing ethical critics rather than Derrida himself who, in their disregard of the classical protocols of reading and writing, help set the stage for the post-truth argumentative practices of someone like Trump and his supporters.

The utopian formulation of dialogue also has a deep kinship with the feminist theory of reading developed by Patrocinio P. Schweickart:

> Because each party must assimilate and interpret the utterances of the other, we still have the introjection of the subject-object division, as well as the possibility of hearing only what one wants to hear. But in a real conversation, the other person can interrupt, object to an erroneous interpretation, provide further explanations, change her mind, change the topic, or cut off conversation altogether. In reading, there are no comparable safeguards against the appropriation of the text by the reader. This is the second moment of the dialectic—the recognition that reading is necessarily subjective. The need to keep it from being totally subjective ushers in the third moment of the dialectic.[46]

Schweickart here also shed light on the deeply masculinist and patriarchal undercurrents of intentionalist (authorial) and opinion-based (affective) non-reading practices. Of course, as Bayard and Derrida would have it, what Schweickart describes here as the indispensable third moment of any dialectic of reading applies to all situations of communication, whether or not the presence of the speaker is available. Any communication risks such an appropriation by its recipient, and this is why the arduous cultivation of listening for an event, the possibility of what we may not already know, becomes so essential.

When non-read in conjunction with our other two utopian texts, this scene in *Fight Club* heightens our awareness of the practice of listening also foregrounded in them. Recall, for example, what we have already forgotten that Bayard writes in his epilogue: "It is necessary to lift these taboos to begin to truly *listen* to the infinitely mobile object that is a literary text. The text's mobility is enhanced whenever it participates in a conversation or a written exchange, where it is animated by the subjectivity of each [non-]reader and his *dialogue* with others, and to *genuinely listen* to it implies developing a particular sensitivity to all the possibilities that the book takes on in such circumstances" (*HT,* 181; emphasis added).

Similarly, bring to mind that in his scathing commentary on the closed-mindedness of too many royal councillors and other intellectuals, Hythlodaeus proclaims, "If anyone, when in the company of people who are jealous of others' discoveries or prefer their own, should propose something which he either has read of as done in other times or has seen done in other places, the *listeners* (*ibi qui audiunt*) behave as if their whole reputation for wisdom were jeopardized" (*U*, 58–59; emphasis added). Elsewhere in his dialogue, Hythlodaeus again raises the problem of listening: "to sum it all up, if I tried to obtrude these and like ideas on men strongly inclined to the opposite way of thinking, to what deaf ears should I tell the tale (*quam surdis essem narraturus fabulam*)!" (*U*, 96–97). Later, in direct contrast to the dystopia figured here by Hythlodaeus, the character of More remembers his beloved friend's earlier words—remembering, in whatever partial form, an indicator of listening having occurred. Moreover, More's sensitivity—that is, his listening—to his friend's current state leads him to decide to defer any premature engagement, waiting and hoping for another day when the opportunity will occur once more "to think about these matters more deeply and to talk them over with him more fully."

At the same time, the entirety of *Utopia* might be understood as a figuration of the utopian potential of listening, as More seems to have taken up the challenge he issues at the end of Book One and has listened to Hythlodaeus so closely, so deeply—at one point in Book One, Hythlodaeus himself proclaims, "Look, my dear More, with how lengthy a tale I have burdened you. I should have been quite ashamed to protract it if you had not eagerly called for it and seemed to listen (*sic uidereris audire*) as if you did not want any part of the conversation to be left out" (*U*, 84–85)—that he is able to recall, or repeat, in its entirety what the latter has said throughout their dialogue. Hythlodaeus's words here recall Byung-Chul Han's claim that "listening always precedes speaking; it is only listening that causes the other to speak. I am already listening before the Other speaks, or I listen so that the Other will speak."[47]

Of course, as everyone from Derrida and Deleuze to Žižek teaches us, repeating always involves "betrayals," happily, thereby making possible creative transformations. Similarly, Paul Goldberger's recent biography of Frank Gehry makes clear that such a listening is foundational to the architect's understanding of his own creative practice: "Couldn't an architect listen carefully to a client's needs, and then respond with an inventive, imaginative form that fulfilled those needs and at the same time brought joy and surprise? In other words, why couldn't creative shapes emerge out of discourse with clients, rather than be presented as if they had sprung full-blown from the architect's head?"[48]

Distinguishing him from the midcentury Los Angeles painters with whom he associated, Goldberger describes Gehry in a way that suggests his kinship with the non-reader theorized by Bayard: "He was a creator, but a creator who had to listen to his clients."[49]

Not surprising, listening turns out also to be an important characteristic of the people of Utopia: "In their devotion to mental study they are unwearied. When they had heard from us about the literature and learning of the Greeks . . . it was wonderful to see their extreme desire for permission to master them through our instruction" (*U*, 181). Abensour points out that for More "it is a matter of making his readers less into adepts at communism and more into Utopians whose intellects have been sharpened by reading."[50] But then might not those whose intellects have been sharpened by reading also in More's view, as it is in Badiou's Plato we discussed in the previous chapter, be on the road to becoming communists? Kendrick similarly notes, "The island's anti-philosophical philosophism, then, amounts to an answer as to what the new literacy means, or ought to mean, if it were properly instituted as a culture."[51] Mastery here should be understood as a listening that enables a repeating or creative writing of these texts in a way, not unlike what Badiou does for Plato's *Republic,* that their truth for the concrete situation of the Utopian people becomes most available.

In addition to being a teacher of literature, Bayard is also a practicing psychoanalyst, and, thus unsurprisingly, what he describes in his book as "non-reading" sounds very much like the practice of "deep listening" pioneered by Theodor Reik and others. In his classic book *Listening with the Third Ear: The Inner Experience of a Psychoanalyst* (1948), Reik maintains:

> The psychoanalyst who hopes to recognize the secret meaning of this almost imperceptible, imponderable language has to sharpen his sensitiveness to it, to increase his readiness to receive it. When he wants to decode it, he can do so only by listening sharply inside himself, by becoming aware of the subtle impressions it makes upon him and the fleeting thoughts and emotions it arouses in him.[52]

Like Bayard, Reik also stresses the deep importance of imagination and creativity in the process of listening or non-reading: "The psychologist who approaches this valuable field [the book that is the patient] as sober as a judge will not capture many data because he will also be as unimaginative as a judge. Only he who is fancy-free and opens all his senses to these impressions will be sensitive to the wealth he will encounter."[53] Reik then concludes his discussion with an acknowledgment, which is again akin to Bayard's and Hythlodaeus's warnings, of the immense challenges involved in such an activity. Recalling a case where he was long stuck at loggerheads until the fiancée of his patient observed what he had repeatedly overlooked, Reik notes:

> Experiences of this kind (I could tell many more) make us psychoanalysts modest about our psychological endowment—or should make us more modest. There was I, who thought myself a trained observer, and I did not recognize what was so obvious. "What is a trained observer?" I asked myself. He is a man [*sic*] who is trained to pay attention to certain things and to neglect others. He is a man who overpays attention to features he expects to see and remains in debt to others that escape his notice.[54]

Again, Reik, like Schweickart, draws our attention to the gendering of deep and not-listening.

In his early essay "Variations on the Standard Treatment" (1955), Jacques Lacan invokes affirmatively Reik's *Listening with the Third Ear*: "The facts rebel first at the level of analytic experience, where no one gives voice to their rebellion better than Theodor Reik."[55] A few years later, in his spring 1964 seminar, Lacan again observes that Reik "maintains that this third ear helps him to hear some voice or other that speaks to him in order to warn him of deceptions—he belongs to the good old days, the heroic days, when one was able to hear what was being said behind the deceptions of the patient."[56] A notion similar to Reik's listening with the third ear is at the heart of Lacan's recasting of psychoanalytic practice, especially in his later seminars where Lacan locates a "deep listening" (*l'écoute*) in the utopian practice of dialogue he names the "discourse of the analyst." Jameson points out in his pioneering 1977 essay on Lacan that the deep listening practiced by the analyst requires "some attention beyond the self or the ego, but one that may need to use those bracketed personal functions as instruments for hearing the Other's desire. The active and theoretical passivity, the rigorous and committed self-denial, of this final subject position, which acknowledges collective desire at the same moment that it tracks its spoors and traces, may well have lessons for cultural intellectuals as well as politicians and psychoanalysts."[57] Han also notes, "The responsible stance of the listener towards the Other expresses itself as *patience*. The *passivity of patience* is the first maxim of listening."[58] Let me only add that I am convinced few cultural intellectuals better exemplify the unity of theory and practice that is deep listening than Jameson himself, and thus there remains a great deal we stand to learn from attending to his ongoing project.

In a recent essay that also touches on the relationship between the four discourses and political action, Žižek further explains the criteria of success in such a practice of analysis or deep listening:

> In his (unpublished) Seminar on "a discourse which would not be that of a semblance," Lacan provided a succinct definition of the truth of interpretation in psychoanalysis: "Interpretation is not tested by a truth that would decide by yes or no, it unleashes truth as such. It is only true inasmuch as it is truly followed." There is nothing "theological" in this precise formulation, only an insight into the properly dialectical unity of a theory and practice in (not only) psychoanalytic interpretation: the "test" of the analyst's interpretation lies in the truth-effect it unleashes in the patient.[59]

This is precisely what occurs in the scene from *Fight Club* when Marla's words invoke from Jack a look of surprised recognition and the repeated affirmation, "Yeah . . . yeah." The second affirmation is crucial, as it marks the reordering of Jack's symbolic universe around such a truth. Indeed, as Lacan puts it in a 1972 talk at Sainte-Anne Hospital in Paris, "Obviously, repetition can only begin with the second time, which turns out to be the one that inaugurates the repetition. If it weren't for the second, there would be no first time."[60] (I will return to the issue of repetition in any act of symbolization in chapter 5.)

A similar notion of deep listening is also at work in the concrete utopia figured by one of the leading practitioners of "engaged spirituality" and one of the greatest living teachers of Buddhism, Thich Nhat Hanh.[61] In a chapter entitled "Deep Listening" in his book *Silence: The Power of Quiet in a World of Noise* (2015), Nhat Hanh observes:

> When we try to have a genuine conversation with someone, we find it difficult to hear and understand the other person. . . . Many couples who have been together for a long time . . . can't hear each other anymore. Sometimes one of the partners will say to me, "It's no use. She doesn't listen." Or "He won't ever change. Talking to him is like talking to a brick wall."[62]

A little later, Nhat Hanh points out, recalling to our ears the words of Hythlodaeus and Marla Singer, "When we give an immediate reply to someone, usually we are just reeling off our knowledge or reacting out of emotion. When we hear the other person's question or comment, we don't take the time to listen deeply and look deeply into what has been shared; we just volley back a quick rejoinder. That's not helpful."[63] Finally, in a parallel with Bayard, Nhat Hanh refers to real listening as a form of the *non-*, in this case, non-action: "Non-action is very important. It is not the same thing as passivity or inertia [not-action]; it's a dynamic and creative state of openness."[64] Nhat Hanh then concludes, "Having the space to listen with compassion is essential to being a true friend, a true colleague, a true parent, a true partner."[65] In short, without deep listening there is no possibility of the material and fundamentally human connection we refer to as love, Badiou's minimal communism.

In the *Fight Club* scene we listened to earlier, Marla seems to fully occupy the subject position of deep listening, and the scene concludes with a therapist encouraging both of them to continue to "share yourself, completely." However, a paradox also emerges in the scene (all great art, as we know, being paradoxical in its structure). When Marla completes Jack's statement, she offers an appearance of listening so deeply that her subjectivity is momentarily emptied out and she is able to channel his innermost self, expressing a truth of him that is far more significant than whatever words he was going to say. This is something very different, keep in mind, than their both speaking simultaneously and, hence, being the same: if this were the case the necessary two for the utopian figure would be collapsed back into the dystopian one.

The same dilemma is at the heart of the great filmic comedy of remarriage of such interest to Bayard—and to which I will return briefly in chapter 6—*Groundhog Day*.[66] In a chapter entitled "Encounters with Someone You Love," Bayard observes:

> There is something frightening in the way Phil sets out to seduce Rita, since it effectively suppresses the uncertainty that is normally part of communication. Endlessly telling the Other the words she wants to hear, being exactly the person she expects, is paradoxically to deny her as an other, since it amounts to no longer being a subject, fragile and uncertain, in her present. (*HT,* 109)

Fortunately, being that this is a concrete utopian film, this initial strategy of seduction fails, resulting in Phil taking up an alternate approach: "In becoming interested in others [that is, by really listening to them instead of just waiting for his turn to talk], [Phil] becomes interesting, and he manages, through his kindness, to win Rita's heart in a single day.... Thus does he manage at last to cross the border, in one unsurpassable moment, that separates his day from the days to come" (*HT,* 110).

However, in *Fight Club,* in order for Marla to demonstrate her deep listening, she is forced to interrupt Jack and speak. And while he does suggest she is correct—thereby acknowledging her capacity, like the analyst, to non-read what is in Jack that is more than Jack himself—in this moment, she nevertheless stops listening. Indeed, the scene reminds us—as does each in their own fashion Bayard, More, Reik, Lacan, and Nhat Hanh—of the fact that most of the time people do not really listen but rather only wait for their turn to speak. The latter situation would be characteristic of what Lacan theorizes as the masculinist discourse of the master, and all masters, Lacan goes on to maintain, require an imaginary other in the form of a hysteric, one who speaks endlessly to a no less imaginary other and to whom the master only listens insofar as he can dominate her or him by telling or commanding her or him how to be. This is precisely what Phil does in his initial attempts to seduce Rita, and we have no guarantee that this is not what Marla is doing here. Moreover, when such a master hides his speaking position under the guise of a single fixed reading, objective truth, or the big Other, who no longer requires an imaginary little other (because everyone has been rendered hysterics), the result is Lacan's final discourse, that of the university.[67] This might be the most devastating dystopian situation, a form of what Badiou names the evil of "disaster," an "absolutization" of truth.[68]

And yet, this is the danger we must always traverse: in order to practice deep listening, non-reading, or love, we have to take the risk of speaking or writing, and hence revealing that we have not-listened, not-read, or not-loved. It is only the most pernicious *anti*-utopians—be they ethical critics of Bayard or More or of any other great utopian thinker—who equate every utopian imaginary, let alone those developed in these rich texts, with the discourses of the master or even university. We can never know whether a real dialogue, a true listening to the other, occurs in the film scene, because the film, as with Bayard's and More's work, offers us only a figure or re-presentation of such a utopian existence, and, again, utopia, like art or love or politics or science, finally can only ever be experienced for ourselves.

Still, the deep effectiveness of the scene and the other works I have discussed lies in their power to educate our desire for the ability to non-read or listen deeply or love. These works also remind us of the tremendous difficulty, indeed some more pessimistic intellectual traditions would say the impossibility, of such a utopian listening or non-reading or loving. Perhaps we can never achieve the attention beyond the self or ego to which Jameson refers, and manifest in Bayard's non-reader, More's Thomas More, Reik's and Lacan's ideal analyst, or Nhat Hanh's deep listener, and all we ever do is encounter in others a mirror of ourselves. Equally important, as these texts all also stress, since such a utopia is not a place but a process, the achievement of such an optimum state will never be secure and must be endlessly, and exhaustingly, renewed and repeated. Every listening, every dialogue, every utopia, is absolutely contingent on the possibility, nay the likelihood, that it will fail.

And yet what all the utopias I have touched on in this chapter teach us is that the throw of the die—the gamble, effort involved, and likelihood of failure—are well worth it. For we always fail; that is, we always fail, until we succeed. If we do succeed, and have earned such an experience, even if for only the briefest of moments, we will be able at last triumphantly to proclaim, as in the scintillating utopian closing lines of one of the greatest English-language novels of the twenty-first century, Junot Díaz's *The Brief Wondrous Life of Oscar Wao* (2007): "So this is what everybody's always talking about! Diablo! If only I'd known. The beauty! The beauty!"[69]

[3]

Beyond Ethical Reading; or, Reading Again the James–Wells Debate

> The important point which I tried to argue with Henry James was that the novel of completely consistent characterization arranged beautifully in a story and painted deep and round and solid, no more exhausts the possibilities of the novel, than the art of Velazquez exhausts the possibilities of the painted picture.
>
> —H. G. Wells, *Experiment in Autobiography*

> Mr. Booth has thus something in common with the object of his criticism: for James also attempted to arrive at the universal laws governing the proper composition of the novel in general, and showed as little awareness of the historically conditioned nature of the form. The difference is that James in doing so reflected his moment in history, whereas Mr. Booth does not.
>
> —Fredric Jameson, *Marxism and Form*

EARLY ON IN HIS REVIEW of David Mitchell's *The Bone Clocks: A Novel* (2014), James Wood acknowledges, "David Mitchell is a superb storyteller. He has an extraordinary facility with narrative: he can get a narrative rolling along faster than most writers, so that it is filled with its own mobile life."[1] Shortly upon the heels of this complimentary observation, however, Wood shifts his tack, querying rhetorically, "Mitchell has plenty to tell, but does he have much to say?" This is Wood's question regarding Mitchell's most celebrated work to date, *Cloud Atlas* (2004): while noting that the novel contains an "impressive narrative parquet," moving as it does across six different generic practices and back again, Wood wonders, "What else was it? . . . *Cloud Atlas* is made up of intricate replications like these, but what do they amount to? Does *Cloud Atlas* do much more than announce and adumbrate a universal, and perhaps not very interesting, interconnectedness?" A similar emptiness, Wood further maintains, is evident in *The Bone Clocks.* In these regards, Mitchell's work becomes symptomatic of a larger shift in modern life:

> As the novel's cultural centrality dims, so storytelling—J. K. Rowling's magical Owl of Minerva, equipped for a thousand tricks and turns—flies up and fills the air. Meaning is a bit of a bore, but storytelling is alive. . . . What becomes harder to find, and lonelier to defend, is the idea of the novel as—in Ford Madox Ford's words—a "medium of profoundly serious investigation into the human case."[2]

Most damning of all is *The Bone Clocks*'s "peculiar cosmology," which, Wood asserts, "has the demented intricacy of science fiction." Science fiction has long been a central aspect of Mitchell's project: as I will suggest in my concluding chapter, *Cloud Atlas* is a reworking of one of the founding texts of modern science fiction, H. G. Wells's *The Time Machine* (1895). The effect of all of this in Wood's eyes is to reverse the history of modern fiction, returning "the secular novel to theological allegory" and the epic form. Moreover, at the heart of this science fictional cosmology is what we might call the "Mitchell Problem": "an unconscious fantasy of the author-god, reinstating the novelist as omniscient deity, controlling, prodding, shaping, ending, rigging." Wood finally concludes his brief with a history lesson and a call to action:

> The novel takes over from the epic not just because inwardness opens itself up as the great novelistic subject but because human freedom asserts itself against divine arrangement. The "human case" refuses to be preordained. The history of the novel can, in fact, be seen as a secular triumph over providential theology: first, God is displaced; then the God-like author fills the theological void; then the God-like author is finally displaced, too. Despite Mitchell's humane gifts as a secular storyteller, *The Bone Clocks* enforces an ordained hermeticism, in which fictional characters, often bearing names from previous Mitchell

fictions, perform unmotivated maneuvers at the behest of mysterious plotters who can do what they want with their victims. Time to redact this particular Script.

Fredric Jameson argues in his early engagement with Wayne Booth's *Rhetoric of Fiction* (1961) that "the ultimate value of Booth's work is that of the conservative position in general: useful as diagnosis, and as a means of disengaging everything that is problematical in the existing state of things, its practical recommendations turn out to be nothing but regression and sterile nostalgia for the past."[3] Much the same can be said of Wood's conservatism in this review essay. The form of the novel that climaxes Wood's capsule history, and to which he nostalgically longs for a return, is that formulated a century ago by Henry James, codified in Percy Lubbock's *The Craft of Fiction* (1921), and that became the dominant practice in U.S. fiction during what Mark McGurl periodizes as "the program era" (which other literary historians have suggested may now be coming to an end, a point I will return to in my Conclusion).[4] Even Wood's judgment of Mitchell's novels as "not very interesting" indicates his investments in a Jamesian aesthetic, for, as Sianne Ngai demonstrates, it is James who singles "out 'interesting' as the idiosyncratic genre's particularly salient, if also particularly minimal, standard of aesthetic worth."[5] Indeed, those who follow in James's footsteps will take up a similar aesthetic, for example, Joseph Conrad in his 1917 author's note to *Lord Jim* (1900) maintains "the postulate must be accepted that the story *was* interesting. It is the necessary preliminary assumption. If I hadn't believed that it *was* interesting I could never have begun to write it."[6] And as Ngai further reminds us, the category of the interesting is always already a "counter-interest," invested over and against others in a particular set of ideological, political, and deeply classed interests.[7]

The great irony at work here is that what is for Wood an object of nostalgia is the target of attack for Booth: "For Booth's book is a defense of the omniscient narrator, the implied author or reliable commentator, who unobtrusively but strategically makes his presence between reader and characters felt in such a way that the former is provided with the standards by which to judge the latter appropriately." Jameson goes on to argue that for Booth, "in the absence of such a figure, and of such absolute standards of moral judgment," the modern novel "ends up in a relativistic subjectivism."[8] In his critical assault on James's formulation of the "universal laws governing the proper composition of the novel," Booth's study in turn becomes a symptom of its historical context, one in which, Jameson archly observes a decade later, James has undergone a "remarkable transformation . . . from a minor nineteenth-century man of letters into the greatest American novelist of the 1950s."[9]

Arguing from self-proclaimed positions of marginality, Wood's and Booth's polemics share another crucial aspect: both take the form of the moralizing ethical criticism that has also long been of major concern for Jameson. At the center of all such ethics, Jameson maintains, stand binary oppositions—in Wood's case, between the novel and storytelling; in Booth's, between the omniscient narrator and Jamesian point of view—that quickly resolve into the Nietzschean terms of good and evil. In *The Political Unconscious,* Jameson further maintains:

> The concept of good and evil is a positional one that coincides with categories of Otherness. Evil thus, as Nietzsche taught us, continues to characterize whatever is radically different from me, whatever by virtue of precisely that difference seems to constitute a real and urgent threat to my own existence. So from earliest times, the stranger from another tribe, the "barbarian" who speaks an incomprehensible language and follows "outlandish" customs, but also the woman, whose biological difference stimulates fantasies of castration and devoration, or in our own time, the avenger of accumulated resentments from some oppressed class or race, or else that alien being, Jew or Communist, behind whose apparently human features a malignant and preternatural intelligence is thought to lurk: these are some of the archetypal figures of the Other, about whom the essential point to be made is not so much that he is feared because he is evil; rather he is evil *because* he is Other, alien, different, strange, unclean, and unfamiliar.[10]

Such an ethical stance, Jameson elsewhere suggests, usually takes the form of an injunction, evident in both Wood's and Booth's arguments "to *stop* doing something" lest one continue down a path of perdition.[11] More recently, Jameson insists, "the challenge remains to avoid that ethical binary, which is the root form of all ideology."[12] This includes the temptation of concluding that it is moralizing ethical criticism itself that "is 'wrong,' that is to say, evil," such that "the ideological closure in question would end up drawing the entire analysis back into itself."[13]

What Jameson points toward here are the four possible positions any critic can take up in relationship to ethical criticism or, indeed, any "dominant and effective" practice. The first, of course, is to embrace it, as do Wood and Booth. The second would involve a full-throated denunciation of the "evils" of an ethical criticism—what we might refer to as an *anti-*ethical criticism.[14] There is nothing in and of itself wrong in such an "anti-" stance, and there are times when it may be a necessary starting point. For example, Gilles Deleuze and Félix Guattari inaugurate their extraordinarily fecund collective project with just such an "anti-": "The task of schizoanalysis goes by way of destruction—a whole scouring of the unconscious, a complete curettage. Destroy Oedipus, the illusion of the ego, the puppet of the superego, guilt, the law, castration."[15] Similarly, this is what William Lloyd Garrison demands in response to "that crime of crimes," slavery: "Why should its existence be prolonged one hour? Is it not evil, only evil, and that continually?"[16] (Unfortunately, as we shall see in the next chapter, Garrison may have been less willing to do all that was necessary to effect such a purging.) The "anti-" can also serve, and this would be the conclusion of Ernesto Laclau and Chantal Mouffe in their classic post-Marxist intervention, as a stance drawing together diverse interests into a coalition, as in the antifascism of the World War II–era Popular Front or in challenges to colonial hegemony: "Thus, a relation of equivalence absorbing *all* the positive determinations of the colonizer in opposition to the colonized, does not create a system of positive differential positions between the two, simply because it dissolves all positivity: the colonizer is discursively constructed as the anti-colonized. In other words, the identity has come to be purely negative."[17]

The problem, as Jameson makes clear, is that if one remains content simply to denounce, the critic adopts, in an inverted form, the stance of the ethical criticism itself—whose enemies it always imagines to be lying somewhere else, nearby and menacing—and thereby remains trapped within the ideological bind meant to be pried open. Moreover, as this critical energy consumes more and more time, making all other reading activities impossible, it transforms itself in a full-blooded ressentiment, a position whose only accomplishment is a corrosive and insistent no: "No to an 'outside,' to a 'different,' to a 'non-self': and *this* No is its creative deed."[18]

The third stance would involve adopting some form of a *not*-ethical criticism, one that proceeds as if a "bad," perhaps even embarrassing, ethical criticism can be tucked away in the corner and ignored. The dilemmas here are likewise twofold. First, the fact is that moralizing ethical criticism, as Clint Burnham and others remind us, very much continues to be part of our world and has very significant consequences in it. Regardless of how much one perceives one's practices as merely "alternative," there is, as Raymond Williams points out, "often a very narrow line, in reality, between alternative and oppositional. A meaning or practice may be tolerated as a deviation, and yet still be seen only as another particular way to live. But as the necessary area of effective domination extends, the same meanings and practices can be seen by the dominant culture, not merely as disregarding or despising it, but as challenging it."[19] At the same, in simply ignoring the ethical criticism, and assuming one continues to be ignored by it, one risks repeating its problems in an even more degraded form.

Finally, there is a position, which I believe is the one Jameson both advocates and puts into practice, that would be the dialectical negation of the negation, the "anti-anti-," what he now terms the "non-anti," or what I will refer to as a *post*-ethical criticism.[20] What distinguishes the "post-" from the "non-" is that any post-ethical criticism, especially in the moment of its theorization, engages in critique, fully acknowledging both the productivity and limitations of earlier practices, tarrying or lingering with them, before proceeding to articulate the axioms or absolute presuppositions of an alternative critical reading strategy, which it then proceeds to demonstrate in action. This "post-" is thus neither the "anti-" of what Nietzsche terms in *On the Genealogy of Morals* "slave morality," nor even the "not-" of the "master morality," but a utopian third stance Nietzsche refers to as *love*:

> Such a human being simply shakes off with a single shrug all manner of worms that dig deeply into others; here alone real "*love* of one's enemies" is also possible—assuming that it is possible at all on earth. How much respect for his enemies has a noble man!—and such respect is already a bridge to love.... For he demands his enemies as his distinction, indeed he toler-

> ates no other enemy than the one in whom there is nothing to despise and *very much* to honor![21]

Of course, as with the "anti-," a good deal of care needs to be taken in the articulation of the "post-," especially in terms of what aspects of an earlier practice are being rejected. Sara Ahmed, for example, points out the dangers inherent in "a postfeminist fantasy: that an individual woman can bring what blocks her movement to an end; or that feminism has brought 'sexism, sexual exploitation or sexual oppression' to an end. . . . We could also think of postrace as a fantasy through which racism operates: as if racism is behind us because we no longer believe in race, or as if racisms would be behind us if we no longer believed in race."[22] This holds as well for the fantasy of postcritique or postinterpretation I touched on the Introduction to this book.

The relationships between the four positions discussed above and their correspondences with Nietzsche's three moralities would appear as in Figure 10. The stance of the post-, or of love, is ideally one any theory needs to occupy in order to establish its own zone of hegemony, regardless of its limits or expansiveness. Jameson helps us recognize that while the royal road of the ethical anti- or slave morality is a permanent temptation in such a process, it is never a necessity.

Such a practice of ethical reading has long been a central aspect of the arsenal of certain champions of James's vision of the novel. Taking up the necessary role of the "Other, alien" in such an imaginary turns out to be none other than the inventor of many of our most fundamental fantasies of the alien Other, one of the founders of modern science fiction and among the leading utopian thinkers of the first half of the twentieth century, H. G. Wells. Wells is cast into this unenviable role largely as the result of an extended exchange between Wells and James unfolding in private letters and public writings between the years 1898 and 1915—from the first meeting of the two men three years after Wells reviewed the disastrous premiere of James's play *Guy Domville* to their final break, less than a year before James's death, on the heels of Wells's nasty "Of Art, of Literature, of Mr. Henry James," printed as the fourth chapter of his satirical broadside *Boon* (1915).[23] During their nearly two-decades-long dialogue, the authors passionately debate what James would describe, in the title of one of his most influential essays, as "the future of the novel."[24] The putative "victory"

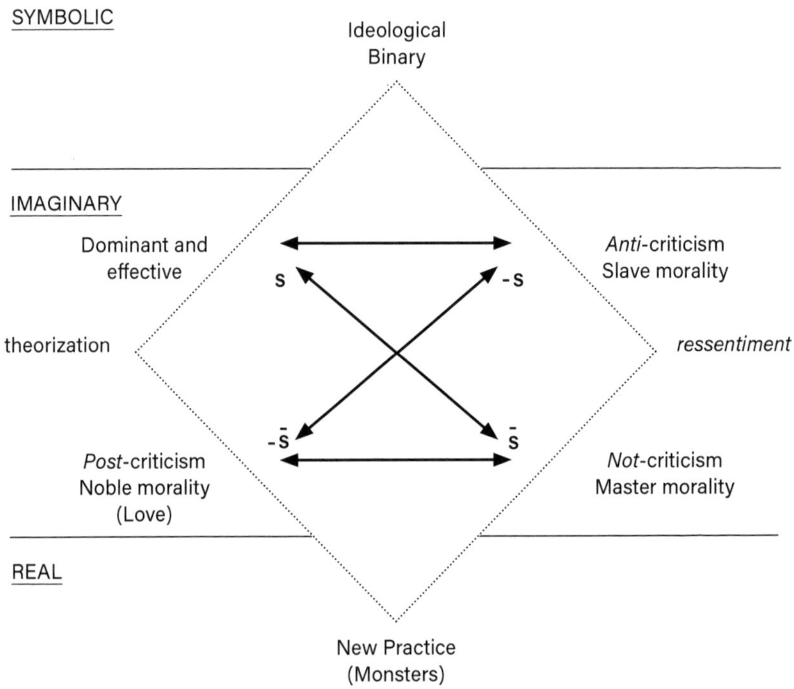

FIGURE 10

of the way forward represented by James long shaped the reading of these two writers, first through some of James's most important heirs, including the British novelists Conrad, Ford Madox Ford, and Virginia Woolf, and then, in the years following the Second World War, by way of the championing of James in the Anglo-American literary academy.

I would like to return to this originary scene, reexamining it through the lens of now more than a half century of writing by Jameson on literature, the novel, and narrative more generally. I do so with the hope that in reading their exchange in terms other than those of an ethical ideology, we might begin to understand in new ways the very different projects executed on each side of the divide—the divide between James and Wells for sure but also, as Wood's review makes abundantly clear, what remains the distinction between the novel and storytelling, "high" and "low" fiction, literature and genre, and, ultimately, art and culture. In rereading the debate in these terms, I also hope we can renew the project called for by Wells in one of the epigraphs to my chapter, expanding our sense of the "possibilities of the novel" in ways that might make this indispensable modern form useful once again for coming to grips with the emerging historical situation we inhabit.

In James's final contribution to their exchange—a letter Leon Edel describes as "one of his finest statements about his view of the artist as the one individual who gives a permanent and enduring shape to a life that is evanescent and perishable"[25]—the novelist writes, "It is art that *makes* life, makes interest, makes importance, for our consideration and application of these things, and I know of no substitute whatever for the force and beauty of its process."[26] This statement effectively encapsulates James's agenda. In his response, Wells maintains, "I don't clearly understand your concluding phrases—which shews no doubt how completely they define our difference" (*HJHG,* 267). The aim of both his critical and fictional output, as James repeatedly emphasizes in private and public forums, is to raise the novel up to the level of Art. In order for this to occur, the novelist must above all be concerned with "method," or what James views as the craft of fiction. Earlier in their exchange James writes, "If literature as life (or life as literature!) is great, Method is [the writer's] prophet—and the more so the more he (the prophet) works behind the veil" (*HJHG,* 171).

Wells's fiction, while admirable in its breadth and intellectual scope, fails in James's estimation because Wells disconnects "method from matter" (*HJHG,* 185). Fiction provides order for a chaotic reality and does so through a process of distillation—or what James describes as the "conception of the extract" (*HJHG,* 209). Wells, along with Arnold Bennett and other writers whom James sees as practicing the "theory of the slice" (of life), follow a different procedure: "They squeeze out to the utmost the plump and more or less juicy orange of a particular acquainted state and let this affirmation of energy, however directed or undirected, constitute for them the 'treatment' of the theme" (*HJHG,* 182–83). The truly successful novel conversely, according to James, focuses on a single theme and forms a completed unity, self-contained and finished, whole unto itself—something not evident in the work of what he refers to in his essay as the "younger generation" of writers.

From our later perspective, James's description of the writer's preoccupation with form represents one of the first and most significant formulations in Anglo-American letters of what will serve as one of the central tenets of high literary modernism. However, there is a second front in his assault on Wells's work—equally influential on the modernist program—that shifts attention from the compositional process to more direct prescriptions as to what constitutes the novel's "proper" contents. For James, the central focus of the novel must be the truthful and "realistic" portrayal of character, or "individual psychology," manifest most effectively in a self-enclosed and rigorously consistent point of view. Here too, he finds Wells's work wanting. The younger writer may make "dear old Dickens turn . . . in his grave" with envy over the "objective vividness and colour" of works like *Ann Veronica* (1909) (*HJHG,* 122). Nevertheless, James notes that even this novel is marred by fundamental shortcomings: "I don't think the girl herself—her projected Ego—the best thing in the book—I think it rather wants clearness and *nuances*" (*HJHG,* 123). Later in his letters, James will claim that Wells is unable to fully realize characters in his works because he cannot achieve distance in them: "I don't think you *get* her, or at any rate give her, and all through one hears your remarkable—your wonderful!—reporting manner and voice (up to last week, up to last night,) and not, by my persuasion, hers" (*HJHG,* 175). It will be James's most notable successors—Conrad, Ford Madox Ford, E. M. Forster, and Woolf, among others—who push this logic to its conclusion and produce in one fell swoop both the full realization of James's dream of the novel as Art and the form's negation. T. S. Eliot observes in his influential 1923 essay, "*Ulysses,* Order, and Myth," "Mr. Joyce has written one novel—the *Portrait*; Mr. Wyndham Lewis has written one novel *Tarr.* I do not suppose that either of them will ever write another 'novel.' The novel ended with Flaubert and with James."[27]

"The novel" Eliot refers to here is, of course, still identified with nineteenth-century realism, and it is to the latter that Jameson has given such profound consideration in his recent study *The Antinomies of Realism* (2013). Realism, for Jameson, is defined according to a series of binary oppositions, which already creates the possibility for the subsequent ethical turn I touched on earlier—"the récit versus *roman,*" "telling versus showing," and most important, "destiny versus the eternal present."[28] The last term in this series, now understood as the omnipresence of the body and the everyday, takes the form in the novel of that new thing, distinct from "the older named emotions," Jameson terms "affect" (*AR,* 44). Jameson further maintains, "what is crucial is not to load one of these dies and take sides for one or the other . . . but rather to grasp that realism lies at their intersection. Realism is a consequence of the tension between these two terms; *to resolve the opposition either way would destroy it*" (*AR*, 26; emphasis added).

It is in James's formulation at the end of the nineteenth century of a new novelistic aesthetic that this tension first begins to lessen: "For James himself, it would seem that mere telling—the récit part of what he describes as a 'double pressure' on the novel—means shirking his job. The narrative summaries and foreshortenings are in effect sheer laziness, they are the sign he has not lived up to his calling, the august vocation he invented for himself (and for others)" (*AR*, 22). Jameson subsequently points out what occurs when the two are finally fully delinked:

> A parting of the ways becomes unavoidable. The "serious" writer—that is, the one who aspires to the distinction of literature—will keep faith with what alone authentically survives the weakening of all the joints and joists, the bulkheads and loadbearing supports, of narrative as such, of the récit on its point of submersion: namely affect as such, whose triumph over its structural adversary is that bodiliness that alone marks any singularity in the everyday, and which now turns to engage its new literary adversary in lyric and language. Its fate is henceforth the fate of modernism, and no longer has any place in this particular story. (*AR*, 184)

Nevertheless, Jameson does return a few pages later to the question of modernism, building on a point he had already made in *The Political Unconscious*: "But who says modernism in the arts also says mass culture, since the two are dialectically and historically interdependent and arise at much the same moment" (*AR*, 187). It will be the new mass culture and genre fictions that then take up the other half of realism's broken dialectic, the récit, or storytelling. This division gives birth to the new binary opposition and the ethical ideology that grows out of it, between the novel (showing, affect, modernism) and storytelling (telling, récit, mass culture) that, as Wood bears out, continues to figure prominently even today.

Interestingly enough, Wells in his part of the dialogue often grants the validity of James's claims. Even decades later, in his *Experiment in Autobiography* (1934), Wells concedes, "The main indictment is sound, that I sketch out scenes and individuals, often quite crudely, and resort even to conventional types and symbols, in order to get on to a discussion of relationships" (*HJHG,* 220). By acknowledging these limits, Wells is able to shift the grounds and argue for another set of possibilities for narrative fiction. In his 1911 essay "The Contemporary Novel," for example, Wells celebrates the powerful "moral persuasive" potential in the form. This possibility emerges only after the novel has been set free from the critical constraints that held the form to be mere "entertainment." And while in his confrontation with the genteel school of criticism Wells concurs with James, he moves in a decidedly different direction when he subsequently proclaims, "I rejoice to see many signs to-day that that phase of narrowing and restriction is over, and that there is every encouragement for a return towards a laxer, more spacious form of novel-writing" (*HJHG,* 137). For Wells, it is the very abandonment of any efforts to constitute a normative canon of novelistic production that opens up these new possibilities: "We are going to write about it all. We are going to write about business and finance and politics and precedence and pretentiousness and decorum and indecorum, until a thousand pretences and ten thousand impostures shrivel in the cold, clear air of our elucidations" (156).

In his declaration of the transformative potential of cultural work more broadly defined, Wells's words resonate with the utopian slogans of a subsequent modernism, from Ezra Pound's "make it new" to Eugene Jolas's "revolution of the word."[29] However, it will be the formal principles elucidated by James—most notably, the emphasis on craftsmanship, individual psychology, and formal closure—that will be selected out as the defining characteristics of "serious" literary fiction.

Three examples of this latter shift, taken from nearly three-quarters of a century of criticism following the end of the debate, bear this out. First, Virginia Woolf, in another of the most influential documents of British literary modernism, the 1924 essay "Mr. Bennett and Mrs. Brown," makes claims for the "proper" work of the modern novel that are strikingly similar to those advanced earlier by James. Woolf offers the axiom that "all novels, that is to say, deal with character, and that it is to express character—not to preach doctrines, sing songs, or celebrate the glories of the British Empire, that the form of the novel, so clumsy, verbose, and undramatic, so rich, elastic, and alive, has been evolved."[30] But this focus is exactly what we do not see in her predecessors, the Edwardian writers Wells, Bennett, and Galsworthy. Their works, Woolf maintains, "leave one with so strange a feeling of incompleteness and dissatisfaction. In order to complete them it seems necessary to do something—to join a society, or, more desperately, to write a cheque."[31] The aims articulated in this essay will come to their fullest realization only three years later in Woolf's extraordinary *To the Lighthouse* (1927), perhaps her most influential work for the development of a later program-era aesthetic. After all, it is her stand-in for the novelist, the painter Lily Briscoe, who echoes the Jamesian values of "distance" and the "interesting" as among the most important criteria for the successful work of art.[32] However, unlike many of her successors, Woolf always deploys such an aesthetic for political ends, never letting us forget who are the beneficiaries, to use Bruce Robbins's term, of the world she portrays, as well as the deep responsibility of these people to instigate repair and change.[33]

Three decades after Woolf's essay, two scholars who played significant roles in the institutional rehabilitation of James's work in the years following the Second World War, Leon Edel and Gordon N. Ray, write in their 1958 introduction to the collected exchange between the two writers that Wells, "whose imagination could soar through space and time and create tales of wonderful new worlds, was yet limited and earthbound when it came to understanding the true nature of art" (*HJHG*, 39). It is James, in their estimation, who stands "on the side of art and responsibility," who possesses a "deep psychological awareness of human motivations and impulses," and who was "reconciled to the man-made hierarchies and wielded his pen as if it were a scepter" (32, 25, 18). Elsewhere, Edel concludes that while James throughout the debate always walks the highroad, Wells's parody of James in *Boon* can be likened "very much as a small boy might reply to an elder's rebuke by leveling a pea-shooter."[34]

Finally, a similar nexus of psychoanalytic and aesthetic criteria are at play in David Bleich's *Utopia: The Psychology of a Cultural Fantasy* (1984). Deploying the tools of a normative developmental psychoanalytic theory, Bleich reads the 1905 fictions by Wells and James, *A Modern Utopia* and *The Golden Bowl,* and concludes that Wells's experimental work remains fixated in "adolescent" fantasy, while James's finely crafted novel was able to "create an adult identity from the same emotional constellation, and perhaps the same fantasy, that paralyzed Wells in adolescence."[35] And what is adolescent in Wells and his work? An unwillingness to "accept" the world as it currently exists.[36]

Despite their different aims and contexts, there is a marked circularity in all three commentaries. Deploying criteria formulated in a large part by James himself, all three evaluate Wells's work and, not surprisingly, find it lacking. Perhaps the most significant difference between these later discussions and James's own engagement with Wells's work is James's readiness to acknowledge the personal and cultural contingency of his own aesthetic values and practices; however, in Edel and Ray's and Bleich's readings in particular, these norms are projected into the mythic domain of a universal and ahistorical "human" psychology.

Moreover, there is another dimension at work in these latter readings that can be brought into sharp relief by a return to one of Wells's replies to James. In a discussion of the origins of the novelistic tradition represented by Walter Scott, Wells writes:

> [Scott] saw events therefore as a play of individualities in a rigid frame of values never more to be questioned or permanently changed. His lawless, romantic past was the picturesque prelude to stability; our current values were already potentially there. Throughout the broad smooth flow of nineteenth-century life in Great Britain, the art of fiction floated on this same assumption of social fixity. (*HJHG,* 222)

For Wells, such a charge applies to James's fiction as well. And indeed, in *Boon,* Wells's narrator describes James's critical writings as "one sustained demand for the picture effect. Which is the denial of the sweet complexity of life, of the pointing this way and that, of the spider on the throne" (*HJHG,* 246). What Wells suggests here is that the kind of introspection, extreme subjectivism, and emphasis on formal technique that we see so centrally at work in the novelistic fiction championed by James can only take place when the stability of the larger social context, or "world," is established in advance. Jameson similarly points out that "realism requires a conviction as to the massive weight and persistence of the present as such, and an aesthetic need to avoid recognition of deep structural social change as such and of the deeper currents and contradictory tendencies within the social order" (*AR,* 145).

What is conviction in the nineteenth century becomes a full-blown agenda in James's work, as he strives ruthlessly to eliminate from his mature fiction anything that threatens the stable picture of the world; or, as Wells puts it, "perceiving the discordant things, he tries to get rid of them" (*HJHG,* 246). Finally then, Wells maintains that in James's perfectly realized fictional worlds, "he omits everything that demands digressive treatment or collateral statement. For example, he omits opinions. In all his novels you will find no people with defined political opinions, no people with religious opinions, none with clear partisanships or with lusts or whims, none definitely up to any specific impersonal thing" (*HJHG,* 247). In short, we witness in James's work, Wells argues, the suppression of anything that might be construed as extra-aesthetic—that is, anything resembling the social or the political.

Wells's commentary can thus help account for the postwar canonization of James's program for the novel. James's agenda, as Wells summarizes it, is one that fit perfectly within the liberal intellectual project of establishing an aesthetic and critical practice purged of the explicitly "political" and other extra-aesthetic concerns that had dominated the modernist 1920s and 1930s. Jameson names this new postwar situation "late modernism," which he describes as "a product of the Cold War, but in all kinds of complicated ways. Thus, the Cold War spelled the end of a whole era of social transformation and indeed of Utopian desires and anticipations. . . . Politics must therefore now be carefully monitored, and new social impulses repressed or disciplined. These new forms of control are symbolically re-enacted in later modernism, which transforms the older modernist experimentation into an arsenal of tried and true techniques, no longer striving after aesthetic totality or the systemic and Utopian metamorphosis of forms."[37] This too is the moment of the rise of the creative writing program, which, McGurl maintains, posits Jamesian notions of craft and the scenic method as the exclusive agenda for all "serious" writing: "After the Second World War, the poetics of 'show don't tell' would gradually evolve into a more general understanding of good fiction as founded on discipline, restraint, and the impersonal exercise of hard-won technique."[38]

At the same time, another crucial distinction is set into place in the moment of late modernism, whose echoes reverberate in Wood's review:

> The autonomy of the aesthetic is not secured by separating the aesthetic from real life. . . . Rather, it is achieved by a radical dissociation within the aesthetic itself: by radical disjunction and separation of literature and art from culture. . . . All the great theorists and ideologists of the autonomy of art, the ideologists of modernism are in agreement that the concept of culture is the true enemy of art as such; and that if one opens the door to "culture," everything currently reviled under the term of cultural studies pours in and leaves pure art and pure literature irredeemably tainted.[39]

Within the dictates of program-era fiction writing, this degraded culture takes the form of "the shoddy inauthenticity of genre fiction of all kinds"[40]—precisely what Wood condemns in Mitchell's writing in a not very subtle judgment of guilt by association (at once, with science fiction, children's literature, J. K. Rowling, and George R. R. Martin). (I will return to the issue of late modernism in chapter 5.)

Now I do not intend at this point simply to reverse older critical conclusions and champion the "superiority" of Wells's fictional or even critical practice—to do so would be to remain trapped in the same ethical binary that I discussed at the outset. Two of the most significant defenses of modernist experimentation—the "replies" offered by Ernst Bloch and Theodor Adorno to Georg Lukács's criticism, the latter not without its own nostalgia, and collected in the volume *Aesthetics and Politics*—already suggest that in modernism—in which we should now include James's late novels—social and political content is not so much evacuated as displaced into form itself.[41] Thus, in the very emphasis on the unique aspects of style and the irreproducibility of the individual work of art we see in both James's critical and fictional practice, as well as in that of his modernist heirs, resistance to the homogenizing aspects of contemporary industrial capitalist and bureaucratic culture (both of the latter on occasion championed by Wells). But, of course, this also points toward the ultimate limits of these achievements: unable to challenge social reality, these works transform weakness into strength and "compensate" by valorizing order exclusively in the work of art.

Rather, I want to stress that in terms of the debate, when read through a lens other than that of an ethical ideology bent on determining winners and losers, what suddenly comes into focus is the fundamental discontinuity in the practices advocated by each writer. Such a focus redirects our attention to the question of the different ways each aesthetic practice "works." Jameson makes a similar point in his most passionate defenses of "other" forms of writing. For example, he begins one of his most hotly debated essays with the following and often overlooked cautionary note:

> Many arguments can be made for the importance and interest of non-canonical forms such as that of the third world, but one is peculiarly self-defeating because it borrows the weapons of the adversary: the strategy of trying to prove that these texts are as "great" as those of the canon itself. The object is then to show that, to take an example from another non-canonical form, Dashiell Hammett is really as great as Dostoyevsky, and therefore can be admitted. This is to attempt dutifully to wish away all traces of that "pulp" format which is constitutive of sub-genres, and it invites immediate failure insofar as any passionate reader of Dostoyevsky will know after a few pages, that those kinds of satisfactions are not present. Nothing is to be gained by passing over in silence the radical difference of non-canonical texts.[42]

The fundamental differences between James's and Wells's practices are already signaled in the debates themselves. In a commentary on the lack of artistic "detachment" fostered by Wells's deployment of a first-person point of view, James writes, "Save in the fantastic and the romantic (*Copperfield, Jane Eyre,* that charming thing of Stevenson's with the bad title—*Kidnapped*?) it has no authority, no persuasive or convincing force—its grasp of reality and truth isn't strong and disinterested. *R. Crusoe,* e.g., isn't a novel at all" (*HJHG,* 128). Now when we bracket aside the normative, ethical tone of James's comment, something quite interesting begins to emerge in his suggestion that Wells's writing might best be understood as part of a parallel tradition. For these works are indeed not "novels," either in the sense of nineteenth-century realism discussed by Jameson or in that of the modernist art novel being formulated by James. Rather, as James suggests, we might far more usefully think of these works as manifestations within the practice of the novel of a narrative tradition that predates both realism and the novel—that of the *romance.*

A still valuable discussion of the romance, contemporary with both Booth's *Rhetoric of Fiction* and Edel and Ray's publication of the exchange between James and Wells, is to be found in Richard Chase's *The American Novel and Its Tradition* (1957). Like Booth, Chase's study aims at a full-blown reevaluation of an older tradition of literary fiction. However, this is motivated for Chase less by nostalgia for what has been lost and more by a deeply historicist recognition of the very different formal practices of American and British literature in the nineteenth century.

Chase's elaboration of the difference between the novel and the romance also coincides in some productive ways with Wells's characterizations of his own practices. Chase suggests that the major difference between the novel and the romance lies in "the way in which they view reality."[43] Whereas the novel is bound to a fairly rigid sense of what is, the romance takes a far looser attitude toward the real and the possible. Similarly, the romance is more formally open, and, in it, the presentation of character takes on far less significance—indeed, the romance, "being less committed to the immediate rendition of reality than the novel, will more freely veer toward mythic, allegorical, and symbolistic forms."[44]

Most interesting for our purposes, Chase claims these particular formal trajectories reflect the quite different contexts in which each emerges. Whereas the novel works best in a relatively stable social context, the romance predominates in far more fluid environments, such as that evident in the United States in the century after its founding: "The American novel has usually seemed content to explore, rather than to appropriate and civilize, the remarkable and in some ways unexampled territories of life in the New World and to reflect its anomalies and dilemmas."[45]

A similar emphasis on the exploratory and mapping—that is, *spatial*—focus of the romance is also stressed by Jameson in his discussion of the practice found in the second chapter of *The Political Unconscious.*[46] Jameson draws upon the phenomenological language of Martin Heidegger to describe romance as "precisely that form in which the *worldness* of *world* reveals or manifests itself, in which, in other words, *world* in the technical sense of the transcendental horizon of our experience becomes visible in an inner-worldly sense."[47] The aim of the romance conceived in this way is to spark a new awareness or self-consciousness of what it means to be-in-the-world by highlighting the specific constructedness of the environments any reader inhabits: the very horizons, as we saw earlier, that Wells argues are occluded in novelistic texts like those of James. If the novel focuses on character, making us aware of complexities of contemporary psychology, the romance concentrates on bringing into purview the historicity of the worlds those characters may inhabit. Character similarly functions very differently in the romance, as "a registering apparatus for transformed states of being, sudden alterations of temperature, mysterious heightenings, local intensities, sudden drops in quality, and alarming effluvia."[48]

In Wells's oeuvre, such an operation is most readily apparent in his celebrated "scientific romances." The mapping or romance aspects of science fiction are also central for Jameson's understanding of the practice. Jameson contends that "whatever our immediate narrative interest in any particular SF plot and its resolutions, we also attend to and derive a readerly gratification from the development of space in SF worlds, in general, a gratification not noticeably damaged by awkwardnesses in the handling of the plot proper."[49] Jameson concludes the essay with the more general proposition, "the collective adventure accordingly becomes less that of a character (individual or collective) than that of a planet, a climate, a weather and a system of landscapes—in short, a map. We thus need to explore the proposition that the distinctiveness of SF as a genre has less to do with time (history, past, future) than with space."[50]

However, the same thing can be said of Wells's more "realist" fictions, and I would hold out as a case in point the work that Wells himself describes as his most "deliberate attempt upon the Novel," *Tono-Bungay* (1909). For this work can be thought of as an heir to the tradition of the picaresque, or what Mikhail Bakhtin describes as the "second stylistic trend" in the novel: a narrative wherein the wanderings of the protagonist serve as a motivating device for the work's goal of mapping different and emergent cultural and social geographies.[51] In *Tono-Bungay,* class and social hierarchies are mapped by way of a geographical or spatial imaginary, much as in *The Time Machine* these hierarchies are extrapolated along a temporal axis until they harden into absolute biological differences (the Eloi and Morlocks). George's wanderings thus provide the reader with a dramatic awareness of the relational historicity of their present in both its geographical—the movement from the manor house ("Bladesover illuminates England"[52]) to the city of London—and temporal dimensions—the uneven development of advertising and finance capitalism within the context of the persistence of older modes of production.[53]

Let me then conclude by suggesting that it is this tradition of the romance novel that is being renewed and transformed by Mitchell and other contemporary artists; and, in so doing, they may very well be marking the end of the hegemony, if not the practices, of the late modernist and program era's ethical version of the Jamesian aesthetic. Wood is right, of course: if you search Mitchell's fiction for a narrow exploration of the "inwardness" of a very particular subject—a historical and classed figure Wood then projects as the universal human—you will be profoundly disappointed. And yet in no way does this mean that Mitchell's work should be understood as lacking a "profoundly serious investigation into the human case."[54] In both *Cloud Atlas* and *The Bone Clocks,* Mitchell offers rich explorations of what it means collectively to inhabit, and act in, an emerging global reality. Not surprisingly, Jameson too ends *The Antinomies of Realism* with a discussion of *Cloud Atlas* as one of the most provocative indicators of what will be necessary to renew another vital tradition of the novel, one whose roots in romance I have also suggested above: that of the historical novel. Mitchell's work shows, Jameson concludes, "for better or worse, our history, our historical past and our historical novels, must now also include our historical futures as well."[55] At the same time, *Cloud Atlas* raises deep questions, as we shall see in my final chapter, of how we might enact an "optimism of the will" in what our intellects cannot help but tell us are profoundly pessimistic times.

However, Jameson also reminds us, "the moment of the aesthetic is not that call but rather is the reminder that all those impulses exist: the revolutionary Utopian one full as much as the immense disgust with human evil, Brecht's 'temptation of the good,' the will to escape and to be free, the delight in craftsmanship and production, the implacably satiric, unremittingly skeptical gaze. Art has no function but to reawaken all these differences at once in an ephemeral instant."[56] *The Bone Clocks* fulfills these criteria, while also taking up the old agenda of the romance, helping us grasp in new ways the complexities of our global space, containing within itself both the traces of the past—slavery and genocide in the south—and the intimations of the future—

the so-called New North. While neither work may do so in ways that James would recognize, or perhaps even approve, both of Mitchell's fictions amply fulfill James's demand that a great work of art "makes life, makes interest, makes importance."

Coda

In the preceding three chapters, I have outlined some of the most significant axioms involved in any practice of close creative non-reading. There may be others, and I would hope that future non-readers will teach me about them. Some less attentive non-readers of these pages, distracted as they are by whatever they find to be pressing moralizing concerns, may perceive paradoxes in some of the claims advanced—every aspect of a text's context potentially must be given equal and complete attention in accounting for meaning as a whole; all non-reading is an inattentive and interested skimming of a text; any criticism of ethical criticism necessarily takes the form of an ethical criticism. However, it is my fundamental presupposition in all that follows that it is precisely through these dialectical tensions, produced by the "impossible" effort to inhabit seemingly incompatible positions, that the creative energies of close non-reading practices, "some thinking of the future," are most effectively marshaled.[57] As I hope the preceding chapters demonstrate, this would be akin to the dialectical non-reading practices characterized by Rebecca Comay and Frank Ruda as "a combination of the most austere formalization and the most undiscriminating attentiveness to the trivial: at once absolutely stupid rigidity and absolutely rigid stupidity."[58] The proof lies in the proverbial pudding—in whatever any other non-reader may find of value in the experiences or encounters to come. "The future can be anticipated only in the form of an absolute danger. It is that which breaks absolutely with constituted normality and can therefore only announce itself, *present* itself, in the species of monstrosity."[59] Is there yet available any more effective characterization of utopia and its unique form of unrepresentability? But then again—aren't we all little monsters?[60]

PART II

Reading Utopia

[4]

John Brown, W. E. B. Du Bois, and Universal History

The general stultification today is the direct result of cutting out utopia. When you reject utopia, thought itself withers away. Thought is killed off in the mere doubling process.

—Theodor Adorno, *Towards a New Manifesto*

Yet utopia as a form is not the representation of radical alternatives; it is rather simply the imperative to imagine them.

—Fredric Jameson, *Archaeologies of the Future*

Courage, brothers! The battle for humanity is not lost or losing. All across the skies sit signs of promise. . . . The morning breaks over blood-stained hills. We must not falter, we may not shrink. Above are the everlasting stars.

—W. E. B. Du Bois, "Address to the Country"

IN 1962, IN HONOR OF the one hundredth anniversary of the Emancipation Proclamation, the great left press International Publishers released a new edition of W. E. B. Du Bois's brilliant and underappreciated historical study *John Brown* (1909), itself originally published exactly fifty years after Brown's failed efforts at Harpers Ferry, Virginia, to spark the revolution that would mark the beginning of the end of the system of slavery.[1] Although on the whole Du Bois left the book largely unchanged, the occasion of this new edition did allow him to add a short second preface concerned with the "bitter debate as to how far force and violence can bring peace and good will";[2] a paragraph at the end of chapter six recalling the genocidal treatment of American Indians by European settlers ("the white man stole and killed and tried to enslave, and their last theft was land");[3] and, most substantially, seven additional pages in the book's final chapter, "The Legacy of John Brown." In the last, Du Bois touches on events that have occurred in the half century since his book's original publication, including the Russian and Chinese Revolutions, and the global expansion of "colonial imperialism":

> The state impelled by the capitalists seized control of colonies using the labor in Asia and Africa and the islands of the seas instead of transporting it to America. . . . The Western world consciously or unconsciously depends for its civilization, comfort and luxury on the low wage of colonial labor and the seizure of colonial land and materials. As a result of this we have war to force new divisions in the ownership of the colonies and war between colonies and imperial powers.[4]

Du Bois then observes, "All this John Brown did not know and could not foresee, but nevertheless he left a clear legacy: First, the right of the enslaved to repeal oppression. Then beyond this a new attitude toward human beings and a belief in the abilities and character of the great mass of mankind."[5]

If Du Bois stresses here the universal lessons of Brown's life and work for contemporary global struggles, one of the most extraordinary aspects of the original study lies in Du Bois's emphasis on the lessons Brown himself takes from earlier revolutionary movements, both in the United States and beyond. Du Bois cites the following testimony from before the U.S. Senate:

> [Brown] had read all the books upon insurrectionary warfare, that he could lay his hands on: the Roman warfare, the successful opposition of the Spanish chieftains during the period when Spain was a Roman province,—how, with ten thousand men, divided and subdivided into small companies, acting simultaneously, yet separately, they withstood the whole consolidated power of the Roman Empire through a number of years. In addition to this he had become very familiar with the successful wars waged by Schamyl, the Circassian chief, against the Russians; he had posted himself in relation to the wars of Toussaint

> L'Ouverture; he had become thoroughly acquainted with the wars in Haiti and the islands round them.[6]

This last event occupies a special place in Du Bois's narrative, something he dramatically underscores in an earlier chapter:

> There was hell in Haiti in the red waning of the eighteenth century, in the days when John Brown was born. . . . John Brown was born just as the shudder of Haiti was running through all the Americas, and from his earliest boyhood he saw and felt the price of repression—the fearful cost that the western world was paying for slavery. From his earliest boyhood he had dimly conceived, and the conception grew with his growing, that the cost of liberty was less than the price of repression. (*JB*, 40)

The epochal upheaval of the Haitian Revolution would have an equally marked influence upon one of the most important intellectual events of the first half of the nineteenth century: the publication of Hegel's *Phänomenologie des Geistes* (1807). This is the claim Susan Buck-Morss advances in her daring 2000 essay "Hegel and Haiti," reprinted along with significant new material in her book *Hegel, Haiti, and Universal History* (2009). Much as Du Bois suggests of Brown, Buck-Morss claims, "we cannot think Hegel without Haiti."[7] She further maintains, "The Haitian Revolution was the crucible, the trial by fire for the ideals of the French Enlightenment. And every European who was part of the bourgeois reading public knew it."[8] This public would very much have included Hegel, a "regular reader" of the journal *Minerva,* which published in 1804–1805 accounts of both events in the island and its longer history. Based upon this evidence, Buck-Morss argues, "Beyond a doubt Hegel knew about real slaves and their revolutionary struggles. In perhaps the most political expression of his career, he used the sensational events of Haiti as the linchpin in his argument in *The Phenomenology of Spirit.* The actual and successful revolution of Caribbean slaves against their masters is the moment when the dialectic of recognition becomes visible as the thematics of world history, the story of the universal realization of freedom."[9] This story occurs in one of the most discussed and influential sections of the text, "Independence and Dependence of

Self-Consciousness: Lordship and Bondage" ("Selbständigkeit und Unselbständigkeit des Selbstbewußtseins; Herrschaft und Knechtschaft"), of which Buck-Morss observes:

> In *The Phenomenology of Mind,* Hegel insists that freedom cannot be granted to the slaves from above. The self-liberation of the slave is required through a "trial by death": "And it is solely by risking life that freedom is obtained. . . . The individual, who has not staked his life, may, no doubt, be recognized as a Person [the agenda of the abolitionists!]; but he has not attained the truth of this recognition as an independent self-consciousness." The goal of this liberation, *out* of slavery, cannot be subjugation of the master in turn, which would be merely to repeat the master's "existential impasse," but rather, elimination of the institution of slavery altogether.[10]

In the final section of her original essay, Buck-Morss asks the question, "Why is it of more than arcane interest to retrieve from oblivion this fragment of history, the truth of which has managed to slip away from us?" Her conclusion would prove to be one of the more controversial of the essay's claims:

> There are many possible answers, but one is surely the potential for rescuing the idea of universal history from the uses to which white domination has put it. If the historical facts about freedom can be ripped out of the narratives told by the victors and salvaged for our own time, then the project of universal freedom does not need to be discarded but, rather, redeemed and reconstituted on a different basis.[11]

Buck-Morss's essay is a product of the dynamic and open historical period of the 1990s—beginning November 9, 1989, with the fall of the Berlin Wall and coming to its conclusion on September 11, 2001—and, in this regard, resonates with a number of other important theoretical projects to appear in its context, that of Michael Hardt and Antonio Negri's *Empire* (1999) being only the most celebrated.[12]

Moreover, as with Hardt and Negri, rather than retreating from these claims in the subsequent situation of the global "war on terror," Buck-Morss reiterates her fidelity to them in her book's second section, "Universal History." The universal history offers, Buck-Morss maintains, "a counter-narrative that does more than criticize the status quo; it inspires action to change it. [Its] explicit aim is to connect today's global resistance to an earlier one."[13] A little further on, she elaborates more fully on her claim:

> The definition of universal history that begins to emerge here is this: rather than giving multiple, distinct cultures equal due, whereby people are recognized as part of humanity indirectly through the mediation of collective cultural identities, human universality emerges in the historical event at the point of rupture. It is in the discontinuities of history that people whose culture has been strained to the breaking point give expression to a humanity that goes beyond cultural limits. And it is our emphatic identification with this raw, free, and vulnerable state that we have a chance of understanding what they say. Common humanity exists in spite of culture and its differences. A person's nonidentity with the collective allows for subterranean solidarities that have a chance of appealing to universal, moral sentiment, the source today of enthusiasm and hope. It is not through culture, but through the threat of culture's betrayal that consciousness of a common humanity comes to be.[14]

It is worth underscoring that Buck-Morss is not concerned in this passage with developing a general theory of universal or global culture, which likely would give "multiple, distinct cultures equal due" and in which people would be "recognized as part of humanity indirectly through the mediation of collective cultural identities." Moreover, as Avram Alpert points out, Du Bois himself elsewhere in his writings imagines an ideal form of global culture based on the exchange between peoples of the "gifts" of ideas and ways of life.[15] Rather, Buck-Morss attempts to think the original form of connection between different groups and cultures that emerges in moments of a universal historical struggle for justice. Finding just such a universal history embodied in the Haitian Revolution of 1791–1804, Buck-Morss argues:

> If we understand the experience of historical rupture as a *moment* of clarity, temporary by definition, we will not be in danger of losing the world-historical contribution of the Saint-Domingue slaves, the idea of an end to relations of slavery that went far beyond existing European Enlightenment thought—and is, indeed, far from realized under today's conditions of a global economy, where sex-slavery is rampant and the bonded labor of immigrants is employed by *all* of the so-called civilizations, and where the myth of "free labor" that Marx called wage-slavery is the reality for millions of members of the working class.[16]

While for Buck-Morss such a moment of danger is always already endemic to global neoliberalism, it takes on an additional resonance in the crisis currently unfolding in the United States and around the world.

Of particular interest in Buck-Morss's characterization of the practices of the universal history is her observation that its universal dimension lies in the identification of a "historical event at the point of rupture." This resonates in some significant ways with Alain Badiou's theorization of the event I discussed in chapter 1. Badiou further maintains that there are four distinct domains, or conditions, in which these kinds of evental encounters with the real occur, and he names these science, art, politics, and love. Each of these conditions further represents one of the fundamental activities through which humans encounter—form or produce—worlds: understanding, representing, organizing, and experiencing. However, Slavoj Žižek argues that of these four conditions, "the first three truth-procedures (science, art, and politics) follow the classic logic of the [Kantian] triad True-Beautiful-Good," while the fourth, love, "stick[s] out from the series, being somehow more fundamental and universal," thereby serving "as a kind of underlying formal principle or matrix of all procedures."[17] In this way, love is akin to what Bruce Fink describes as the impossible doubleness of the Lacanian real, as both one of the four conditions *and* the material a priori of this open dialectic: in short, love is the traumatic real, or the truth of the truth procedures themselves.[18] As a result, Žižek maintains, Badiou's fourfold schema should really be understood as "*three plus one.*"[19]

A similar logic of "three plus one" is also at work in the dialectical revision of the Greimasian semiotic square I elaborated in chapter 1. Of the four terms mapped in that discussion—the complex term, or

Lacan's symbolic; the middle opposition of the imaginary; and the real of Greimas's neutral—it is this last, the "plus one," that takes on a singular significance, as it marks the place of a materialist opening in what is more conventionally understood as a closed structuralist schema. Strictly speaking, however, my presentation bears out the fact that the distribution would be more along the lines of 1 (Symbolic) +2 (Imaginary) +1 (Real). Bruno Bosteels helps clarify the special status of the condition of science, the privileged expression of which for Badiou is mathematics:

> In short, if we return to the title of Badiou's major work, mathematics is operative both on the side of being and on the side of the event. This double inscription is what gives mathematics a unique status, completely distinct from politics, art, or love, which operate only at the level of truth procedures as conditions for philosophy.[20]

Likewise, Burhanuddin Baki notes, "mathematics, whose corresponding propositions are not mere formal representations for metaphysical conclusions, is precisely ontology itself and its conditional relationship with metaontology is not simply that of whimsical metaphorical induction or provocation."[21] It is precisely because it unfolds as a rigorous formal or symbolic language—what Louis Althusser identifies as "a discourse without a subject"—that science or mathematics can be uniquely operative on the side of being; or to put this another way, it is in speaking from this condition or within this discourse that emerges the possibility of re-presenting any particular situation.[22]

If science or mathematics, like the Greimasian semiotic square considered strictly as a symbolic presentation, offers a formalization of ontology, marking both its being and becoming, then the truth condition of love—in my Greimasian presentation, the real of the four generic procedures—is the dialectical inverse of science in that it unveils the real, the sheer unrepresentability of all events, or all utopias, and the fact that, as Badiou himself maintains, they can only ever be "encountered." Love thus at once makes apparent the foundational subjective and interpersonal or collective dimension of the other conditions—the objective side being the situation or open multiplicity, codified by the axioms of set theory, into which the newly constituted subject of a truth intervenes—and serves as a placeholder for a radically other way of being and acting in the world. This recognition also explains why in his hypertranslation of Plato's *Republic* Badiou characterizes the tyrant—effectively figured in the Trump-era blockbusters *Avengers: Infinity War* (2018) and *Avengers: Endgame* (2019)—as "the person who has lost the power to love and thus can only wield the sterile power to doom both himself and others to death."[23] Death in this case stands as a figure, as is also the case in the great dystopia of Yevgeny Zamyatin's *We* (1921), for the end of history itself; as Fredric Jameson puts it, "what characterizes death is precisely its structure as that instant in which no future (and no hope) is any longer possible."[24] In Jo Walton's *Lent* (2019), this is the definition of hell: "As he slams into it suddenly there is no hope, no change, no breath, no friendship, no God. He is tormented by everything he said, everything he tried to do, and the ultimate futility of it all that ends here."[25]

In a follow-up to my rethinking of the Greimasian semiotic square that I undertake in *Periodizing Jameson,* I show how Greimas's semiotic square in turn helps us understand in a whole new way the radical breakthrough that occurs in Jacques Lacan's 1969–1970 seminar, *The Other Side of Psychoanalysis,* wherein Lacan shifts the core focus of his thinking from the triad of the imaginary, symbolic, and the real that had dominated his work until this point, and formulates the fourfold schema of the discourses, those of the university, master, hysteric, and analyst.[26] I further show in this essay that there is another productive correspondence to be posited between Badiou's four conditions and Lacan's discourses. Finally, I would add here that there exist homologies between Lacan and Badiou's respective fourfold schemas and the four forms of critical practice—dominant and effective, not-, anti-, and postcriticisms—and Friedrich Nietzsche's three moralities—master, slave, and noble—that I touched on in the previous chapter. A mapping of these correspondences would appear as in Figure 11.

Each of these four conditions and discourses also has a specific narrative practice by which its consequences and traces are most effectively given expression. These four practices make up what I name in *Shockwaves of Possibility: Essays on Science Fiction, Globalization, and Utopia* (2014) the "evental genres" ("genres événementiels"): the *universal history*; *science fiction,* at the center of attention in *Shockwaves of*

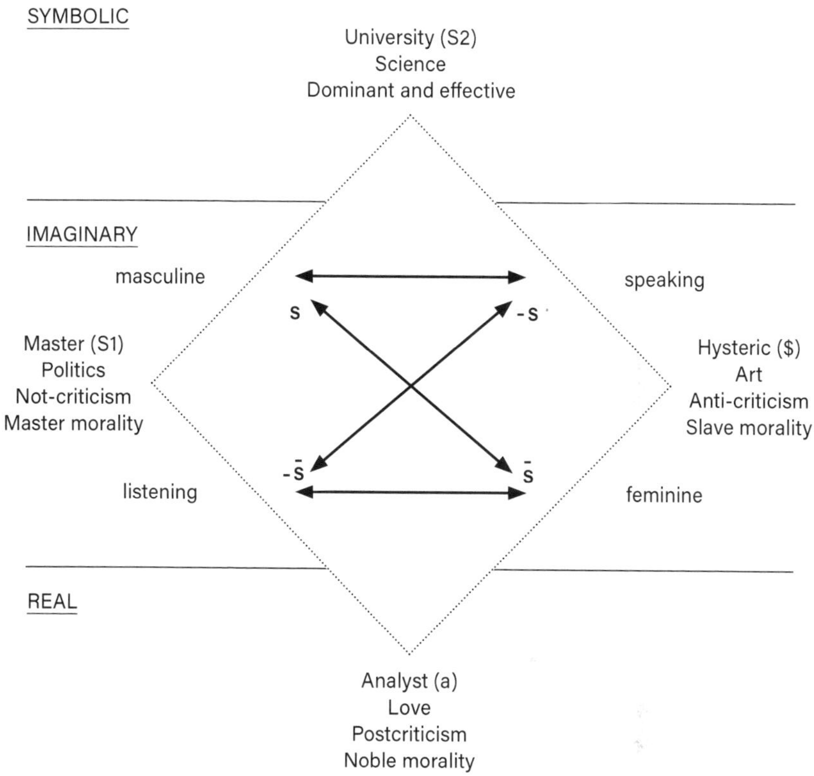

FIGURE 11

Possibility; the *Künstlerroman,* or artist narrative, discussed further in the next chapter; and what Stanley Cavell theorizes in his great book *Pursuits of Happiness* (1981) as the *comedy of remarriage,* to which I will return in chapter 6.[27] Crucially, works in these genres are not usually artistic events in the sense in which Badiou formulates it, texts that punch a hole in reigning discourses and reorder the field around them—it is precisely this sense of the work of art itself as an event that I examine in a discussion of James Joyce's breakthrough 1907 story "The Dead."[28] Rather, the evental genres take up the vital labor of all utopian texts, educating their readers' desires, highlighting the human necessity of fidelity to events when they irrupt along the void of any situation. It is exactly this radical alternative form of historical narration, and its accompanying political pedagogy, that we find realized in Du Bois's landmark reading of Brown's life and achievements.

Having studied in Berlin for two years, Du Bois was deeply familiar with Hegel's writings, and a significant body of scholarship has arisen in recent years that explores the ways Du Bois draws upon Hegel's *Phenomenology* in composing his earlier masterpiece of dialectical thinking, *The Souls of Black Folk* (1903). Stephanie J. Shaw reminds us that not only did Du Bois's "arrival at Friedrich Wilhelms Universität in 1892 coincide with a European/German revival of interest in Hegel (with one of Hegel's most devoted followers, whose lectures Du Bois attended, teaching at the university where Hegel himself spent a significant portion of his professional career), but there was an equally important and comparable movement in America that was already generations old."[29] Shaw further contends that in writing *The Souls of Black Folk,* Du Bois drew deeply upon his reading of Hegel's work, and in fact the book's opening and middle chapters can be understood as both paralleling and reworking the narrative arc of *The Phenomenology of Spirit* so as to think "the movement of the souls of black folk from Consciousness to Self-Consciousness to Reason."[30] Of special interest in our context, Shaw maintains that "Hegel's discussion of 'Self-Consciousness,' . . . finds parallels in Du Bois' 'Of the Meaning of Progress,' where nearly all the personalities who appear are involved in an unmistakable 'Lordship and Bondage' type of struggle."[31] Shaw contends that Du Bois nonreads and writes Hegel in this way in order both to establish black folk's "*humanity* and their rightful placement in the narrative of the World Soul's journey to freedom and to knowledge."[32]

George Ciccariello-Maher argues that for all of its tremendous significance, Du Bois's achievement in *The Souls of Black Folk* is nevertheless limited by a "Hegel-inspired faith in progress and a palpable ambiguity toward the 'terrible' Maroons, John Brown, Nat Turner, and Toussaint L'Ouverture."[33] Elsewhere, Ciccariello-Maher contends that the book's idealism and its overemphasis on the transformative power of "a higher education in the humanities" may account for the fact that this early book has "attracted more attention than the entirety of Du Bois's intellectual production during the next 60 years."[34] Ciccariello-Maher further observes that by the time of his monumental 1935 study, *Black Reconstruction in America, 1860–1880,* Du Bois has rediscovered "revolutionary Black agency where it was invisible to master dialecticians, through a transposition of slaves with workers and slavery with capitalism as a global system."[35] While I concur readily with Ciccariello-Maher's claims, I maintain that such a transformed perspective is already fully evident in *John Brown.*

Du Bois's breakthrough in *John Brown* to his own form of universal history is as much a product of the particular situation of the book's composition as it is of Du Bois's reading and education. In the opening of his introduction to the 2001 republication of *John Brown,* David Roediger points out that in 1906—the year Du Bois was working on his book and of his visit for the second meeting of the predecessor to the NAACP, the Niagara Movement, which took place in Harpers Ferry—Du Bois stood at the site of Brown's "failed" insurrection "as both a militant pilgrim and as Brown's academic biographer."[36] As a result, Roediger argues, Du Bois was "torn" in his work on the book "between what might now be called advocacy and scholarship."[37] (Shaw similarly notes that Du Bois worked in a moment "when narrow, disciplinary boundaries were not clearly established, and when intellectuals were more multidimensional than they are now.")[38] Du Bois had earlier been asked to write a biography of Frederick Douglass, which would also encompass "material on the Fugitive Slave Law, slave trading, and the Underground Railroad," only to have the commission withdrawn when Booker T. Washington belatedly made the decision to write the book himself. Du Bois in turn proposed a book on Nat Turner, the leader of the infamous 1831 Virginia slave rebellion; however, "questioning both the availability of sources and Turner's importance, the editor balked" and suggested that Du Bois instead write on Brown, this despite the fact there was a general resistance in this moment to "historical writing on whites by black historians."[39]

Bill V. Mullen argues that another important influence on Du Bois's intellectual and political development at this time was "the 1904–1905 Russo-Japanese War and its political aftermath. It is *this* event, rather than his trip to Russia in 1926, that instantiated Du Bois's participation in wider world-revolutionary struggle."[40] Mullen further maintains that this event remained an important touchstone for Du Bois's evolving thought; indeed, in 1950 Du Bois notes "that it was the Russo-Japanese War and Russia's subsequent first revolution that inspired him to consider for the first time the historical parallels between Russia's peasantry under the tsar and African American slaves, peasants, and sharecroppers in the American South—the subject of his flurry of economic studies at Atlanta University between 1903 and 1910."[41] This complex interaction of factors would shape in an immediate way the original experimental form of Du Bois's book.

Du Bois crafts his study as a response to two trends in his moment coming to dominate both the representations of the post–Civil War period of Reconstruction and of Brown himself. The former was codified in the Dunning School, named after its founder, the conservative and deeply influential University of Columbia historian William Archibald Dunning, who, drawing upon then widespread social Darwinist ideologies, characterizes Reconstruction as follows:

> A tragic epoch of misrule, a time when political corruption dominated southern politics, and a time when ignorant freedmen gained undue political rights and exercised undue political influence over the defeated southern whites. The tragedy of Reconstruction was that northern idealists engaged in a revolution to forge an interracial society out of the maelstrom of civil war. Dunning complained that these idealists succeeded only in relegating southern whites to unnaturally subjugated peoples, elevating blacks well beyond their capabilities, and denying the American people an opportunity to realize their true, national identity by reuniting the sections in a sensible and realistic manner. Dunning and his acolytes, therefore, universally judged Reconstruction a complete failure.[42]

Du Bois would confront Dunning's thought head-on at the end of 1909, when he presented to an American Historical Association audience that included Dunning himself "Reconstruction and Its Benefits," an essay that would later blossom into *Black Reconstruction in America*.

Du Bois invokes directly the social Darwinism at the basis of Dunning School ideology in *John Brown*'s stirring concluding chapter:

> A step has been taken in America fraught with the gravest social consequences to the world, and threatening not simply the political but the moral integrity of the nation: that step is denying black men the validity of those evidences of culture, ability, and decency which are accepted unquestionably in the case of other

> people; and by vague assertions, unprovable assumptions, unjust emphasis, and now and then by deliberate untruth, aiming to secure not only the continued prescription of all these people, but, by caste distinction, to shut in the faces of their rising classes many of the paths to further advance. (*JB*, 227)

Du Bois then continues, "When a social policy, based on a supposed scientific sanction, leads to a moral anomaly, it is time to examine rather carefully the logical foundations of the argument" (227). This is precisely the task Du Bois undertakes in his book, in order to disprove the presupposition of a lack of collective agency on the part of peoples of color not only in the United States but worldwide.

At the same time, Du Bois challenges the fundamental assumptions about Brown and his actions being set into place by liberal and even progressive white historians and writers. It is this view that is given its fullest expression in *The Nation* publisher Oswald Garrison Villard's *John Brown 1800–1859: A Biography Fifty Years After* (1910), a work first published within months of Du Bois's book. Villard was the grandson of the abolitionist leader William Lloyd Garrison, and it is perhaps the negative portrayal in Du Bois's text of Garrison that so greatly upset Villard. For example, Du Bois notes, "For the Abolitionist of the Garrison type Brown had a contempt, as underserved as it was natural to his genius. To recognize an evil and not strike it was to John Brown sinful" (*JB*, 204). After the failure of the Harpers Ferry assault, Du Bois further maintains that "some, impulsive, eager to justify themselves, rushed into print. To Garrison, the non-resistant, the sword of Gideon was abhorrent; Beecher thundered against John Brown and Seward bitterly traduced him" (212). In this way, Garrison, Beecher, and Seward become precursors to those "political moderates" who in the later civil rights struggle counseled Martin Luther King Jr. to abandon the path of "nonviolent direct action" and, in our own moment, those who are, in Ibram X. Kendi's brilliant turn of phrase, "more devoted to order than justice."[43]

In his own exhaustive study of Brown's life and work, David S. Reynolds notes that Villard, "narrated the facts of Brown's life but did not link them to larger historical currents. A committed pacifist, Villard decried Brown's use of violence, especially at Pottawatomie [Kansas]. More surprisingly, given his closeness to Du Bois and the NAACP, he had little to say about Brown's progressive racial agenda. He was dismissive, for instance, of Brown's provisional constitution, which gave blacks complete citizenship rights."[44] Indeed, Villard wrote that this constitution stood as "a chief indictment of Brown's saneness of judgment and his reasoning powers."[45] Moreover, Roediger gives evidence that Villard orchestrated a damaging review campaign aimed at discrediting Du Bois's book, going so far as to pen "an extremely damaging unsigned review of Du Bois's *Brown,* and published it just before the appearance of his own Brown book . . . in both the *Evening Post* and in *The Nation*. . . . Villard's review was almost relentlessly negative. . . . Villard then dismissed even the original sources used by Du Bois, including Franklin Sanborn's biography with documents and Osborne P. Anderson's account of the raid at Harper's Ferry, as unreliable because they were partisan."[46] (The journalist and abolitionist Sanborn was one of the chief financial supporters of Brown, and Anderson was the only African American member of Brown's party at Harpers Ferry to survive.) Villard subsequently helped block publication of Du Bois's response to his review.

Du Bois challenges in two fundamental ways the assumptions that underlie Villard's book. First, he evaluates in a radically new way the strategies pursued by Brown and Garrison. Du Bois begins by noting the deep connection between the two men: "Few Americans recognized in 1839 that the great central problem of America was slavery; and of that few, fewer still were willing to fight it as they knew it should be fought. Of this lesser number, two men stood almost alone, ready to back their faith by action—William Lloyd Garrison and John Brown" (*JB*, 51). However, Du Bois then points out the significantly different forms of action advocated by each leader:

> They were alike only in their intense hatred of slavery, and spiritually they crossed each other's paths in curious fashion, Garrison drifting from a willingness to fight slavery in all ways or in any way to a fateful attitude of non-resistance and withdrawal from the contamination of slaveholders; John Brown drifting from non-resistance to the red path of active warfare. (51)

In the subsequent pages of his study, Du Bois not only argues that Brown's decision was the more productive one, he shows that violence on the part of those fighting against slavery was a self-defensive response to the original inhuman violence that was part and parcel of the system of slavery: "American slavery was the foulest and filthiest blot on nineteenth century civilization. As a school of brutality and human suffering, of female prostitution and male debauchery; as a mockery of marriage and defilement of family life; as a darkening of reason, and spiritual death, it had no parallel in its day. . . . Four things make life worthy to most men: to move, to know, to love, to aspire. [Might these four correspond to Badiou's conditions of, respectively, art, science, love, and politics?] None of these was for the Negro slave" (41).

Moreover, Du Bois's analysis shifts from Garrison's and Villard's ethical framework to a political one in order to show how even the most violent acts of Brown and his followers, and especially the massacre at Pottawatomie, Kansas, were carefully considered and absolutely necessary interventions in their particular and concrete situations. These events represent what Georg Lukács will later theorize as the *Augenblick*:

> What is a "moment" [*Augenblick*]? A situation whose duration may be longer or shorter, but which is distinguished from the process that leads up to it in that it forces together the essential tendencies of that process, and demands that a *decision* be taken over the *future direction of the process*. That is to say the tendencies reach a sort of zenith, and depending on how the situation concerned is handled, the process takes on a different direction after the "moment." Development does not occur, then, as a continuous intensification, in which development is favorable to the proletariat, and the day after tomorrow the situation *must* be even more favorable than it is tomorrow, and so on. It means rather that at a *particular* point, the situation demands that a decision be taken and the day after tomorrow might be too late to make that decision.[47]

Du Bois argues that until Brown's action, "it seemed inevitable that Kansas would become a slave state, with a code of laws which made even an assertion against the right of slaveholding a felony punishable with imprisonment" (*JB*, 78). Du Bois subsequently characterizes the situation in which Brown intervenes in this way:

> The deed was done. Kansas was a slave territory. The free state program had been repudiated by the United States government and had broken like a reed before the assaults of the pro-slavery party. There were mutterings in the East but the cause of freedom was at its lowest ebb. Then suddenly there came the flash of an awful stroke—a deed of retaliation from the free state side so bloody, relentless and cruel that it sent a shudder through all Kansas and Missouri and aroused the nation. In one black night, John Brown, four of his sons, a son-in-law and two others, the chosen executors of the boldest free state leaders, seized and killed five of the worst of the border ruffians who were harrying the free state settlers, and practically swept out of existence the "Dutch Henry" pro-slavery settlement in the Swamp of the Swan. . . . The deed did not make Kansas free—no one, least of all John Brown, dreamed that it would. But it brought to the fore in free state councils the men who were determined to fight for freedom, and it meant the end of passive resistance. The carnival of crime and rapine that ensued was a disgrace to civilization but it was the cost of freedom, and it was less than the price of repression. (79)

Without this act at this precise moment, Du Bois maintains, history would have moved in a very different direction.

What such an alternate history would look like is figured in Russell Banks's novel of John Brown and his moment, *Cloudsplitter* (1998). Banks's narrator in this scene and throughout the book is Brown's real-world son, Owen, who would survive the events at Harpers Ferry and ultimately die in 1889 at the age of sixty-four and be buried in the desert outside Pasadena, California. Decades later, Owen reflects:

> I believe that I am further responsible, and to nearly the same degree, for the bloody acts that night of my father and brothers, too. For without my having instigated the attack and then goaded them when they grew timorous and frightened by the idea, they would not have done it.
>
> Simply, I showed them at the time and afterwards that if we did not slay those five pro-slave settlers and did not do it in such a brutal fashion, the war in Kansas would have been over. Fin-

> ished. In a matter of weeks, Kansas would have been admitted to the Union as a slave-state, and there would have been nothing for it then but the quick secession of all the Northern states, starting with New England, and the wholesale abandonment of three million Negro Americans to live and die in slavery, along with their children and grandchildren and however many generations it would take before slavery in the South was finally, if ever, overthrown. There would have been no raid on Harpers Ferry, certainly, and no Civil War, for the South would not have objected in the slightest to the break-up of the Union. Let them go. We will happily keep our slaves.
>
> When we went down to the Pottawatomie, I believed all that. And in spite of my guilty feelings, I believe it still. . . . On that dark May night in '56, I truly thought that we were shaping history, that we were affecting the course of future events, making one set nearly impossible and another very likely, and I believed that the second set was morally superior to the first, so it was a good and necessary thing, what we were doing.[48]

Owen then adds, in an echo of Du Bois's claims, "If we had learned anything over the last decade, it was that there was no other way to defeat slavery, except with a willingness to die for it. We had learned what the Negroes long knew. And thus we merely did what the Negroes themselves had done over and over in the past—in Haiti, in the mountains of Jamaica, and in the swamps of Virginia."[49] It would thus have been a failure to act in this moment, far more than the violence involved in the acting, that, both Du Bois and Banks's fictional Owen Brown maintain, future generations would have been unable to forgive.

Another more explicitly science fiction alternate history fiction, Terry Bisson's *Fire on the Mountain* (1988), bears out the universal dimension of Brown's actions at Harpers Ferry by imagining a comedic "what if" scenario concerning the raid's success. Bisson, who acknowledges the influence of Du Bois on his novel, imagines the success of Brown's actions leading to an explosion of revolutionary upheaval across the globe: "Many people date the formal beginning of the Independence War from Lee's Christmas defeat at Roanoke, because it marks the entry of Garibaldi and Mexico, Haiti and the Cherokee, Douglass's proclamation, and the internationalization of the conflict."[50]

A little further on, one of Bisson's characters, who is a direct witness to the aftermath of the events at Harpers Ferry, proclaims, "In California, the Chinese, imported to slog the Railroads like the Irish here in the East, have joined with the Republicans, to re-raise the Bear Flag. The Irish in Baltimore are refusing to load tobacco for England. Emily, our dear Abolitionism has taken on an International as well as a Revolutionary character!"[51] As a result of these unexpected events, not only is an independent nation, Nova Africa, established in what had been the southern United States, James Connolly leads a successful uprising in Ireland, the Paris Commune flourishes, revolutions erupt in Russia and Egypt, and socialism is established throughout Africa.[52] Moreover, in Bisson's alternate history, Abraham Lincoln stands on the wrong side of history, precisely because of his efforts to recontain this struggle as exclusively one of national provenance:

> Lincoln was a Whig, backed by U.S. Capital, who had organized a fifth column of Southern whites to support an invasion of Nova Africa in 1870, right after the Independence War. If the whites couldn't keep the slaves, they at least wanted the land back. Though the invaders had been routed at the Battle of Shoat's Bend without crossing the Cumberland River, "One nation indivisible" had become a rallying cry for white nationalists on both sides of the border.[53]

Returning to Du Bois's text, it is in the line of *John Brown* that immediately follows the contrast of the different paths pursued by Garrison and Brown where the radicality of Du Bois's intervention and his book's novel formal and generic breakthrough into the universal history become fully evident:

> Nowhere did the imminence of a great struggle show itself more clearly than among the Negroes themselves. Organized insurrection ceased in the South, not because of the increased rigors of the slave system, but because the great safety-valve of escape northward was opened wider and wider, and the methods were gradually coordinated into that mysterious system known as the Underground Railroad. The slaves and freedmen started the work and to the end bore the brunt of danger and hardship; but

> gradually they more and more secured the cooperation of men like John Brown, and of others less radical but just as sympathetic. (*JB*, 51–52)

In a single stroke, Du Bois here undermines a system of representation that would locate Brown's efforts, either hagiographically or in order to vilify, as those of an isolated individual or as an extreme along the continuum of white abolitionist activities. Indeed, it is precisely his "unconditional affirmation of universal rights" and "intransigent politics of conviction" that led more moderate reformers and the slave-owning aristocracy alike to label Brown a *fanatic*:[54]

> "To set them free would sacrifice the life of every man in this community."
> "I do not think so."
> "I know it; you are fanatical." (*JB*, 209)

Du Bois, however, reframes these actions within the context of transnational black actions to overturn the "most daring and insolent system of human repression," violence, and *exploitation* known as slavery (231)—and crucially not, as a liberal representation of Villard's type would have it, to liberate *dominated* American slaves.[55] Du Bois makes clear early on that the systemic nature of slavery results in its debilitating consequences, though by no means equally, for all parties involved: "While the Negro slaves sank to listless docility and vacant ignorance, their masters found themselves whirled in the eddies of mighty movements: their system of slavery was twisting them backwards toward darker ages of force and caste and cruelty, while forward swirled swift currents of liberty and uplift" (*JB*, 4). Only by obliterating the system itself, Du Bois maintains, can these effects be overcome.

In a way that directly connects his narration to Buck-Morss's formulation of the universal history, Du Bois argues that the world historical event of the Haitian Revolution sparked similar efforts across the globe:

> The flaming fury of their mad attempts at vengeance echoes all down the blood-swept path of slavery. In Jamaica they upturned the government and harried the land until England crept and sued for peace. In the Danish Isles they started a whirlwind of

> slaughter; in Haiti they drove their masters into the sea; and in South Carolina they rose twice like a threatening wave against the terror-stricken whites, but were betrayed. Such outbreaks here and there foretold the possibility of coordinate action and organic development. To be sure, the successful outbreaks were few and spasmodic; but the flare of Haiti lighted the night and made the world remember that these, too, were men. (*JB*, 43)

Bisson creates a similar image in his fiction in relationship to the successful assault at Harpers Ferry: "We were far enough up in the valley now to see the famous fires—one on the Blue Ridge, one on Signal Knob, and two on the Cumberlands to the west. . . . Beautiful they were, like stars, and indeed they had drawn me here like the Christ star; and others from around the world, as well. I was musing on how very far they were visible (poetically), all the way from England, Italy, Greece, even Africa."[56]

In Du Bois's view, not only does Brown learn from these historical examples, he was extraordinarily rare among white abolitionists in that he understood the vital role of radical black activist, freed person or slave, in the Americas or beyond, in the present struggle:

> Of all this development John Brown knew far more than most white men and it was on this great knowledge that his great faith was based. To most Americans the inner striving of the Negro was a veiled and an unknown tale: they had heard of Douglass, they knew of fugitive slaves, but of the living, organized, struggling group that made both these phenomena possible they had no conception. (*JB*, 146)

It is thus in his very actions that, as Ted A. Smith points out, "Brown's life displayed the shape of a new social imaginary, a new America marked by equality and love between people of all races. He even wrote a constitution for this new America. The violence done to and by him played a crucial role in creating this community."[57]

In her examination of Du Bois's appropriation in *The Souls of Black Folk* of Hegel's *Phenomenology of Spirit*, Shaw argues that "just as Hegel's 'curtain' had to be 'drawn away' to reveal what was behind it, Du Bois had to 'raise' the veil—the middle term of 'appearances'—that stood between *America's* divided (double) consciousness."[58] Similarly, in *John Brown,* Du Bois removes the veils, the appearances constructed by the presuppositions and formal demands of national histories, be they liberal or conservative, that mask the global and universal aspects of the struggles underway as much in Brown's moment as in our own. However, crucially, as Buck-Morss suggests of the other great examples of this genre, "universality emerges in the historical event at the point of rupture."[59] That is, it is only John Brown's interventions, at Pottawatomie even more than at Harpers Ferry, that reveal the full universality of earlier and contemporary global histories of struggle. With this, the radicality and originality of Du Bois's dialectic become fully evident: John Brown's actions can only be understood when resituated in the context of the global activism of people of color, while this unknown history is itself fully unveiled only in terms of the point of rupture created by Brown's actions.

In closing, there is one final dimension of Du Bois's universal history to which I would like to draw attention. Du Bois is not content simply to celebrate the past successes of Brown and, lest we forget again, the larger global collective struggles of which he was always already a part. Michelle Cliff's extraordinary novel, *Free Enterprise* (1993) makes a similar point when the real-world radical black activist Mary Ellen Pleasant, whose gravestone in California was long marked simply "She was a Friend of John Brown," bristles at "everyone referring to our enterprise as 'John Brown's Raid on Harper's Ferry'" and points out that from the perspective of a larger global movement, "J. B. was a splendid ally; no more, no less."[60] In their local and immediate contexts, these successes were significant, and Du Bois readily acknowledges them. However, within the larger global framework of a universal history, Du Bois maintains that they must ultimately be understood as failures. This is because of the fact that, as Du Bois suggests, while the particular institution of Southern American slavery may have come to its end in the events of the U.S. Civil War, the universal system or structural violence of racial division and economic exploitation, of which the institution was a particular manifestation, remains in place. Indeed, Du Bois writes that in his own moment, "The price of repressing the world's darker races is shown in a moral retrogression and an economic waste unparalleled since the age of the African slave-trade" (*JB,* 230). As the news reminds us almost every day, such retrogression and waste continue into our millennium, piling wreckage upon wreckage ever higher at our feet.

And yet, failure too is a constitutive aspect of the dialectical narrative Du Bois develops in his book. Jameson writes:

> It is the failure of imagination that is important, and not its achievement, since in any case all representations fail and it is always impossible to imagine. This is also to say that in terms of political positions and ideologies, all the radical positions of the past are flawed, precisely because they failed. The productive use of earlier radicalisms . . . lies not in their triumphant reassemblage as a radical precursor tradition but in their tragic failure to constitute such a tradition in the first place. History progresses by failure rather than by success, as Benjamin never tired of insisting; and it would be better to think of Lenin or Brecht (to pick a few illustrious names at random) as failures—that is, as actors and agents constrained by their own ideological limits and those of their moment of history—than as triumphant examples and models in some hagiographic or celebratory sense.[61]

Ted A. Smith similarly argues:

> Du Bois described a divine violence made manifest at Harpers Ferry that shattered the system of relations that legitimated the violence of the Commonwealth of Virginia and the United States as well as the moral obligations that bound their citizens. In breaking the death grip with which slavery and their nation held one another, it did not become a warrant for later action. It *did* open space for a new freedom in relation to that which had been destroyed. That freedom is not abstract and absolute. It is pointed and particular. And it invites responses that recognize its particularity.[62]

And yet, never is this stance intended to drive the reader to pessimism or cynical despair (a theme to which I will return again in my concluding chapter). The central goal of the counternarrative Du Bois offers is, as Buck-Morss notes of the universal history more generally, to do "more than criticize the status quo; it inspires action to change it. [Its] explicit aim is to connect today's global resistance to an earlier one."[63] "This, then, is the truth," Du Bois proclaims on his book's final page:

> The cost of liberty is less than the price of repression, even though the cost be blood. Freedom of development and equality of opportunity is the demand of Darwinism and this calls for the abolition of hard and fast lines between races, just as it called for the breaking down of barriers between classes. Only in this way can the best in humanity be discovered and conserved, and only thus can mankind live in peace and progress. (*JB*, 237)

Three decades later, in the context of a rising tide of fascism, Lukács maintains "that every honest intellectual who takes the problems of the popular front and the liberation of his people from the real or threatened yoke of Fascism seriously must come up against the problem of socialism in practice as soon as he examines any question concretely."[64] Similarly, Bhaskar Sunkara points out that today, "dealing seriously with oppression means distributing wealth and power (currently held by economic elites and not less oppressed workers) to the working-class victims of racism and sexism. That means confronting corporate interests. . . . If liberals want to fight oppression they need to start talking about how to revive our unions and turn them into vehicles for a majoritarian movement for justice. Until they do that, we shouldn't take anything they say about racism and sexism seriously."[65]

It is this still unfulfilled universal demand that makes Du Bois's book, and the story it tells, as important for us today as it was a century ago—as Buck-Morss reminds us one final time, "Radical antislavery is a human invention that belongs to no one, because it belongs to everyone. Such ideas are the residues of events, rather than the possession of a particular collective, and even if they fail, they can never be forgotten."[66]

[5]

Politics, Art, and Utopia in "Babette's Feast"

> A certain readiness to perish is not so very rare, but it is seldom that you meet men whose souls, steeled in the impenetrable armour of resolution, are ready to fight a losing battle to the last; the desire of peace waxes stronger as hope declines, till at last it conquers the very desire of life.
>
> —Joseph Conrad, *Lord Jim: A Tale*

> The event exists in the situation only through its name.
>
> —Burhanuddin Baki, *Badiou's "Being and Event" and the Mathematics of Set Theory*

THIS CHAPTER READS the underappreciated late modernist short story "Babette's Feast" by the Danish writer Karen Blixen, better known by her pen name of Isak Dinesen. I take up Dinesen's tale both as an example of the second of the evental genres—the *Künstlerroman* or artist narrative—and in terms of its fidelity to one of the supreme universal historical events of the latter part of the nineteenth century: the 1871 Paris Commune, which Alain Badiou describes as "the striking, and totally unforeseeable, beginning of a rupture (true, still without concept) with the very thing that had established the norms of its appearing."[1] "Babette's Feast" was originally published in English in the June 1950 issue of the *Ladies' Home Journal*—the story goes that Dinesen wanted to place a story in a major U.S. magazine and a friend recommended she write about food because "Americans are obsessed with food"[2]—and reprinted eight years later in the final collection to appear during her lifetime, *Anecdotes of Destiny* (1958). The story would also serve as the basis for a widely acclaimed 1987 film adaptation directed by

Gabriel Axel, which went on to become the first Danish film to win the Academy Award for Best Foreign Language Film.

Dinesen's tale opens in an isolated fishing village in the far north of Norway. Early on, we are told that twelve years prior, on "a rainy June night of 1871," a disheveled and dispirited French woman, "a friendless fugitive, almost mad with grief and fear," appears at the home of two sisters, Martine and Philippa.[3] The two women are the elderly and unmarried daughters of "a Dean and a prophet, the founder of a pious ecclesiastic party or sect, which was known and looked up to in all the country of Norway. Its members renounced the pleasures of this world, for the earth and all that it held to them was but a kind of illusion" (*BF,* 3). Their unexpected guest, named Babette Hersant, becomes the sisters' "French maid-of-all-work" (4).

As time passes, the community discovers that Babette is an extraordinarily gifted chef—even more astonishing is the revelation that in her earlier years she "was once cook at the Café Anglais" (*BF,* 44). The Café Anglais was an actual historical restaurant located at the corner of Boulevard des Italiens and Rue de Marivaux in Paris, its celebrated supper room 16, Le grand seize, as the *New York Times* put it on the occasion of its closing in 1913, "the centre of the fashion and elegance of that brilliant period, the Second Empire."[4] The restaurant's most well-known chef, Adolphe Dugléré, was the creator in 1869 of potage Germiny—named in honor of Charles Gabriel Le Bègue, comte de Germiny and head of the Banque de France—and, a year later, of pommes Anna, reputed to be named after the famed courtesan Anna Deslions, nicknamed Lionne des Boulevards ("lioness of the boulevards"), who served as a significant inspiration for Émile Zola's *Nana* (1880).[5]

Years later, Babette unexpectedly receives a letter informing her that she has won ten thousand francs in the French lottery. She decides to spend all of her winnings on the preparation of an extravagant meal for the sisters and other members of their community: "A dinner for twelve at the Café Anglais would cost ten thousand francs," Babette informs the confounded Martine and Philippa after the meal has been consumed (*BF,* 46). The story climaxes with the following exchange:

> But Philippa's heart was melting in her bosom. It seemed that an unforgettable evening was to be finished off with an unforgettable proof of human loyalty and self-sacrifice.

> "Dear Babette," she said softly, "you ought not to have given away all you had for our sake."
>
> Babette gave her mistress a deep glance, a strange glance. Was there not pity, even scorn, at the bottom of it?
>
> "For your sake?" she replied. "No. For my own."
>
> She rose from the chopping block and stood up before the two sisters.
>
> "I am a great artist!" she said.
>
> She waited a moment and then repeated: "I am a great artist, Mesdames."
>
> Again for a long time there was a deep silence in the kitchen.
>
> Then Martine said: "So you will be poor now all your life, Babette?"
>
> "Poor?" said Babette. She smiled as if to herself. "No, I shall never be poor. I told you that I am a great artist. A great artist, Mesdames, is never poor. We have something, Mesdames, of which other people know nothing." (46–47)

Babette's final words concern her fellow artist, the renowned opera singer Monsieur Papin, who decades earlier had been the mentor and very nearly the lover of the gifted Philippa, and who later would be responsible for sending Babette to the sisters:

> "It was like that with Monsieur Papin too," she said.
>
> "With Monsieur Papin?" Philippa asked.
>
> "Yes, with your Monsieur Papin, my poor lady," said Babette. "He told me so himself: 'It is terrible and unbearable to an artist,' he said, 'to be encouraged to do, to be applauded for doing, his second best.' He said: 'Through all the world there goes one long cry from the heart of the artist: Give me leave to do my utmost!'" (48)

The utopianism of the Künstlerroman is the focus of a magisterial pair of essays by Ernst Bloch, "Philosophische Ansicht des Detektivromans" ("A Philosophical View of the Detective Novel") and "Philosophische Ansicht des Künstlerroman" ("A Philosophical View of the Novel of the Artist") (1965). Early on in the second essay, Bloch suggests the dialectical link between the practices of the detective and artist novels when he notes, "Whereas the detective novel requires a process of collecting evidence, penetrating backward to a past crime, the novel of the artist requires recognition of and interest in the creative person who brings out something new instead of something past."[6] Near the essay's conclusion, Bloch again reiterates:

> If the action of the detective story—from the beginning of *Oedipus*—is concerned with revealing *a past crime*, with revealing it, then the action of the *artist* story—from the beginning of *Prometheus*, even to the legend of the *building of the tower* of Babel—concerns itself with the *formation of the human*, with revealing this. The detective story depends on penetrating and digging up material, while the inventive story depends on revealing and shaping it in the not-yet and out of the not-yet that arises before us as that of the work.[7]

Bloch further notes, "That which moves one in the novel of the artist itself, as one which ultimately, like the genuine Faust material, concerns all of humankind, even without the respective epithets, is the desire to break new ground, with knights, death, and the devil, to head for the envisioned utopian castle or to that which corresponds to its formation in shape, sound, or word."[8] Earlier, in an insight that resonates with the climactic exchange from "Babette's Feast" I cited above, Bloch also points out, "Art must be grasped by the artist, not by people who experience, receive, or even categorize it."[9]

Throughout the essay, Bloch draws upon his fundamental distinction between "abstract" and "concrete" utopias: between, on the one hand, wish fulfillments, happy endings, and reassuring idealist dreams and, on the other, figures that are of a truly "anticipatory kind."[10] (A related distinction, between a "subjunctive"—and hence passive—"should have been" and the historical and materialist "could have been" is at the heart of Charles Yu's first novel, *How to Live Safely in a Science Fictional Universe* [2010].)[11] In her own significant engagement with Bloch's work, Ruth Levitas notes, "the distinction between abstract and concrete utopia is fundamental to Bloch's project. The rehabilitation of utopia depends upon the removal of the abstract elements which clutter up the concrete core. Concrete utopia must be winnowed out, stripping wishful thinking of that which is purely fantastic, compensatory and escapist."[12]

However, the authentic Künstlerroman maintains a fidelity to the concrete utopia in a paradoxical fashion, by way of an acknowledgment of a certain failure in its project: the failure to represent the new thing, the work of art itself, which, Fredric Jameson maintains in his discussion of Bloch's essays, "confers upon the novel's hero his right to be called an artist." Jameson continues, "For Bloch, however, this emptiness of the work within a work, this blank canvas at the center, is the very locus of the not-yet-existent itself; and it is precisely this essentially fragmentary and aesthetically unsatisfying structure of the novel of the artist which gives it its ontological value as a form and figure of the movement of the future incomplete before us."[13] Conversely, if this work does appear in the text—as, say, in the villanelle Stephen Dedalus composes in the final chapter of James Joyce's *A Portrait of the Artist as a Young Man* (1917)—then we have either fallen back into the abstract utopia or, as is the case in Joyce's open-ended fiction, we have a sign that the becoming of the artist is not-yet (and may never be) complete.

It is in its very unrepresentability that the work of art at the heart of the Künstlerroman becomes another figure for Badiou's event. Badiou argues that language is deeply embedded within the known. "The name of the event," however, "is supernumerary, and so it does not belong to the language of a situation."[14] Thus, Badiou maintains, an event "cannot be communicated [*ne se communiqué pas*]." Rather, it is *encountered*: "The Immortal that I am capable of being cannot be spurred in me by the effects of communicative sociality, it must be *directly* seized by fidelity. . . . To enter into the composition of a subject of truth can only be something that *happens to you*."[15]

In such an encounter a person is presented with the opportunity to become more than an individual or multiple. Badiou argues:

> If there is no ethics "in general," that is because there is no abstract Subject, who would adopt it as his shield. There is only a particular kind of animal, convoked by certain circumstances to *become* a subject—or rather, to enter into the composing of a subject. That is to say that at a given moment, everything he is—his body, his abilities—is called upon to enable the passing of a

> truth along its path. This is when the human animal is convoked [*requis*] to be the immortal that he was not yet.[16]

A little further on, Badiou notes, "the subject, therefore, in no way pre-exists the process. He is absolutely nonexistent in the situation 'before' the event. We might say that the process of truth *induces* a subject."[17] Then, in a paragraph that has special resonance for the evental genre of the comedy of remarriage that I will discuss in my next chapter, Badiou continues:

> It is important to understand that the "subject," thus conceived, does not overlap with the psychological subject, nor even the reflexive subject (in Descartes's sense) or the transcendental subject (in Kant's sense). For example, the subject induced by fidelity to an amorous encounter, the subject of love, is *not* the "loving" subject described by the classical moralists. For this kind of psychological subject falls within the province of human nature, within the logic of passion, whereas what I am talking about has no "natural" pre-existence. The lovers as such enter into the composition of *one* loving subject, who *exceeds* them both.[18]

In *Being and Event,* Badiou further maintains that "the essence of the event is to be undecidable with regard to its belonging to the situation."[19] Hence an event requires on the part of the subject a "decision with respect to its belonging to the situation," a decision that is at the basis of any "intervention" in the world.[20] Badiou argues that one is a subject, or what he also refers to as an immortal, only as long as one maintains what he calls a *fidelity* to the original "evental" (*événementiel*) encounter: "To be faithful to an event is to move within the situation that this event has supplemented, by *thinking* (although all thought is a practice, a putting to the test) the situation 'according to' the event. And this, of course—since the event was excluded by the regular laws of the situation—compels the subject to *invent* a new way of being and acting in the situation."[21]

The four evental genres I have been discussing in these chapters—the universal history, Künstlerroman, comedy of remarriage, and science fiction—can further be understood as modernist inversions of what Jameson identifies in *The Antinomies of Realism* as the great realist genres of the nineteenth century: the historical novel, "a hypostasis of this inner historical reality: isolating the virus of historical change as though in a test tube"; the bildungsroman, "an instrument for the exploration of the new possibilities of bourgeois society"; the novel of adultery, "the very space of negativity in nineteenth-century bourgeois life"; and naturalism, "a more general narrative paradigm, which could be described as the trajectory of decline and failure, of something like an entropy on the level of the individual destiny."[22] A Greimasian presentation of the relationships between the evental and realist genres would appear as in Figure 12. The distinction between the realist and evental genres further underscores a point already implicit in Bloch's essays: rather than being, as usually assumed, a subspecies of the bildungsroman—although there are bildungsroman of the artist, Balzac's *Illusions perdues* (*Lost Illusions*) (1843) being a case in point—the authentic Künstlerroman represents a distinct practice, with its own unique genealogy.

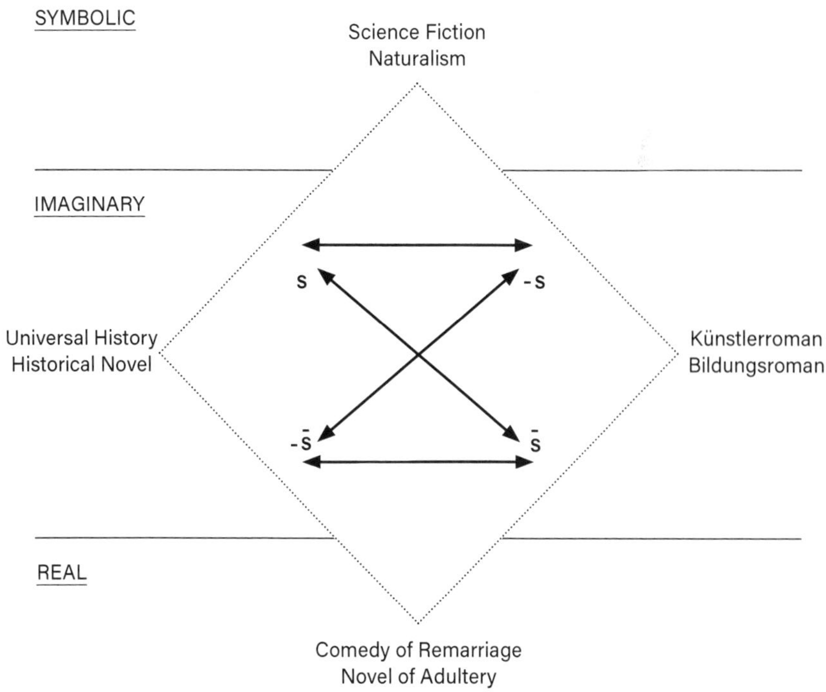

FIGURE 12

Both the bildungsroman and the Künstlerroman originate in the context of German Romanticism and in particular from within the fecund intervention of Goethe. If the paradigm of the bildungsroman is to be located in Goethe's *Wilhelm Meisters Lehrjahre* (*Wilhelm Meister's Apprenticeship*) (1795), the seeds of the Künstlerroman appear in his earlier international sensation *Die Leiden des jungen Werthers* (*The Sorrows of Young Werther*) (1774). However, because Werther is a proto-artist, his real fidelity being located in the condition of love, the first full-blown Künstlerroman is, as Bloch suggests, to be found in E. T. A. Hoffmann's *Lebensansichten des Katers Murr, nebst fragmentarischer Biographie des Kapellmeisters Johannes Kreisler in zufälligen Makulaturblättern* (*The Life and Opinions of Kater Murr, along with a Fragmentary Biography of Kepellmeister Johannes Kreisler on Random Sheets of Waste Paper*) (1819–1821). In Hoffmann's narrative, the reader is presented directly with the doggerel poetry of Kater Murr—who characterizes his own "wonderful sonnet" as "a model of its kind, an effusion from the deepest depths of my soul"—while the authentic art of Kreisler is only invoked indirectly: "But soon both voices rose on the waves of the song like shimmering swans, now aspiring to rise aloft to the radiant, golden clouds with the beat of rushing wings, now to sink dying in sweet amorous embrace in the roaring current of chords."[23] As Maurice Beebe also points out in his classic study of the practice, the Künstlerroman subsequently falls into neglect during the moment of realism only to reemerge in the latter part of the nineteenth century and become a central concern of modernism, as exemplified by such diverse works as Joyce's *A Portrait of the Artist as a Young Man,* James Weldon Johnson's *The Autobiography of an Ex-colored Man* (1912), Willa Cather's *The Song of the Lark* (1915), Virginia Woolf's *To the Lighthouse* (1927), and, of most importance to Bloch, Thomas Mann's *Doktor Faustus* (1947).[24]

Dinesen's story appears only three years after the publication of Mann's novel, and Dinesen acknowledged her admiration of it, even comparing herself to the novel's doomed artist, Adrian Leverkühn.[25] Both Mann's novel and Dinesen's story also share, as I will suggest in my Conclusion, a place in the situation of postwar late modernism. However, unlike *Doktor Faustus,* for many people today, if they are at all familiar with Dinesen's story, it is only indirectly, as the inspiration for Axel's film adaptation. Although relocating the action from northern Norway to Denmark's rural west coast, Axel's version appears at first glance to be relatively faithful to Dinesen's original. However, even this change of setting introduces incongruities into the film narrative. For example, as a result of siding with Napoleon in his war with Great Britain, Denmark was forced in 1814 to cede control of Norway to the Swedish crown, which would remain the case until Norwegian independence in 1905. This accounts for the fact that in Dinesen's story, a young aristocrat, whom I will introduce momentarily, serves in the Swedish and not the Danish court. The fact, then, that he is also a colonial subject might offer a clue to his course of action in the story. This simple change thus has the effect of evacuating the narrative's concrete historical content, transforming it into that quintessential postmodern genre of the "nostalgia film (or what the French call *la mode rétro*)," which Jameson characterizes in the following manner: "the nostalgia film was never a matter of some old-fashioned 'representation' of historical content, but instead approached the 'past' through stylistic connotation, conveying 'pastness' by the glossy qualities of the image, . . . by the attributes of fashion."[26]

At the same time, a series of seemingly more minor changes in the film transforms in a significant way the overall vision. In his essay "Adaptation as a Philosophical Problem," Jameson elaborates what might be referred to as the axioms of all film adaptations: "the novel and its film adaptation must not be of equal quality," and in the exceptional cases when they are, "the film must be utterly different from, utterly unfaithful to, its original."[27] (I would add a Žižekian corollary: the most apparently faithful adaptation can be the deepest betrayal, while only in a dramatic variation on the first text is there a chance of remaining true to the original's spirit.)[28] Jameson goes on to demonstrate the second proposition through a close reading of Stanisław Lem's *Solaris* and Andrei Tarkovsky's 1972 film adaptation of the same name. The two texts I am looking at here conversely bear out his first proposal, and the changes that take place in the film adaptation of "Babette's Feast" have the effect of transforming Dinesen's concrete utopianism into the abstract.

After winning an Academy Award, Axel's adaptation gave rise to a veritable cottage industry, evidence of which you can still find online, of efforts to re-create the sumptuous meal staged in the film. However, it is precisely the film's visual representation of the meal that marks a significant departure from Dinesen's story and the beginnings of the film's slide into an abstract utopianism. In Dinesen's "Babette's Feast," the only thing we are told about the central dish of the meal is its name. One of the guests at the dinner, General Lorens Loewenhielm, who years earlier as a young officer had visited the village and fallen in love with Martine only later to leave her to pursue an immensely successful career in service of the Swedish court, has the following recollection:

> General Loewenhielm stopped eating and sat immovable. Once more he was carried back to that dinner in Paris of which he had thought in the sledge. An incredibly recherché and palatable dish had been served there; he had asked its name from his fellow diner, Colonel Galliffet, and the Colonel had smilingly told him that it was named "Cailles en Sarcophage." He had further told him that the dish had been invented by the chef of the very café in which they were dining, a person known all over Paris as the greatest culinary genius of the age, and—most surprisingly—a woman! "And indeed," said Colonel Galliffet, "this woman is now turning a dinner at the Café Anglais into a kind of love affair—into a love affair of the noble and romantic category in which one no longer distinguishes between bodily and spiritual appetite or satiety! I have, before now, fought a duel for the sake of a fair lady. For no woman in all Paris, my young friend, would I more willingly shed my blood!" General Loewenhielm turned to the neighbor on the left and said to him: "But this is Cailles en Sarcophage!" The neighbor, who had been listening to the description of a miracle, looked at him absentmindedly, then nodded his head and answered: "Yes, Yes, certainly. What else would it be?" (*BF*, 38)

In this regard, the miracle that is "Cailles en Sarcophage" (Quails in coffins) functions as what Saul Kripke theorizes as a *name,* a rigid designator, which, independent of any "description or cluster of descriptions," functions to "*fix the referent* then that . . . will be the referent . . . in all possible worlds."[29] Also lost in the film translation then is the rigorous dialectical sequence in Dinesen's story of dishes, moving as it does from a universal category, "turtle-soup," through a named particular preparation, "Blinis Demidoff," to an entry that exists only in the singular individual form of its name (36, 38).[30] This scene and its vision of the singularity of the authentic work of art is prefigured earlier in the story, when Martine witnesses bottles being wheeled into the kitchen in preparation for the meal: "'What is there in this bottle, Babette?' she asked in a low voice. 'Not wine?' 'Wine, Madame!' Babette answered. 'No, Madame. It is Clos Vougeot 1846!'" The scene concludes, "Martine had never suspected that wines could have names to them, and was put to silence" (25).

The effects of the encounter with the event of the dinner are presented in the story in this way. First, at the meal's conclusion, Dinesen relates that the elderly guests "realized that the infinite grace of which General Loewenhielm had spoken had been allotted to them, and they did not even wonder at the fact, for it had been but the fulfillment of an ever-present hope. The vain illusions of this earth had dissolved before their eyes like smoke, and they had seen the universe as it really is. They had been given one hour of the millennium" (*BF*, 42). Shortly thereafter, they depart the sister's home: "The guests from the yellow house wavered on their feet, staggered, sat down abruptly or fell forward on their knees and hands and were covered with snow, as if they had indeed had their sins washed white as wool, and in this regained innocent attire were gamboling like little lambs. It was to each of them, blissful to have become as a small child" (43). The film's conclusion similarly suggests that the meal has worked its magic on the elderly members of the party by showing them joining hands outside the home in a redemptive song and dance in the street and under the stars. Crucially, however, a little earlier Dinesen notes, "Of what happened later in the evening nothing definite can here be stated. None of the guests later on had any clear remembrance of it" (41).

It is in its portrayal of what occurs following the evental encounter that the film begins to depart in significant ways from the story. First, in the story when Babette informs the sisters that she will not be returning to Paris, the following exchange occurs:

> "No," said Babette. "What will I do in Paris? They have all gone. I have lost them all, Mesdames."
>
> The sisters' thoughts went to Monsieur Hersant and his son, and they said: "Oh, my poor Babette."
>
> "Yes, they have all gone," said Babette. "The Duke of Morny,

> the Duke of Decazes, Prince Narishkine, General Galliffet, Aurélian Scholl, Paul Daru, the Princess Pauline! All!" (*BF,* 45)

Crucially, these are all figures who stood against the Commune: for example, of the playwright and journalist, Aurélian Scholl, the French Wikipedia site notes that he opposed the Commune to the extent that, "in a letter of denunciation addressed to the police, he indicated the whereabouts of a certain Lavalette who had participated in the Commune. This Lavalette was married to his wife's sister."[31] In the film adaptation, however, this list of names is omitted, Babette breaking off after declaring that there is no one waiting for her in Paris. Moreover, immediately afterward, in the scene I cited earlier when the sisters confront Babette about her expenditure for the dinner of all her funds, her response is changed in the film, almost imperceptibly, from Dinesen's "'For your sake?' she replied. 'No. For my own,'" to "In fact, I did not do it just for you" (*BF,* 46).

The most significant change, however, occurs in the long monologue, which begins with Babette's repeated affirmation of herself as a "great artist" and concludes with her final recollection of Papin's words. In Dinesen's story, inserted between these two passages is the following exchange between Philippa and Babette:

> "But all those people whom you have mentioned," she said, "those princes and great people of Paris whom you named, Babette? You yourself fought against them. You were a Communard! The General you named had your husband and son shot! How can you grieve over them?"
>
> Babette's dark eyes met Philippa's.
>
> "Yes," she said, "I was a Communard. Thanks be to God, I was a Communard! And those people whom I named, Mesdames, were evil and cruel. They let the people of Paris starve; they oppressed and wronged the poor. Thanks be to God, I stood upon a barricade; I loaded the gun for my menfolk! But all the same, Mesdames, I shall not go back to Paris, now that those people of whom I have spoken are no longer there."
>
> She stood immovable, lost in thought.
>
> "You see, Mesdames," she said, at last, "those people belonged

> to me, they were mine. They had been brought up and trained, with greater expense than you, my little ladies, could ever imagine or believe, to understand what a great artist I am. I could make them happy. When I did my very best I could make them perfectly happy." (*BF*, 47–48)

In this exchange, Philippa refers to Papin's original letter of introduction to the two sisters, in which the singer writes:

> The bearer of this letter, Madame Babette Hersant, like my beautiful Empress herself, has had to flee from Paris. Civil war has raged in our streets. French hands have shed French blood. The noble Communards, standing up for the Rights of Man, have been crushed and annihilated. Madame Hersant's husband and son, both eminent ladies' hairdressers, have been shot. She herself was arrested as a Pétroleuse—(which word is used here for women who set fire to houses with petroleum)—and has narrowly escaped the blood-stained hands of General Galliffet. She has lost all she possessed and dares not remain in France. (13)

In the film, the entire passage on the Commune disappears, while Papin's letter is shortened to "The bearer of this letter, Madame Babette Hersant, like my beautiful Empress herself, has been forced to flee from Paris. Civil War has been raging in our streets. Madame Hersant's husband and son were killed like rats. She herself narrowly escaped the blood-stained hands of General Galliffet. She has lost everything and dares not remain in France." The only direct reference to the Commune that remains in the film is a brief image of the execution of the Communards that appears on screen during the reading of Papin's letter.

Dinesen herself was deeply familiar with the events of the Commune, as her father, Wilhelm Dinesen, was in the city during its unfolding and later published his memoirs in Danish under the title *Paris under Communen* (*Paris under the Commune*) (1873). (His book was the source for the Norwegian author Nordahl Grieg's play *Nederlaget* [*The Defeat*] [1937], which in turn was adapted by Brecht as *The Days of the Commune* [1955].)[32] In his book, the elder Dinesen makes clear his enthusiasm for the Commune and his disappointment at its defeat, concluding, "But I had seen enough. I was weary, body and soul, and soon left Paris."[33] The introduction to the French translation of the book points out, "Karen Blixen inherited the spirit of freedom and nonconformity of her father."[34] The fact that in her tale, Dinesen repeatedly underscores the brutal role in the Commune's suppression played by General Galliffet—Gaston Alexandre Auguste, Marquis de Galliffet, a man later known by the sobriquet "Fusilleur de la Commune" (Executioner of the Commune)—and the unfounded accusation that Babette was a pétroleuse are likely also derived from her father's book. Near its conclusion, the elder Dinesen archly notes, "The reputation for bravery and cruelty, which General Galliffet had acquired in Mexico City and in Algiers, was confirmed during the capture of Paris."[35] Of the Commune's aftermath, he then reports, "With each passing day, the number of prisoners at Satory, near Versailles [today, the site of a French military weapons testing facility], increased: processions of 'assassins' and 'pétroleuses' passed daily before the gates."[36]

What, then, are we to make of the film's erasure of Babette's affirmation of her participation in the Commune, as well as Papin's enthusiastic endorsement of the event? Of the few critics who even acknowledge the excision from the film of the story's repeated invocations of the Commune, a number see it as a positive change. This is put the most succinctly in an early discussion, which claims, "This change the film makes in the original story is an improvement, because it distances Babette's story from the political and particular and gives it a greater universality by focusing it on the relation of art and grace in Babette's story."[37] Not only does such a reading elide the significant place of the concrete experience of the Commune in Dinesen's tale, it takes as one of its unspoken assumptions the notion of a fundamental divide between art and politics, of the universal and particular. And yet, it is this division that the story itself calls into question. Understanding art and politics, as does Dinesen, as inseparably—that is, dialectically—linked thus casts the events that unfold during the dinner in a whole new light.

A number of significant things take place during Babette's climactic monologue. First, Babette announces a double fidelity on her part, at once in Badiou's conditions of politics and art. This underscores too what Badiou shows to be the deep relationship between all four conditions. But there is also another form of doubling that occurs here. In both her declarations, Babette repeats her assertion:

> "I am a great artist!" she said.
>
> She waited a moment and then repeated: "I am a great artist, Mesdames."
>
> . . .
>
> "Yes," she said, "I was a Communard. Thanks be to God, I was a Communard!" (*BF,* 46–47)

In a passage from which I have taken inspiration in different ways in my first two books, Žižek underscores the importance of such redoubling: "The crucial point here is the changed symbolic status of an event: when it erupts for the first time it is experienced as a contingent trauma, as an intrusion of a certain non-symbolized Real; only through repetition is this event recognized in its symbolic necessity—it finds its place in the symbolic network; it is realized in the symbolic order."[38]

Moreover, another such redoubling occurs earlier in the story in the accusation that Babette was a pétroleuse: shortly after Papin notes as much in his letter, the sisters speculate, "Perhaps after all she had indeed been a Pétroleuse" (*BF,* 18). In her classic study of the important role of women in the Commune, Edith Thomas underscores the fact that such figures were the invention of the forces of reaction after their seizure of the city: "In this mass hysteria, pétroleuses were to be found everywhere. In the areas occupied by the Versailles army, it was enough that a woman be poor and ill-dressed, and that she be carrying a basket, box, or milkbottle."[39] However, the original French title of Thomas's study is *Les pétroleuses,* a decision the author justifies in this way: "The term '*pétroleuse*' was coined in 1871 to designate the women who were accused of having set fire to Paris. I am using it in a much wider sense: it applies to all the women who were involved in the revolutionary movement of 1871. In no way is its use pejorative."[40] It is only in Thomas's more expansive and transvalued sense then that Babette can be said to be a pétroleuse.

Even more significantly, through these redoublings Dinesen helps the reader grasp that the dinner is itself to be understood as another repeating: a repeating not only of her work as an artist, but also of the radically original experience of the production and consumption of art briefly realized in the Commune. In no way then does the dinner commemorate the Commune; rather, it engages in what Badiou calls in *The Communist Hypothesis* its "reactivation."[41]

In her study *Communal Luxury: The Political Imaginary of the Paris Commune* (2015), Kristin Ross explains the significance of the terms in her title in this way:

> It is the proof that one participates in another life. When Marx says that the greatest accomplishment of the Paris Commune was "its own working existence" he is saying much the same thing. More important than any laws the Communards were able to enact was simply the way in which their daily workings inverted entrenched hierarchies and divisions—first and foremost among these the divisions between manual and artistic or intellectual labor. The world is divided between those who can and those who cannot afford the luxury of playing with words or images. When that division is overcome, as it was under the Commune, or as it is conveyed in the phrase "communal luxury," what matters more than any images conveyed, laws passed, or institutions founded are the capacities set in motion. You do not have to start at the beginning—you can start anywhere.[42]

Ross's observation offers an extraordinary framework for viewing the event of Babette's feast as a concrete utopian figure of both the "impossible" work of art and the working existence of the Commune, the activity that Ross characterizes as communal luxury of undermining long entrenched hierarchies and divisions of labor. Even the cook Babette's declaration of herself as an artist should be understood as underscoring her fidelity to the experience of the Commune, where, as Ross points out, the "overcoming of the division between fine and decorative artists" served as "the principle dimension of its revolutionary arts program."[43] That such an achievement is limited in time and space is acknowledged by both Ross and Dinesen; however, whatever the briefness of its duration it is a concrete reality nonetheless, one that can be learned from, modeled upon, and, in Ross's term, "prolonged" into the future.[44] Moreover, Ross underscores the "universal historical" dimensions of the Commune when she writes:

> The scale of the Commune as an "audacious act of internationalism" can thus be measured not just by the number of Poles or Italians under its flag but by the conduits it enabled of theory

> and practice across national borders. . . . Like the *obshina,* the terms *citoyen, universal republic,* and *commune,* though borrowed from the national past, could be distilled through the internationalist aims and culture of the communal laboratory, and put to immediate use dissolving state bureaucracy.[45]

Interestingly, the third of Badiou's four conditions, that of love, appears in the story by way of its failure to be actualized, in the aborted relationship of the young Loewenhielm and Martine. Loewenhielm's initial encounter with Martine is described by Dinesen in language that confirms its status as an evental site: "But at this one moment there rose before his eyes a sudden, mighty vision of a higher and purer life, with no creditors, dunning letters or parental lectures, with no secret, unpleasant pangs of conscience and with a gentle, golden-haired angel to guide and reward him" (*BF,* 6). Of course, to have been truly faithful to the utopian promise of this encounter would have meant that he too would have had to change his existence entirely and break completely with his, and his class's, established ways of living. This is what he ultimately fails to do, deciding instead to return to the conventional path laid out before him. He first informs Martine, "I am going away forever! . . . I shall never, never see you again! For I have learned here that Fate is hard, and that in this world there are things which are impossible!" Shortly thereafter, Dinesen writes, "he pulled himself together, and in the greatest effort of his young life made up his mind to *forget* what had happened to him in Berlevaag. From now on, he resolved, he would look forward, not back. He would concentrate on his career, and the day was to come when he would cut a brilliant figure in a brilliant world" (7–8; emphasis added). In his assertions that he has no control over his destiny and miraculous events are impossible, and in his willed "forgetting," Loewenhielm fails to become a subject, instead opting for the form of "evil" Badiou names *betrayal*: persuading himself that the event of his encounter with Martine and "the Immortal in question *never existed,* and thus rally to opinion's perception of this point—opinion, whose whole purpose, in the service of interests, is precisely this negation."[46]

A similar betrayal of utopian subjective potential, this time in the condition of art, occurs in the case of Philippa, who refuses to leave her home and develop her gifts, which decades earlier had been encountered, and equally significantly named, by Papin:

> She would, he said, rise like a star above any diva of the past or present. The Emperor and Empress, the Princes, great ladies and *bels esprits* of Paris would listen to her, and shed tears. The common people too would worship her, and she would bring consolation and strength to the wrong and oppressed. When she left the Grand Opera upon her master's arm, the crowd would unharness her horses, and themselves draw her to the Café Anglais, where a magnificent supper awaited her. (*BF*, 10)

Later Papin kisses Philippa while caught up in the passion of a performance of the duet in the second act of Mozart's *Don Giovanni*—a song in which, Bloch notes, "life itself is thrusting at Zerlina."[47] Dinesen writes that he did so "solemnly, as a bridegroom might kiss his bride before the altar" (*BF*, 11). The shocked young woman shortly thereafter breaks off her training. Of the consequences of her decision, Dinesen writes, "In the Dean's house Martine felt that the matter was deeper than it looked, and searched her sister's face. For a moment, slightly trembling, she too imagined that the Roman Catholic gentleman might have tried to kiss Philippa. She did not imagine that her sister might have been surprised and frightened by something in her own nature" (12). It is the stirring of her nascent subjectivity, in the condition of art, and perhaps that of love, from which, Dinesen suggests, Philippa flees.

The brief reunion of Loewenhielm and Martine at the dinner and the recalling of Papin to Philippa function in Dinesen's story as reminders of the tragic nature of these figures, like Joyce's earlier Gabriel Conroy, as alternate histories for Babette (and, as in Joyce's case, perhaps Blixen herself) in their failure to become subjects to truth when a rare opportunity to do so opened up to them.[48] As they separate once again, Loewenhielm tells Martine:

> "I have been with you every day of my life. . . .
>
> "And," he continued, "I shall be with you every day that is left to me. Every evening I shall sit down, if not in the flesh, which means nothing, in spirit, which is all, to dine with you, just like tonight. For tonight I have learned, dear sister, that in this world anything is possible." (*BF*, 42)

This scene is reproduced almost verbatim in the film. However, its valence in each narrative is again radically different. In the film, it becomes a romantic cliché of redemption, another manifestation of the compensatory, abstract utopia. Conversely, for Dinesen, as Sara Stambaugh beautifully puts it, "the path to spirit lies through the flesh."[49] Thus, in Dinesen's story, Loewenhielm's words are to be understood as an extension of his initial betrayal of the truth of their encounter and a reinforcement of the self-justifying illusions that sustain it. For, in simple truth, he has *not* been with her every day, nor will he be in the future: to do the latter would be to introduce another of the evental genres, the comedy of remarriage, into Dinesen's short tale. This possibility, and even more so the failure to realize it, underscores the fact that true events, as in the meal itself and the "working existence" of the Commune, are always a matter of the material and affective, of how we live, of what we do in our bodies, and not of what we think silently, believe, or feel in our hearts.

The closing lines of both the film and novel, addressed by Philippa to Babette, once again appear nearly identical: "'Yet this is not the end! I feel, Babette, that this is not the end. In Paradise you will be the great artist that God meant you to be! Ah!' she added, the tears streaming down her cheeks. 'Ah, how you will enchant the angels!'" (*BF,* 48). In this Philippa cites nearly verbatim the conclusion to Papin's early letter (14). Is there a more apt figure of the abstract utopia than that of the religious paradise, the idealist compensation for all we do not dare do in this fallen world—the only world, of course, in which we live (Brecht's bad new days)? Again, however, the difference in the two texts is that Dinesen has fully prepared her readers by this point to recognize, or more precisely to experience, this truth—and the fact the Philippa may do so as well is signaled by tears she sheds; while the film encourages us once again to imbibe the numbing opiate that such a declaration of faith entails. The desperate retreat at the story's conclusion is in fact intended by Dinesen to be understood as deeply ironic, as a figure of Babette's death—if not of her body, then of the momentary Phoenix-like revival of her existence as an authentic subject in both the artistic and political conditions.

The final question left on the table here concerns Babette's claim, also removed from the film, that to be an artist she "needs" the elites of

Paris, however monstrous their actions may have been. These people are literally embodied at the dinner in figure of Loewenhielm, whose mention of dining in Paris at the Café Anglais with his fellow officer, Colonel Galliffet, not only underscores his active involvement in their social world but even hints at the more monstrous possibility that he had taken part in the murder of the Communards—among them, Babette's husband and son. What Dinesen thus means to bear out in her tale is that Loewenhielm is the one person at the dinner table, besides the artist Babette of course, who truly grasps the evental nature of his experience and hence becomes capable of naming it—naming, as Badiou shows, being fundamental to the procedure that follows an event. This distinction is again born out during the dinner when the guests are served champagne. Dinesen describes the scene in this way: "This time the Brothers and Sisters knew that what they were given to drink was not wine, for it sparkled. It must be some kind of lemonade." The General's response is quite different: "Loewenhielm again set down his glass, turned to his neighbor on the right and said to him: 'But surely this is a Veuve Cliquot 1860?' His neighbor looked at him kindly, smiled at him and made a remark about the weather" (*BF*, 37).

In a reading of "Babette's Feast" as a figure of the individual's proper work of mourning, Esther Rashkin maintains that Babette's traumatic double loss—that of her family and of the community that understood her artistic genius—"conflict with each other."

> To mourn her husband and son would mean recognizing that the society for which she lived and that gave her life and love as an artist was oppressive and murderous. To mourn the loss of this society and of her position as a culinary genius within it would be to express her love for those who murdered her husband and son and wronged the poor. Caught in an impossible, unspeakable double bind where mourning is tied to shameful love, Babette's solution during her twelve years in Berlevaag is to mourn no one: to keep secret the drama of her loss, and to exclude from language any expression of her suffering.[50]

Rashkin thus concludes that the "therapeutic" preparation of the dinner enables this long-deferred mourning process to take place, enabling Babette to "introject" properly her losses.[51] At this moment, Rashkin maintains, Babette, "finally separates the past from the present and is, in effect, 'reborn in Norway.' Now finally, she will be able to reconcile herself to the ascetic world in which she has existed for twelve years. Now, at last, she should be able to share wholly in the simple pleasures and self-denial of these people, all of which she has borne stoically these past years, but has never made her own."[52]

In Rashkin's conclusions we see evidence of the deep divide between an American ego psychotherapy and the radical Lacanian "return to Freud," first broached in the period in which Dinesen writes her story and so fundamental to Badiou's project:

> I won't go back over the function of my "mirror stage" here, the first strategic point I developed as an objection to the supposedly "autonomous ego" in favor of psychoanalytic theory, whose academic restoration justified the mistaken proposal to strengthen the ego in a type of treatment diverted thereafter toward successful adaptation—a phenomenon of mental abdication tied to the aging of the psychoanalytic group in the Diaspora owing to the war, and the reduction of an eminent practice to a *Good Housekeeping* seal of approval attesting to its suitability to the "American way of life."[53]

Rashkin's reading of the dinner as a therapeutic scene ending with Babette's long-deferred "successful adaptation" to her new life exemplifies such an understanding of the role of analysis. However, approaching the story in terms of its larger historical contexts, which I have shown that Dinesen's story goes to great lengths to underscore and which Axel's adaptation likewise obscures, casts a very different light on this mourning work. From this perspective, any such "separation from the past" and "reconciliation" would be the greatest betrayal imaginable of Babette's subjectivity, a giving way on her desire, and a failure in her obligation to both communities. What all of this underscores is Babette's kinship with another figure, central for Lacan's theorizations, who refuses to give way on her desire: Sophocles's Antigone.[54] (Imagine Antigone being expected to come to a similar reconciliation with Creon and the Theban state.)

Revealingly, Rashkin must pass over in her reading all the positive assertions by Babette of who she *is* that occur in her final monologue.

Keep in mind that Babette twice claims she is an artist and a Communard. Moreover, what Rashkin characterizes as the "impossible, unspeakable double bind" in which Babette is caught is, in the story's larger allegory, the very condition of the artist in the modern world. The only real resolution to this contradiction, as in Sophocles's play as Hegel reads it, would thus lie in changing the world itself: precisely what Babette, her family, and her comrades strive to achieve in the concrete working existence of the Commune. (Of course, as we already saw in chapter 2, such a desire is characterized by some forms of ego psychology as arrested "adolescent" fantasy.) The fact that they had been defeated and the recollection of what might have been had they succeeded (the "could have been") are what is being celebrated in the dinner: "*even the dead* will not be safe from the enemy if he is victorious," Walter Benjamin contends, adding, "and this enemy has never ceased to be victorious."[55] In her final act as both artistic and political subjects, Babette becomes like Benjamin's historical materialist, for whom nothing should be lost.

Throughout the narrative, and in particular in Babette's concluding monologue, Dinesen develops a tragic, late modernist vision of the work of art that resonates in a number of ways with that of her contemporaries in the New Critics I discussed in chapter 1 and in Theodor Adorno, for whom all authentic art stands as a "*promesse de Bonheur.*" As Jameson puts it, for Adorno, "art is not bliss, but rather the latter's promise."[56] Early in the story, the dinner guests from the village react to Babette's preparations for the exotic meal with profound horror, taking it to be "a witches' sabbath," and they vow to "be silent upon all matters of food and drink," so that "on the day of our master we will cleanse our tongues of all taste and purify them of all delight or disgust of the senses" (*BF*, 26–27).[57] In this response, they remain like the figures in Max Horkheimer and Adorno's brilliant allegory of the fate of the work of art in the modern world, the rowers on Odysseus's boat, their ears stuffed with wax, knowing "only of the danger of the song, not of its beauty." Conversely, Loewenhielm and the other earlier elite patrons at the Café Anglais are akin to Odysseus himself, able to experience the true miracle of the event only at the price of binding themselves impotently to the mast: "What he hears has no consequences for him."[58] The problem Dinesen's story so brilliantly illustrates thus lies not in the experience of art but rather in its "expense": the systemic violence—psychological, ideological, and, as in the case of the Commune, physical—that guarantee its continued access only to a chosen few, what Jameson refers to as "the sheer guilt of Art itself in a class society, art as luxury and class privilege."[59] It will only be in a concrete utopia such as that actualized in the Commune that the Babettes and Papins will be given leave to do their utmost and that all the guests at Babette's feast will have the resources—the education, experience, cultivation, and time—necessary to recognize and name the miracle they have experienced.

Dinesen's story also expresses a kinship with the dystopian side of Adorno's vision (and to that of another even more grim contemporary, George Orwell's *Nineteen Eighty-Four* [1949]): the fear that the political catastrophes of the twentieth century, combined with the emergence of a global consumer "culture industry"—that which continuously encourages and rewards artists to do their second best—have rendered impossible events in the conditions of both politics and art (and perhaps even science and love, as Orwell's total dystopian nightmare suggests).[60] And yet, in Dinesen's and Adorno's cases at least, rather than a justification for a retreat into despair or nihilism—for Adorno the fundamental form of all ideology—this situation makes the authentic work of art more significant than ever.

This expression on Dinesen's part of a persistent fidelity to utopian hope becomes even more remarkable when we recall, as Susan Hardy Aiken so movingly reminds us, that she composes her story "at a time when her own body was consumed by incurable illness."[61] Aiken later notes:

> In the years before her death her body was increasingly ravaged by the pain and debilitation of the syphilis contracted from her husband, which attacked the spinal nerves that control digestion, ultimately causing her to die of starvation. The comic transcendence of her oblique self-reference in "Babette's Feast" appears the more stunning when we recall that she wrote the celebration of transformative consumption at a time when her own body was literally devouring itself.[62]

The authentic work of art in Dinesen's story, as much as in Adorno's aesthetics, teaches us to refuse to become like the fish in Dinesen's fable

"The Diver," also reprinted in *Anecdotes of Destiny,* who "rest quietly" and "run no risks," and who query the man who converses with them, "How can equilibrium be obtained by a creature which refuses to give up the idea of hope and risk?"[63] Fidelities to the truth of the work of art and the Commune are precisely what disrupt any such equilibrium and encourage us, in the words of Badiou's singular ethical maxim, to "Keep going! [*Continuer!*]," lest their concrete promise perish with us.[64]

[6]

Repetition, Love, and Concrete Utopia in *50 First Dates*

It is not until an act occurs within the landscape of the past and the future that it is a human act. Loyalty, which asserts the continuity of past and future, binding time into a whole, is the root of human strength; there is no good to be done without it.

—Ursula K. Le Guin, *The Dispossessed*

For there are these three things that endure: Faith, Hope and Love, but the greatest of these is Love.

—Aramaic Bible, 1 Corinthians 13:13

IN THIS CHAPTER, I read (or, more precisely, non-read) the Adam Sandler and Drew Barrymore vehicle *50 First Dates* (2004) as an example of the evental genre of the "comedy of remarriage," a term coined by Stanley Cavell in *Pursuits of Happiness* (1981). Such a decision to examine this particular film in this particular fashion will inevitably raise some eyebrows (and indeed, has already done so) among more moralizing judgmental critics. This is the second film to pair Sandler and Barrymore; their earlier hit, *The Wedding Singer* (1998), established them as a leading screen couple. Something that links these films and makes them attractive to those of us from Sandler's generation is their soundtracks, the earlier replete with 1980s new wave classics and the later with hip-hop and reggae remakes of other 1980s pop tunes (such as will.i.am's catchy cover of Spandau Ballet's "True"). But with this confession, the reader might further, and rightly, ask, What would make a highly theoretical reading of this particular film anything more than what Slavoj Žižek characterizes as an academic's "excuse for indulging" in one's deeply, and even shamefully, personal "idiotic enjoyment of popular culture"?[1] A "disposable" canon, indeed.

I might try to justify my choice by declaring that I have been interested in contemporary comedies of remarriage for some time, having already published an essay on *Notting Hill* (1999); briefly discussed *Groundhog Day* (1992) in the first chapter of *Life between Two Deaths* and in chapter 2 of this book; and included a chapter in *Shockwaves of Possibility: Essays on Science Fiction, Globalization, and Utopia* (2014) on the unexpected comedy of remarriage to be found in the climax of Andrei Tarkovsky's *Stalker* (1979).[2] This last example especially should underscore that the definition of "comedy" I am using here is not its contemporary popular one—even though most of the examples I invoke fit that loose commercial generic classification as well—but rather the classical Greek meaning, referring to a theatrical agonistic practice whose resolution differs significantly from that of tragedy and that Northrop Frye defines in this way: "At the end of the play the device in the plot that brings the hero and heroine together causes a new society to crystallize around the hero, and the moment this crystallization occurs is the point of resolution in the comedy, the comic discovery, *anagnorisis* or *cognitio*."[3] Fredric Jameson maintains, "anagnorisis is thus in this sense as much the identification or production of a community or collectivity, as it is the simple revelation of a name or of a family relationship."[4] Finally, like Frye, Cavell stresses, "the genre of remarriage is an inheritor of the preoccupations and discoveries of Shakespearean romantic comedy, especially as that work has been studied by, first among others, Northrop Frye."[5] (I will return to the importance of Frye's argument for Cavell in the conclusion of this chapter.)

However, to include *50 First Dates* within what few would now argue against as an important film genre would itself be considered something of a scandal for those critics who champion a return to disciplinarity in film studies and for whom Cavell has reemerged as a reigning figure.[6] After all, Cavell's major objects of study—*It Happened One Night* (1934), *The Awful Truth* (1937), *Bringing Up Baby* (1938), *The Philadelphia Story* (1940), *His Girl Friday* (1940), *The Lady Eve* (1941), and *Adam's Rib* (1949)—are products of the classic Hollywood period of the 1930s and 1940s and are now accepted, thanks in large part to readers such as Cavell, as filmic masterpieces directed by some of the most important Hollywood auteurs (Frank Capra, George Cukor, Howard Hawks, Leo McCarey, and Preston Sturges); while *50 First Dates* is understood to be forgettable, or at best a mildly amusing bit of mass-cultural distraction, directed by the eminently obscure Peter Segal, whose other credits include *Naked Gun 33 1/3: The Final Insult* (1994), *Tommy Boy* (1995), *Nutty Professor 2: The Klumps* (2000), *Get Smart* (2008), *Grudge Match* (2013), and two less distinguished entries in the Sandler canon, *Anger Management* (2003) and the remake of *The Longest Yard* (2005).

There is a certain irony in such a stance, as Cavell concludes *Pursuits of Happiness* with an appendix focusing on the dubious status in the academic context of the late 1970s of writing about and teaching any "idiotic"—read: Hollywood—film. Imagining a course that would bring together Buster Keaton comedies and Martin Heidegger's writings, Cavell muses, "It is not unlikely that a department of philosophy as well as a department of film studies would object to such a proposal. Then I should interpret their objection—apart from matters of personality—as a denial either of the legitimacy of studying film, or of the legitimacy of studying philosophy, or of the legitimacy of studying Heidegger, or all three."[7] Moreover, Žižek's rejoinder to the claim cited above, paraphrasing "De Quincey's famous propositions concerning the art of murder," also has special resonance for any discussion of this film:

> If a person renounces Stephen King [read here as "low" popular culture of the ilk of *50 First Dates*], soon Hitchcock himself [canonical popular culture achievements like the classic Hollywood comedies of remarriage] will appear to him dubious, and from here it is just a step to a disdain for psychoanalysis and to a snobbish refusal of Lacan. How many people have entered the way of perdition with some fleeting cynical remark on Stephen King, which at the time was of no great importance to them, and ended by treating Lacan as a phallocentric obscurantist![8]

I would like to think that both of these pathbreaking readers would thus share Theodor Adorno's fundamental axiom of all dialectical thinking, that is, of all theory and interpretation: "everything is equally close to the center, which is why any truly consistent dialectical thought can begin from what looks like the most obscure and ephemeral of phenomena."[9] In the opening paragraph of his essay, Cavell thus paints a very different picture of our scholarly labors:

> Isn't a university the place in our culture that enables us now to teach one thing today and learn another tomorrow, to hunt for time to write in the morning, fish for a free projector in the afternoon, try to raise money for projects in the evening, and after a seminar read criticism? To some this will not seem a Utopian set of activities, but in the meantime, and for those with a taste for this particular disunity, why not have it?[10]

In the particular disunity that follows, I hope to realize something of the grand utopian vision for which Cavell here so eloquently calls.

The utopian charge of the figure of marriage is established by Ernst Bloch in the first volume of his magnum opus, *Das Prinzip Hoffnung* (*The Principle of Hope*) (1954). Bloch writes:

> Thus marriage appears as the utopia of one of the most friendly and most strict expressions of the substance of human life. . . . Marriage initiates and survives the fire-ordeal of truth in the life of the partners, of the steadfast befriending of gender in everyday life. Guest in the house, peaceful unity in fine, burning otherness, this therefore becomes the imago of marriage and the nimbus it undertakes to win. Often making the wrong choice, as is well-known, with resignation as the rule, with happiness as the exception, almost even as mere chance. And seldom does marriage become the outbidding truth of what was initially hoped for, therefore deeper, not merely more real than all the songs of the bride. Nevertheless it has its utopian nimbus with justification: only in this form does the by no means simple, the cryptic wishful symbol of the house work, is there any prospect at all of good surprise and ripeness. Just as the pain of love is a thousand times better than unhappy marriage, in which there only remains pain, fruitless pain, so too the landlocked adventures of love are diffuse compared with the great sea voyage which marriage can be, and which does not end with old age, not even with the death of one partner.[11]

Cavell focuses his analytic light more specifically on the utopian horizons of the comedy of remarriage. Flourishing in the Hollywood studio system of the mid-1930s to the late 1940s, the classic comedies of remarriage are defined by Cavell in this way:

> Our films may be understood as parables of a phase of the development of consciousness at which the struggle is for the reciprocity or equality of consciousness between a woman and a man, a study of the conditions under which this fight for recognition (as Hegel put it) or demand for acknowledgment (as I have put it) is a struggle for mutual freedom, especially of the views each holds of the other. This gives the films of our genre a Utopian cast. They harbor a vision which they know cannot fully be domesticated, inhabited, in the world we know. They are romances. Showing us our fantasies, they express the inner agenda of a nation that conceives Utopian longings and commitments for itself.[12]

What distinguishes these particular works from other screwball and romantic comedies are the structures of repetition found in them: the unions, breakups, and reunions that characterize both classic Hollywood comedies of remarriage and contemporary expressions of the genre such as, in addition to those referred to above, *When Harry Met Sally* (1989), *High Fidelity* (2000), *Kissing Jessica Stein* (2001), *Eternal Sunshine of the Spotless Mind* (2004), *Shrek Forever After* (2010), and *The Adjustment Bureau* (2011). Cavell argues that these narratives thus aim to verify the proposition "that the validity of marriage takes a willingness for repetition, the willingness for remarriage. . . . Put a bit more metaphysically: only those can genuinely marry who are already married. It is as though you know you are married when you come to see that you cannot divorce, that is, when you find that your lives simply will not disentangle. If your love is lucky, this knowledge will be greeted with laughter."[13] The practice's fundamental lesson is thus that to be a subject is to be married; and of course, to be truly married, the couple must again and again encounter and negotiate the concrete potential to be divorced and remarried, for only in this way can the truth of the marriage be renewed each and every day. It is this activity of inventing and reinventing, together, new ways of being and acting in the world that we see so marvelously on display in *50 First Dates.*

Cavell's characterization of remarriage resonates in a number of ways with Badiou's description of the foundational evental condition of love, or minimal communism. In his dialogue with Nicholas Truong, published under the title *Éloge de l'amour* (*In Praise of Love*), Badiou begins by noting, "In today's world, it is generally thought that individuals only pursue their own self-interest. Love is an antidote to that."[14] We need first, however, Badiou maintains, to "reinvent" the concept of love, reframing it more rigorously in terms of the notions of "separation or disjuncture based on the simple difference between two people and their infinite subjectivities"; and of the encounter or event, "namely of something that doesn't enter into the immediate order of things."[15] Badiou further maintains, stressing the process or temporal dimension of and the labor involved in all truth procedures, that love needs to be understood as "a quest for truth . . . truth in relationship to something quite precise: what kind of world does one see when one experiences it from the point of view of two and not one? What is the world like when it is experienced, developed and lived from the point of view of difference and not identity?"[16] Similarly, George Ciccariello-Maher observes that Enrique Dussel "defines metaphysics as 'knowing how to ponder the world from the exteriority of the other.'"[17] For this reason, Badiou claims that the "two scene" of a "love that is real is always of interest to the whole of humanity, however humble, however hidden, that love might seem on the surface."[18]

It is the deeply material and affective dimensions of the evental encounter of love that marks its difference from friendship:

> But surrendering your body, taking your clothes off, being naked for the other, rehearsing those hallowed gestures, renouncing all embarrassment, shouting, all this involvement of the body is evidence of a surrender to love. It crucially distinguishes it from friendship. Friendship doesn't involve bodily contact, or any resonances in pleasures of the body. That's why it is a more intellectual attachment, and one that philosophers who are suspicious of passion have always preferred. Love, particularly over time, embraces all the positive aspects of friendship but love relates to the totality of the being of the other,

> and the surrender of the body becomes the material symbol of that totality.[19]

In short, if friendship, at least as it has been classically imagined, is at its core an ethical relationship, aimed at maintaining the world as it currently exists, love is political, and its point, as with all four conditions, is to change the world.[20] At the same time, while Badiou reasserts the importance of maintaining a rigorous distinction between the truth procedures of politics and love, he also notes a "secret resonance that is created, in the most intimate individual experience, between the intensities life acquires when a hundred per cent committed to a particular Idea and the qualitatively distinct intensity generated by the struggle with difference in love. It is like two musical instruments that are completely different in tone and volume, but which mysteriously converge when unified by a great musician in the same work."[21] As with the commitment, or fidelity, involved in the unfolding of a truth of politics (or art or science), Badiou thus means here to develop "a concept of love that is less miraculous and more hard work, namely a construction of eternity within time, of the experience of the Two, point by point."[22] This is possible because love—and again this is a fundamental axiom of all the truth procedures—is only realized in the world through repetition, by a constant reenactment of a fidelity to the event by those whose subjectivity is constituted by it.

The earlier comedy of remarriage *Groundhog Day* shares a number of features with *50 First Dates.* First the two films, as in the case of Isak Dinesen's "Babette's Feast" discussed in the previous chapter, highlight the fluidity and deep interrelationship between the evental genres. Both films stage the event of artistic creation: in *Groundhog Day,* this takes the form of Phil Connors's production of a stunning ice sculpture of Rita and his virtuoso piano performance, skills developed through a long fidelity to both practices; and in *50 First Dates,* one of our two partners in the marriage plot, Lucy Whitmore (Barrymore), creates a veritable survey of art historical representations of the individual who, she tells us, is quite literally "the man of her dreams." Moreover, both films self-reflexively foreground the structure of repetition that is characteristic of this evental genre. Indeed, *50 First Dates* unfolds by staging a sharp contrast between negative, even destructive, individualistic cycles of repetition and life-affirming and deeply human collective ones.

At the opening of the film we are introduced to Henry Roth (Sandler), a marine biologist residing in Hawaii. The film begins with a montage of characters recalling to friends their recent vacations and reveals to us the initial empty repetitions within which Henry is trapped as he engages in a seemingly endless series of devious and unfulfilling sexual encounters with tourists—interestingly, shown to be black and white, young and old, and even female and male. In this vision, the film actualizes a point Ursula K. Le Guin makes in her own deep meditation on love and marriage found in her landmark utopia *The Dispossessed* (1974), which also provided one of the epigraphs for this chapter: "The search for pleasure is circular, repetitive, atemporal. The variety seeking of the spectator, the thrill hunter, the sexually promiscuous, always ends in the same place. It has an end. It comes to the end and has to start over. It is not a journey and return, but a closed cycle, a locked room, a cell."[23] Henry acts in this way in order to avoid entanglements that would put in jeopardy his real dream: to sail to Alaska on a ship he is repairing in order to study firsthand the mysterious undersea behavior of Pacific walruses. However, it is the leap into the void of scientific discovery represented by this voyage that too seems as if it will never come: we are shown repeatedly that there always seems to be one more repair Henry needs to make before he can leave and begin his "real" life.

It is also in these opening moments that we meet Henry's coworkers, an offensive gathering of clichéd ethnic, racial, and gender stereotypes. First, there is Henry's stoner sidekick, the Polynesian Ula (Rob Schneider), father of a gaggle of endearing children and married to a woman he now finds physically repulsive. Ula constantly complains of his domestic situation and expresses the vicarious pleasures he gets from Henry's tales of sexual conquest. Next, there is the Russian émigré, Alexa (Lusia Strus), who tells Henry of her sexual frustrations and about whom Henry repeatedly informs all around him that he is unsure whether she is a man or a woman. Treated with far more affection and dignity are Henry's animal companions, a preternaturally intelligent walrus and a small penguin. These figures, along with a number of other minor characters—a foul-mouthed older Asian man (Glen Chin) who frequents the same island café as Lucy; Doug Whitmore (Sean Astin), the diminutive, steroid-popping, and (again) sexually frustrated younger brother of Lucy; the happy-go-lucky Samoan giant and short-order cook, Nick (Pomaika'i Brown); and the brain-damaged hospital resident, Ten Second Tom (Allen Covert)—all serve as the butts of the jokes in a series of broad slapstick encounters. For example, Henry induces his walrus companion to soak Alexa in vomit; Ula is beaten with a baseball bat by Lucy after Henry and Ula trick her into thinking Ula is mugging a tourist; the old Asian man refers to everyone as "dipshits"; hospital patients and staff greet with hilarity the revelation of Doug's frequent nocturnal emissions; and Ten Second Tom engages in an endless series of reintroductions to all around him. It is these aspects that compose what Ruth Levitas refers to as the "dross" of such films, the contingencies of its particular historical situation in which its real utopian content remains "dressed up"—after all, this is a Sandler vehicle, and it appears in part to have been scripted to appeal to the comedian's core demographic audience of adolescent boys.[24]

This should also remind us that the classic Hollywood comedies of remarriage are no less popular Hollywood products, with their own fair share of dross, as in their reprehensible representations of racial others (recall here Chinua Achebe's pointed query to scholars of Joseph Conrad's *Heart of Darkness* "whether a novel which celebrates this dehumanization, which depersonalizes a portion of the human race, can be called a great work of art"[25])—but then again, this is also true of Shakespeare's equally popular entertainments, and we might benefit from thinking about them again in this estranging light. "There is no document of culture which is not at the same time a document of barbarism," Walter Benjamin stresses in a fundamental axiom of any materialist cultural criticism;[26] but then, perhaps, might not this observation have the corollary that there are documents of barbarism that also have their own redeeming core of "culture"? If this is the case, it is our task as engaged readers to tease it out.

It is here that I need to acknowledge one of the most significant recent critiques of Cavell's discussion of this heuristic genre, that found in David R. Shumway's *Modern Love: Romance, Intimacy, and the Marriage Crisis* (2003). Shumway maintains:

> Screwball comedies respond not so much to the fears of social collapse articulated by the moralists as to the fears of individuals about the fate of their own current or future marriages. The project of the comedies of remarriage is to reaffirm the romantic view of marriage in the face of its failure. Hollywood films

> take up this cultural work not only out of patriarchal interest and ideology but also for the coincident reason that films that participated in this ideology were popular. A majority of the film audience doubtless found it pleasurable to be reassured about the possibilities of marriage. The movies were the obvious place for such reassurance to be offered.[27]

It is not that I find fault with Shumway's assessment of the historical and ideological labor of these films. Moreover, Shumway acknowledges that "because screwball comedies typically focus on the interaction and conversation of the central couple—and often a pair who seem to know each other too well—these films represent a step toward the discourse of intimacy."[28] However, by focusing too much on these limitations, Shumway's historicist reading, as I suggested in chapter 1 of similar significant historicist readings of the New Criticism, talks past Cavell, bypassing altogether the concrete anticipatory essence, or truth, of another way of being in the world that might be extricated from the dross of these degraded and degrading films.

The more utopian dimensions of *50 First Dates* begin to come to the fore when Henry and Lucy accidently meet each other for the first time early one morning in November. From this initial *encounter*—and I mean this in the deepest Badiouian sense of the term—the chemistry between the two figures is evident as they engage in playful flirting, witty repartee, and honest conversation. In short, we witness in this new couple the reciprocity that Cavell claims is so significant: "Talking together is for us the pair's essential way of being together, a pair for whom, to repeat, being together is more important than whatever it is they do together."[29]

However, the budding relationship encounters its first crisis the very next day when Henry returns to the café to meet with Lucy once again. To his bewilderment, Lucy denies she even knows who he is and screams for help. When things settle down, the proprietor of the café, Sue (Amy Hill), informs Henry that this particular young woman is "very different from other people." Sue relates that a year earlier Lucy was involved in a car accident and as a consequence lost her short-term memory: while she can recall with perfect clarity the events of her life up through the day before the accident, every day when she goes to sleep she forgets everything that happened to her that day. As a result, she is fated to relive, apparently indefinitely, the same Sunday in October when she was injured—her doctor (Dan Aykroyd) later informs Henry and the film's viewers that her condition, while stable, is "likely permanent." The next scene bears this out, as we see Doug and Lucy's father, Marlin (Blake Clark), engage in an elaborate ritual designed to hide from Lucy the fact that any time has passed. This includes having a shed full of copies of the Sunday newspaper that was delivered on the morning of the accident and a whitewashing every evening of the workshop walls that the art teacher Lucy has spent the large part of her day painting with elaborate colorful murals. It is thus not only Lucy but also her family who seem to have been fated, like Henry, to live an empty, repetitious existence. Conversely, on hearing this story, Ula tells Henry that Lucy is the perfect girl for him, as no commitment would be required—when he tires of her and leaves, she will not remember he ever existed.

However, it is precisely here that the film, like its predecessor *Groundhog Day,* begins to take up a metafictional relationship to the classic comedies of remarriage, as this film literalizes the sequence of couplings, breakups, and reunions that characterize the practice. It is here too that what Badiou would call Henry's deep fidelity to the initial event of their encounter first becomes apparent, as does the interminable and strenuous work necessary on the part of the subject-to-the-event to sustain it. Badiou again defines this fidelity in a way that resonates deeply with what we see staged in the film: "It is clear that under the effect of a loving encounter, if I want to be *really* faithful to it, I must completely rework my ordinary way of 'living' my situation. . . . An evental fidelity is a real break (both thought and practiced) in the specific order within which the event took place (be it political, loving, artistic or scientific . . .)."[30] Henry first returns to the café every day to try to convince Lucy to have breakfast with him—and, often as not, he fails to do so. And yet he perseveres, thereby embodying Badiou's fundamental "ethical maxim 'Keep going!' [*Continuer*]."[31] Later, after following Lucy home, Henry meets Marlin, who, fearing Henry's intentions and telling him that Lucy "can't have a *normal* relationship with a man," warns him to stay away from the café. Henry decides to honor his agreement in a literal fashion and stages a new set of "first" meetings on the roadside between the house and the café (this is where the beating of Ula occurs). After this second series continues for another indeterminate duration, Marlin and Doug relent and agree to bring Henry back to the house, where they show him Lucy painting and singing. Marlin tells him, "She only sings on days she meets you." He then asks Henry, "What's in it for you, what do you get out of this?" to which Henry replies, "I don't know." His words bear out the fact that, as Badiou would have it, what has happened to Henry, his "experience" of an encounter with truth, "cannot be communicated."[32]

If it cannot be communicated, however, the film's viewers can bear witness to the transformative effects of the couple's evental encounter. Immediately afterward, the film presents a traumatic interruption of Lucy's fantasy scenario, as she accidently discovers the truth (the real) of her condition. After spending a long day with the family helping to calm Lucy, Henry proposes to her father another plan. The next day he delivers to her lilies and a videotape cassette labeled "Good Morning, Lucy." The videotape humorously narrates to Lucy her accident, the current status of her developing relationship with Henry, and everything else that has happened in the world since the accident. In the video, Henry tells her, "I like you and you like me. Most days. Every day is different." Although Lucy remains upset, her reaction is not as dramatic as in the previous scene, and she recovers her equilibrium within a few hours. Even more importantly, this shift in approach enables significant further developments in their relationship to occur. In the next scene, Henry notes, "I never hung out with you in the afternoon like this." A few scenes later, Lucy asks Henry if he loves her, and Henry responds, "Well, love is a very loaded word. Let's see, I go to this restaurant every morning, and I see you there reading, and . . . I love you, very much, probably more than anybody could love another person." The couple then embraces, and Lucy responds, "Nothing beats a first kiss," a line that is then repeated in a number of different settings, all authentic kisses now understood as first kisses.

Here we arrive at the paradox on which this film is structured. While at the beginning of the film Henry's encounters vary every day, he is in fact caught in the repetitious structure of what Benjamin characterizes as "homogenous, empty time."[33] Conversely, while later voluntarily reenacting the same scenes every day—as one of Lucy's friends puts it on first meeting Henry, in a veritable summary of the narrative dynamic of the comedy of remarriage, "So every day you help her to realize what happened, and then you wait patiently for her to be OK with it, and then you get her to fall in love with you again"—Henry and Lucy become subjects capable of real freedom, change, and growth, breaking the cycles within which both had, in different ways, remained trapped. This too resonates with another insight in *The Dispossessed*:

> A promise is a direction taken, a self-limitation of choice. As Odo pointed out, if no direction is taken, if one goes nowhere, no change will occur. One's freedom to choose and to change will be unused, exactly as if one were in jail, a jail of one's own building, a maze in which no one way is better than any other. So Odo came to see the promise, the pledge, the idea of fidelity, as essential in the complexity of freedom.[34]

(I will return to Le Guin's novel again in the next chapter.)

The true brilliance of this film, however, and its significance for both our understanding of this evental genre and its importance more generally, lies in its concluding sequence. Lucy, after overhearing a conversation between Henry and her family, decides to end their relationship. She tells Henry she is doing so for his own good: "You had plans and a life before you met me, and now all you have time for is to make me fall in love with you again every day." From this dystopian recasting of their situation, she concludes with the apparently antiutopian sentiment, "You have to understand that there is *no future* with me." In a scene that brings to mind the contemporary and more properly science fictional comedy of remarriage *Eternal Sunshine of the Spotless Mind*, Lucy and Henry then proceed to erase him from her "memory" by removing all references to him from her notebook that she began keeping right after Henry first gave her the video (she informs him, in a scene that underscores the film's vision of full mutuality in their relationship, that sometimes when watching the tape, she "feels like I am being told my life by somebody else, and when I read this it's like I'm telling myself"). Their joint action literalizes the form of ethical failure Badiou names "betrayal": "Betrayal is not mere renunciation. . . . I must always convince myself that the Immortal in question *never existed*."[35] Soon after, Henry decides that he can no longer bear to remain on the island and departs, alone, for his sea voyage to Alaska.

Henry, however, quickly comes to realize that his flight is a mistake, and he returns to encounter Lucy once-more-for-the-first-time at the brain trauma institute where she now resides (her father earlier informed Henry that she had decided to move there so she would no longer be a burden on her family). Henry asks Lucy, "Do you have any idea who I am?" and she answers in the negative. But she then brings him up to her studio, where we see the hundreds of renditions of Henry's face to which I referred above. Lucy says, "I don't know who you are, Henry, but I dream about you almost every night. Why?" Henry then confesses, "You erased me from your memories because you thought you were holding me back from having a full and happy life, but you made a mistake; being with you is the only way I can have a full and happy life. You're the girl of my dreams, and apparently I'm the man of yours." She says, "Henry, it's nice to meet you," and he responds, "Lucy, it's nice to meet you too." They then embrace for the first time once again as the screen fades to white.

Immediately, though, the scene returns to Lucy awakening in her bed as if from a dream. She sees the "Good Morning, Lucy" videocassette, plays it, and relearns once again of her accident and her life since—with the additional revelation that she and Henry are now married. The video ends with Henry telling her, "It's very cold outside, so when you're ready, put on a jacket and come have breakfast with me. Love ya." Lucy looks out her window only to discover that they are on Henry's sailboat in an Alaskan bay. She goes up top, sees Henry and her father, and "meets" her young daughter. She picks up the child and looks lovingly at her as the camera pulls back and circles the boat, Israel Kamakawiwo'ole's moving rendition of "Somewhere over the Rainbow" playing in the background as the screen fades to black. After a brief scene of four walruses kissing, the credits roll, images, photos, and words from Lucy's renewed diary passing by in the background.

The very setting of this climactic scene, located literally on a great sea voyage, recalls the passage from *The Principle of Hope* that I cited earlier in this chapter and offers an inversion of the "green world" setting of most classic romantic comedies: "The green world charges the comedies with the symbolism of the victory of summer over winter."[36] There is another Blochian resonance of this scene, for it offers us in condensed form the film's utterly unexpected movement from what Bloch calls "abstract" to "concrete" utopian horizons: that is, as we saw in the previous chapter, from a merely compensatory utopian figure to one of an "anticipatory kind."[37]

FIGURE 13. *Closing scene from* 50 First Dates.

In order to grasp more effectively the way in which the film undertakes this winnowing, it is worth repeating here an exercise in which my graduate seminar students and I engaged, contrasting the actual ending of the film with other, more conventional possible ones—alternate endings that would enact the operation of "symbolic containment" that Jameson describes in his 1979 essay "Reification and Utopia in Mass Culture."[38] The first and the most abstract, in Bloch's terms, would have been to end the film with the fade-out following the reunion and kiss. The fact that the screen fades to white at this point recalls the conclusion of Paul Verhoeven's earlier scathing science fiction indictment of the false abstract utopianism of contemporary mass culture, *Total Recall* (1990): in Verhoeven's film, this conventional Hollywood ending becomes a figure of the death of the imagination, as the cynical viewer concludes that the fade-out, or more precisely here the burn-out, signals the playing out of the preprogrammed fantasy scenario, "Blue Skies on Mars," that the protagonist, Douglas Quaid (Arnold Schwarzenegger), has been inhabiting the length of the narrative, resulting in the "schizophrenic embolism" he had been warned would occur if he followed the narrative through to its bitter climax. With this, *Total Recall*'s conclusion comes very near to those of the great dystopias of Yevgeny Zamyatin's novel *We* (1921) and Orwell's *Nineteen Eighty-Four* (1949) or, perhaps even more apt here, Terry Gilliam's film *Brazil* (1985). This also suggests an equally dystopian possible conclusion to *50 First Dates*: that the entire series of events really was only Lucy's dream.

More concretely, the film could have given us the coda that, I must confess, on my first viewing of the film I assumed was going to follow, showing us that "somehow" the magic of their love has broken the curse and "cured" Lucy, so that the couple would be free to live happily, and conventionally, ever after. This would have made the coda equivalent to the operations of recontainment performed not only by fairy tales but also by numerous Victorian novels and classic Hollywood films, all of which work to legitimate a normative middle-class household and domestic reality. However, it is precisely this resolution that the film refuses, confirming Marlin's earlier claim that Lucy cannot have a "normal" relationship. This offers a wholly different reading of Lucy's earlier assertion that Henry can have "no future" with her: she is correct if we understand the notion of no future in Lee Edelman's sense of a rejection of "reproductive futurity" of the status quo.[39] Through these labors of transvaluation, the film thus presents us not only with a moving allegory of the fidelity required to continue a loving relationship in a situation involving the severe disabling of one of the partners but also with a concrete figure of the day-by-day labors, the unending process of remaking, renewal, and reinvention, and the ceaseless "deep listening" (*l'écoute*) that, as I suggested in chapter 1, Lacan finds fundamental to the utopian discourse of the analyst and that is required in any authentic "marriage."

This points as well toward the gender dynamic at work in this film. Cavell opens his book by invoking an essay by Frye:

> In his early "The Argument of Comedy," Frye follows a long tradition of critics in distinguishing between Old and New Comedy: while both, being forms of romantic comedy, show a young pair overcoming individual and social obstacles to their happiness, figured as a concluding marriage that achieves individual and social reconciliations, New Comedy stresses the young man's efforts to overcome obstacles posed by an older man (a senex figure) to his winning the young woman of his choice, whereas Old Comedy puts particular stress on the heroine, who may hold the key to the successful conclusion of the plot, who may be disguised as a boy, and who may undergo something like death and restoration. What I am calling the comedy of remarriage is, because of its emphasis on the heroine, more intimately related to Old Comedy than to New, but it is significantly differ-

> ent from either, indeed it seems to transgress an important feature of both, in casting as its heroine a married woman; and the drive of its plot is not to get the central pair together, but to get them *back* together, together *again*. Hence the fact of marriage in it is subjected to the fact or the threat of divorce.[40]

While the welcome transformations in the understanding, practices, and institution of marriage over the course of the last seventy-five years make it readily apparent why the genre no longer requires the couple to be married in a strictly legal sense, this film, given that the central actor of *50 First Dates* is Henry, would seem to depart even further from the genre as Cavell characterizes it. However, to come to this conclusion is to collapse together the biological and the gendered nature of the two positions at work in the contemporary comedy of remarriage. Badiou, in describing the disjunctive positions necessary for the condition of love, notes, "Man is he (or she) who does nothing. I mean nothing for and in the name of love, because he considers that once something is won it stays won without having to be proved again. Woman is she (or he) who makes love voyage, and wants her word to be reiterated and renewed."[41] Henry is the one who most fully occupies the position of the woman in this even newer comedy of remarriage. Badiou concludes by stressing the importance of this gendered position in making the immediate intersubjective encounters of love, and hence the comedy of remarriage, the foundation of the entire edifice of truth (and, as a consequence, of my heuristic metageneric system): "Stating that H [Humanity] is a virtual composition of the four types of truths also makes it possible to argue that, for the woman position, love type *knots the four together*, and that it is only as conditioned by love that H, that is, humanity, exists as a general configuration."[42]

Moreover, in its closing pocket utopian mise-en-scène, the film presents us with a truly "queer" kinship structure, one composed of both the central couple and three generations of family, engaged together in the noncommercial everyday labors of building and rebuilding their human community. Cavell similarly comments on the odd place of children in the classics of the genre: "Children, if they appear, must appear as intruders. Then one's obligation would be to make them welcome, to make room for them, to make them be at home, hence to transform one's idea of home, showing them that they are not responsible for their parents' happiness, nor for their parents' unhappiness. This strikes me as a very reasonable basis on which to work out a future."[43] In light of this scene in *50 First Dates,* we might expand Cavell's notion to include parents and other members of older generations and even of nonbiological, elective kinship structures, which replace "the blood tie as the basis for kinship with consensual affiliation"—what Armistead Maupin more recently names the "logical family."[44] This reading is driven home especially forcefully when we recall that Leo McCarey, the director of *The Awful Truth* (1937)—named by Cavell the "best, or the deepest, of the comedies of remarriage"[45]—also directed in the same year the devastating tragedy *Make Way for Tomorrow.* The latter becomes the dystopian inversion of *The Awful Truth* precisely when an elderly couple's married adult children fail in their obligation to welcome and make room in their homes for their parents in the latter's moment of greatest need.

Finally, the fact that the voyage is also one of scientific inquiry—which Doug describes, upon first hearing of Henry's intent, as "kinda fruity" (another operation of queering here)—adds an additional level of resonance, as Kim Stanley Robinson suggests in his landmark utopian science fiction novel *Red Mars* (1993): "That is utopia, John, especially for primitives and scientists, which is to say everybody. So a scientific research station is actually a little model of a prehistoric utopia, carved out of the transnational money economy by clever primates who want to live well."[46] It is in this labor of concrete utopian figuration that *50 First Dates* becomes a significant one for anyone interested in the problem of how we too, as clever primates, might live life otherwise and thereby become truly human subjects, once again for the very first time.

[7]

Conditions of Utopia in *2312* and *The Best of All Possible Worlds*

Love—some kind of leap of the imagination. Inexplicable.
—Kim Stanley Robinson, *2312*

Without understanding, love is an impossible thing.
—Thich Nhat Hanh, *True Love: A Practice for Awakening the Heart*

NEAR THE CONCLUSION of his discussion of the "aesthetics of utopia" in his groundbreaking 1970 study *The Shape of Utopia: Studies in a Literary Genre,* Robert C. Elliott speculates that "the same substantive problems which have plagued writers trying to imagine what utopia would be like will face those who try, once utopian conditions are established, to create their own literature." In expanding upon his claim, Elliott turns to an often-invoked scene in the most influential utopian fiction of the late nineteenth century, *Looking Backward, 2000–1887* (1888), wherein Edward Bellamy's time-traveling protagonist, Julian West, is presented with a copy of the new world's greatest literary "masterpiece," Berrian's *Penthesilia.* Julian reflects:

> The story writers of my day would have deemed the making of bricks without straw a light task compared with the construction of a romance from which should be excluded all effects drawn from the contrasts of wealth and poverty, education and ignorance, coarseness and refinement, high and low, all motives drawn from social pride and ambition, the desire of being richer or the fear of being poorer, together with the sordid anxieties of any sort for one's self or others; a romance in which there

> should, indeed, be love galore, but love unfretted by artificial barriers created by differences of station or possessions, owning no other law but that of the heart.[1]

West soon assures his readers that these challenges have indeed been surmounted, and as a result, "the reading of *Penthesilia* was of more value than almost any amount of explanation would have been in giving me something like a general impression of the social aspect of the twentieth century."[2] However, Elliott notes, "Berrian's achievement we must take on faith."[3] This is because in *Looking Backward* not even the most bare bones description of *Penthesilia* is forthcoming: like the miracle of Babette Hersant's "Cailles en Sarcophage" that I discussed in chapter 5, *Penthesilia* remains only a name, what Saul Kripke terms a rigid designator. In this way, Bellamy honors in his utopian novel the prohibition Ernst Bloch levies on the representation of the work of art in the evental genre of the Künstlerroman.

In her 1971 review of Elliott's book, Joanna Russ dismisses his discussion of the utopian narrative's aesthetic problems as "rather routine."[4] However, it is not her moralizing assessment of Elliott's claims that makes her review such an interesting document. Rather, it is because the very problems Elliott highlights in his analysis are precisely those Russ herself grapples with at this moment, as the review appears only months before the first publication of her award-winning short story "When It Changed" and as she works on her breakthrough "critical utopia," *The Female Man* (1975). Indeed, shortly following her dismissal of Elliott's treatment of these challenges, Russ points toward what she thinks may be a solution to them:

> Non-Utopian science fiction seems to be finding all sorts of ways of dealing with lyric (or "static" material), which Utopian novelists might well imitate. After all, Finding Out is itself a process, and perception is an act. Samuel Delany believes that in modern fiction the center of narrative interest has switched from the passions to perceptions; if this is true, it might well rescue Utopian fiction. And it's possible to see the irruption of the lyric mode into prose narrative as typical of what has been called the post-realistic novel.[5]

The making of bricks without straw or the successful staging of lyric material within prose narrative—these can stand as apt characterizations of the miraculous narrative labor undertaken in two of the most interesting utopian fictions to appear in the last few years: Kim Stanley Robinson's *2312* (2012) and the second novel by the Barbadian author Karen Lord, *The Best of All Possible Worlds* (2013). Robinson is widely regarded as among the most significant science fiction and literary authors of the last half century. Nalo Hopkinson compares favorably Lord's achievement with that of one of the greatest of the early twenty-first-century works of fiction, Junot Díaz's *The Brief Wondrous Life of Oscar Wao* (2007): "As with *Oscar Wao, The Best of All Possible Worlds* is in part a declaration of pedigree, a dual love letter to science fiction/fantasy and to African diasporic cultures and realities. The novel explicitly invokes Ray Bradbury and Indiana Jones, echoes writers such as Ursula K. Le Guin, and filters it all through a creolized landscape."[6] The significance of Hopkinson's insights will become evident momentarily.

Robinson's *2312* reads as a sequel of sorts—he has told me in conversation that he considers it, as well as all of his fictions, to be set in different universes—to his celebrated and deeply influential utopian Mars trilogy (1993–1996).[7] The events in the novel are set three hundred years in the future—the first decades of the twenty-first century (2005–2060) ruefully periodized as "the Dithering. . . . These were wasted years"—and sometime after the story related in the Mars trilogy, which concerned what is indexed in *2312* as the "terraforming of Mars and subsequent Martian revolution."[8] However, Mars itself appears only in the novel's closing pages, as *2312* expands the "world" of the earlier works to the solar system as a whole, the action literally ranging from Mercury to Pluto and Charon.

The plot of *2312* is equally expansive. The novel opens in Terminator, the mobile city on Mercury, which first appeared in Robinson's earlier solar-system-spanning novel *The Memory of Whiteness* (1985). Robinson's Terminator is the inverse of James Cameron's more well-known technological figure of the same name, whose film debut occurred only a year prior to the publication of *The Memory of Whiteness*: both are all enframing (*Ge-stell*) mobile technologies, but whereas Cameron's represents the epitome of alienation, Robinson's expands the possibilities of human being and doing in the world.[9] In *2312,* Terminator is destroyed in an unprecedented "terrorist" attack, its track is bombed and the city incinerated when exposed to the ferocity of the Mercurial sun—an image that cannot help but invoke the September 11, 2001, attacks on the World Trade Center: "In their final transmissions, the cameras had recorded the city igniting in the sunlight—burning, melting, exploding, and so forth, until the recording instruments had failed" (*2312,* 191). Later, denizens of the other worlds, named the "spacers," both successfully seed the Earth with specimens of its extinct animal species and instigate a massive project of terraforming the environmentally devastated planet. And finally, a wide-scale conspiracy is uncovered, involving the Venusian production and dissemination of artificial intelligent humanoids, who, we learn, are responsible for the attack on Terminator and other related acts of mass destruction.

Lord's *The Best of All Possible Worlds* similarly narrates events that occur in an interplanetary network of human worlds, including our own. However, because our planet, Terra, remains under quarantine, ostensibly to protect it from meddling, we actually never see what life is like on our planet. The reader is informed early on that "Terra was the newest of the crafted worlds and Terrans the youngest breed of humans in the galaxy, but what they lacked in technology and mental development, they made up for in sheer evolutionary potential."[10] Instead, the novel largely focuses on the aftermath of a genocidal assault on the home world of a powerful humanoid species, the Sadiri, "whose fleet of mindships has been the backbone of galactic law, diplomacy, and scientific discovery for centuries" (*BA,* 13).

Although in her closing acknowledgments, Lord tells us that her inspiration for the plot came from reading reports of the distressing aftermath of the Indian Ocean tsunami of December 26, 2004, she is, as Hopkinson underscores, deeply familiar with the traditions of science fiction, and there are striking similarities of the novel's central event to the destruction of the Vulcan home world portrayed in the 2009 J. J. Abrams's *Star Trek* reboot. Indeed, much of Lord's characterizations of the Sadiri suggest their deep kinship with the Vulcans. They are described as "impassive," deeply dedicated to logic, and practitioners of mind disciplines, with the ability to telepathically connect to others—they even "raise an eyebrow" when surprised (*BA,* 12). However, *The Best of All Possible Worlds* differs in a significant way from the *Star*

Trek film, and indeed most popular science fiction portrayals of planetary disasters—think, for example, of Princess Leia's (Carrie Fisher) response in *Star Wars* (1977) to General Vanden Willard's (Eddie Byrne) expression of concern over the recent destruction of her home world of Alderaan and the murder of those she has known up to this point as her entire family and community: a curt "We have no time for sorrows, Commander." Instead, the novel delves into the event's devastating psychological and emotional impact on a handful of mostly male survivors as they desperately struggle to reestablish some version of their culture and way of life on the alien world of Cygnus Beta.

With all that takes place in these two rich and ambitious novels, in what follows, I want to focus on what may strike some as insignificant moments of "fancy" in them: the burgeoning romance and ultimate marriage in *2312* of the Triton denizen Wahram and the Mercurial artist Swan Er Hong and the similar love story involving the Sadiri survivor Dllenahkh and the Cygnian native and linguist Grace Delarua.[11] Both *2312* and *The Best of All Possible Worlds* offer readers romances that meet Julian West's criteria of a "love unfretted by artificial barriers created by differences of station or possessions, owning no other law but that of the heart." In this way, both books not only cast new light on the deep significance of the often-derided romance plot in twentieth-century narrative utopias, ranging from that in *Looking Backward* to Le Guin's *The Dispossessed* (1974) and Delany's *Stars in My Pocket Like Grains of Sand* (1984), they develop profound meditations on what is involved in composing a narrative that today can most effectively begin to educate readers' "desire for utopia."

Robinson's Wahram and Swan first encounter each other on Mercury, shortly after the death of Swan's grandmother, Alex, the planet's titular head and a major player in the world-spanning confederation of the Mondragon Accord: "Swan spotted Mercury, down by the sun, small and red. The Mondragon members were all red, making a constellation of red dots scattered through the system—all small, but there were a lot of them" (*2312*, 82). When they first meet, Swan is far from taken with Wahram: "He's slow, he's rude, he's autistic. He's boring" (30). Later, the couple is unexpectedly thrust together again when Terminator is attacked, and they are forced to spend more than three weeks hiking in a tunnel beneath the track encircling the planet, a time during which Swan nearly dies from radiation poisoning. At first, they pass time on their journey whistling "some very stirring duets. It definitely passed the time in ways that it hadn't passed before. You needed the gift of time, he thought, to explore a pleasure like this" (159). Subsequently, after becoming "all whistled out," Swan requests of Wahram, "Tell me a story. Tell me your story, I want to hear more things that I don't know about you" (170). Her willingness to listen expressed here will become foundational to their future relationship.

Over the coming years, the pair encounters one another on a number of different worlds, deepening the complex bond that had been established in the tunnel journey. Late in the novel, they find themselves once again stranded alone together in outer space near Venus. It is during this last experience that they talk about their relationship, and Wahram informs Swan that he loves her. This leads Swan to meditate, in one of the most moving passages in recent fiction:

> It was hard for her not to feel that a person loving her was making a big mistake. . . . And yet it was precisely that misplaced love she wanted. Someone who likes you despite yourself, someone more generous to you than you are. That was how Alex had been. And when you see that, when you feel that—feel loved beyond justice, from some kind of generosity—that sets off certain other feelings. A kind of a glow. A spillover. It caused something to start that felt reciprocal. A mutual recognition. . . . But something else, some kind of . . . pairing, like Pluto and Charon, with the center of gravity between the two. Not a single supra-organism, but two working together on something not themselves. A duet. A harmony. (*2312*, 498–99)

A little further on in the novel, the act of marriage is characterized in similar terms: "Maybe that's what a marriage is. . . . Whistling together. Some kind of performance. I mean, not just a conversation, but a performance" (543). Swan's words resonate deeply with Slavoj Žižek's contemporary characterization of love:

> And here love enters: the most radical moment of love is not the belief of others which sustains the subject in its existence, but the subject's own counter-gesture, the terrifyingly daring act of fully accepting that its very existence depends on others. . . . love

> occurs when the loving subject discovers that the treasure in the beloved is just a deceiving fetish, that the true treasure is the fragile beloved himself, perplexed, at a loss, unable to relate his subjectivity to the treasure the beloved sees in him.[12]

The love plot concerning Grace Delarua and Dllenahkh comes to its climax with a similar performative declaration, in this case by Grace: "Reader, I married him" (*BA*, 296). As some of these readers may recognize, Lord here cites the famous opening line of the thirty-eighth and concluding chapter of Charlotte Brontë's *Jane Eyre* (1847). Lord does so to underscore not only the parallels between the romance plots of these two novels—for example, in both, the late revelation of an earlier marriage nearly derails the betrothal—but also the way *The Best of All Possible Worlds* challenges long-standing European assumptions about the Caribbean, assumptions in no small way set into place by works like Brontë's novel. In her acknowledgments, Lord makes this aim clear in stating, "The Caribbean is to me the new cradle of humanity. It was easy for me to imagine an entire planet just like it, with people from every corner of the world" (*BA*, 306). If we understand Jean Rhys's great novel *Wide Sargasso Sea* (1966) as a late modernist estrangement of the colonial imaginary underlying Brontë's realist text, then *The Best of All Possible Worlds* figures a fully post-postmodern utopian alternative to it.

This too points toward another link between the utopian imaginaries at work in Robinson's and Lord's fictions, as both present us with breathtaking examples of what Fredric Jameson describes as the necessary form of any "new global Utopia," as "so many islands: a Utopian archipelago, islands in the net, a constellation of discontinuous centers, themselves internally decentered."[13] The main plot of *The Best of All Possible Worlds* follows the journey of the Sadiri and their companions to a range of different communities on Cygnus Beta, a world "reputed to have some of the most complex and vibrant cultures in the galaxy," in their hopes of finding people genetically and culturally compatible with them and, even more importantly, willing to assist them in rebuilding not only their lost culture but their very race (*BA*, 11). Throughout, the novel will underscore the fact that such a rebuilding will not involve anything like a return but rather the utopian project of constructing the utterly new.

This plot device serves as the excuse, what the Russian formalists call the motivation of the device, for Lord's extraordinarily imaginative mapping of a diverse variety of ways humans might consent to live together. For example, one of the odder communities they visit takes the form of a role-playing matriarchal version of Edmund Spenser's *The Faerie Queene* (1596):

> Reports are sketchy. Faerie has been closed for more than a century, because visitors tended to treat it a bit like a theme park. . . . But they say that for centuries the land was populated by two taSadiri clans who were constantly at war with each other. They had endured a particularly bad run of hostilities when a strange Cygnian turned up with an intriguing solution to their problem. Since the main cause of their war was a question of which clan's rituals and dialectic should take precedence, the compromise was for both clans to learn an entirely new identity. (*BA*, 121)[14]

At the same time, the novel raises profound questions concerning the limits that might be imposed on such variety and our obligation to intervene when those limits have been transgressed. When Grace encounters on a remote island a society that practices slavery, she finds her innermost values thrown into question: "I suppose up to that point I had wanted to disbelieve. The idea that trafficking could take place right under the nose of the Cygnian government, that we were no more immune from oppression than any other planet—it shook me" (*BA*, 171–72). Grace subsequently decides to intervene and expose these practices even though she is informed that her actions are, in another echo of the *Star Trek* universe, "a direct violation not only of our mission protocols but of the General Code *and* the Science Code" (174). Furthermore, she is told that if she follows through on her promise, she will effectively end her career. Nevertheless, she does proceed and afterward wonders to Dllenahkh if she acted properly. He responds, "Legalities notwithstanding, to *not* wonder indicates a dangerous lack of awareness of the nearly infinite array of choices presented by life" (176).

It is during the course of this journey that Grace and Dllenahkh develop their own deep and unique bond, which crosses the gulf of their cultural and personal differences. At the center of this development once again lies the practice of dialogue, of both speaking and the deep and sustained listening that I discussed in chapter 2. Early on, Grace notes that Dllenahkh's "Standard was better than my Sadiri, needless to say, so many times I just did a lot of listening while he talked with the homesteaders, and then afterward he'd summarize for me so I wouldn't miss a thing. I didn't expect them to speak Standard to me. When you've been almost exterminated, language is the first thing you cling to, one of the main roots of identity" (*BA*, 10).

Later during their voyage, when they are stranded alone together, she again observes, "I forgot my cooling tea and listened avidly. I had never dared ask any Sadiri about their life before the disaster, and though I knew Dllenahkh better than any of them, all my knowledge of him was newly minted, scarcely over a year old" (108). Following a moment of telepathic contact between the couple, Grace further confesses, "During our close communication, I had seen myself through Dllenahkh's eyes. It had been disconcerting, even alien" (217). This last claim recalls Badiou's notion that love involves "a quest for truth . . . truth in relationship to something quite precise: what kind of world does one see when one experiences it from the point of view of two and not one? What is the world like when it is experienced, developed and lived from the point of view of difference and not identity?"[15]

Their ultimate union, sealed as is the Sadiri custom by the establishment of a permanent telepathic bond between them, is described in the novel's closing pages:

> She had imagined her mind would be bare before his, naked under a scorching desert sun, with neither shelter nor refuge. Instead, it was like playing hide-and-seek in the light and shadow of a forest, discovering and inventing a new language of double meaning, subtlety, poetry, and image. As a linguist, she was captivated; as a lover, she was enraptured. Nothing could be said the same way twice. (*BA*, 301)

The Best of All Possible Worlds then concludes in a way, as I will suggest momentarily, that signals that their bond has remade their shared world.

The emphasis in these two novels on the continuous performative dimension of love and marriage indicates that at work in both is the narrative paradigm of the "comedy of remarriage" discussed in the previous chapter. That marriage can be an event, even in utopia, is borne out by Robinson's Swan when she reflects that marriage seems "a concept from the Middle Ages, from old Earth—an idea with a strong whiff of patriarchy and property. Not meant for space, not meant for longevity. . . . At least so it seemed to her, and to many others she knew. It was the current structure of feeling in her culture and time." However, she then concludes, "structures of feeling were cultural, historical; they changed over time like people did; the structures themselves went through their own reincarnations" (*2312*, 543–44). Swan's formulation here echoes what Judith Butler refers to as the act of "resignification" she undertakes in her own efforts to pry out the utopian core of the notions of "family" and "kinship."[16] The repetitious structure of fidelity in love, or any of Badiou's four truth procedures for that matter, is named by Wahram the *good pseudoiterative*: "The pattern of the day might be the same, in other words, but the individual events fulfilling the pattern were always a little bit different. Thus there was both pattern and surprise" (*2312*, 51). Only in this good pseudoiterative fashion can the truth of the marriage be renewed each and every day.

While I suggested in the previous chapter that there is a great deal of overlap between the four evental genres, one of the most interesting aspects of Robinson's and Lord's novels lies in the way they bring into focus a distinction between the more specific practices of the evental genre of science fiction—the practice located in the place of the symbolic in my Greimasian presentation because it makes explicit the formal protocols of the four genres as a whole—and those of the utopia proper. This occurs in a way that reverses Darko Suvin's classic formulation of the modern utopia as the "sociopolitical subgenre of SF."[17] If science fiction centers on events, or what Bloch and Suvin refer to as a *Novum*, that occur specifically in the material condition of science—even, or especially, when these have consequences for the larger social and cultural whole—the totalizing formal drive of the utopian narrative requires that it figure possible events in all four conditions before it can come to a satisfactory conclusion. In Bloch's and Suvin's terms, utopia thus marks the shift from the *Novum* to the *Ultimum*, the "total leap out of everything that previously existed."[18]

A recognition of this narrative dynamic changes in a fundamental way our reading of the achievement of Bellamy in his romance *Looking*

Backward: for now it becomes evident that *Looking Backward* already undertakes the presentation of the traces of events in all four conditions. I discussed in the opening of this chapter Bellamy's ingenious solution to the problem of the figuration of the event of art. A similar operation takes place in terms of the domain of science, through the book's allusive descriptions of technological marvels and, especially, the new cityscape:

> It was the first interior of a twentieth-century public building that I had ever beheld, and the spectacle naturally impressed me deeply. I was in a vast hall full of light, received not alone from the windows on all sides, but from the dome, the point of which was a hundred feet above. Beneath it, in the center of the hall, a magnificent fountain played, cooling the atmosphere to a delicious freshness with its spray. The walls and ceiling were frescoed in mellow tints, calculated to soften without absorbing the light which flooded the interior. Around the fountain was a space occupied with chairs and sofas, on which many people were seated conversing.[19]

The event in the third domain, that of politics, occurs with the founding of the utopian community itself, which Bellamy assures his readers can come about without violence: "The solution came as the result of a process of industrial evolution which could not have terminated otherwise. All that society had to do was to recognize and cooperate with that evolution, when its tendency had become unmistakable."[20]

Finally, the romance of Julian and Edith, with its repeated separations and reunions and its resolution in the green world—"a place in which perspective and renewal are to be achieved"[21]—can now be understood as a comedy of remarriage, the practice that most effectively presents events in the condition of love:

> When at length I raised my bowed head and looked forth from the window, Edith, fresh as the morning, had come into the garden and was gathering flowers. I hastened to descend to her. Kneeling before her, with my face in the dust, I confessed how little was my worth to breathe the air of this golden century,

> and how infinitely less to wear upon my breast its consummate flower. Fortunate is he who, with a case so desperate as mine, finds a judge so merciful.[22]

I would argue, then, that it is the figuration of the redemptive possibility of such events in each of these domains, far more than the plan outlined for the Nationalist Industrial Army, which made *Looking Backward* so deeply attractive for its numerous late nineteenth-century readers. In these labors, Bellamy establishes a narrative paradigm that will be taken up again and with renewed vigor in the great revival of utopian fiction that occurs in the 1970s.

Moreover, a similar figuration of events in the four conditions takes place in one of the most important works of fiction in the twentieth century, and one that we might now read as a narrative utopia, James Joyce's *Ulysses* (1922). *Ulysses* is a work structured around four questions—"How long is Haines going to stay in this tower?"; "Can you work the second for yourself?"; "What is the word known to all men?"; and "Now who is that lankylooking galoot over there in the macintosh?"—the answers to which mark encounters with an event in each of the four conditions.[23] It is no coincidence too that late in *Ulysses,* Joyce invokes (without perhaps fully grasping) Cantor's set theory: "To reflect that each one who enters imagines himself to be the first to enter whereas he is always the last term of a preceding series even if the first term of a succeeding one, each imagining himself to be first, last, only and alone whereas he is neither first nor last nor only nor alone in a series originating in and repeated to infinity."[24]

In this light, it becomes possible to read anew the major plot developments of *2312* as motivations of the device for this figurative operation to unfold. For example, early on, one of the novel's numerous scientific events is presented to the reader in a dramatic fashion through the Mercurial city, Terminator:

> Terminator rolls around Mercury just like its sunwalkers, moving at the speed of the planet's rotation, gliding over twenty gigantic elevated tracks, which together hold aloft and push west a town quite bigger than Venice. The twenty tracks run around Mercury like a narrow wedding band, keeping near the forty-fifth latitude south, but with wide detours to south and

> north to avoid the worst of the planet's long escarpments. The city moves at an average of five kilometers an hour. The sleeves on the underside of the city are fitted over the track at a tolerance so fine that the thermal expansion of the tracks' austenite stainless steel is always pushing the city west, onto the narrower track still in the shade. A little bit of resistance to this movement creates a great deal of the city's electricity. (*2312*, 27)

Equally magnificent are Robinson's invocations of the various terraria, worlds manufactured in hollowed-out asteroids:

> The interior space in the *Wegener* was pretty substantial, about twenty kilometers long and five across, spun to a one-g equivalent. The great majority of the interior space was park, with a few small towns scattered mostly fore and aft. The mix of savanna and pampas was very attractive, Wahram thought as he walked toward the first village, looking up at the land overhead. Grass prairie and patches of forest arched like a giant Sistine Chapel overhead, a Sistine on which Michelangelo had painted a version of Eden—a savanna, the first human landscape, appealing to something very deep in the mind. (42)

Another more subtle presentation of the scientific event takes place when Swan, in a passage I cited above, mediates on changes in any "structure of feeling." The notion of a structure of feeling was first formulated by one of the most significant theorists of the twentieth century, Raymond Williams, in his books *The Country and the City* (1973) and *Marxism and Literature* (1977).[25] Elsewhere in the novel, Robinson invokes another pair of Williams's central concepts—"in residual-emergent models, any given economic system or historical moment is an unstable mix of past and future systems. Capitalism therefore was the combination or battleground of its residual element, feudalism, and its emergent element—what?"[26] There are also scattered throughout references to notions of Jacques Derrida, Jean-Paul Sartre, and others.[27] In fact, Robinson deploys this strategy throughout his fiction: for example, in *Red Mars*, the psychologist Michel Duval sketches a series of Greimasian semiotic squares, and in *The Years of Rice and Salt*, references are made to Hayden White's theorization of the various modes of historical emplotment.[28] In *Valences of the Dialectic,* Robinson's teacher, Jameson, maintains, in what is also one of the central themes of my book as a whole:

> the dialectic is not a thing of the past, not some chapter in the history of philosophy, but rather a speculative account of some thinking of the future which has not yet been realized. . . . A way of grasping situations and events that does not yet exist as a collective habit because the concrete form of social life to which it corresponds has not yet come into being.[29]

Robinson's off-the-cuff introduction of these theoretical concepts into his character's dialogue hints that, in these imaginary futures at least, the concrete forms of social life that would enable just such a collective practice of thinking have come into being.

Moreover, throughout the novel we encounter traces of diverse artistic events, a number of which are produced by Swan herself: "Much of her landscape and performance art is devoted to it, and these days she spends most of her time making goldsworthies and abramovics on the land and her body"; and again, "At Rilke she had erected a circle of Göbekli T-Stones, which looked very contemporary even though they were based on something over ten thousand years old" (*2312,* 3, 16). Shortly before the destruction of Terminator, the couple attends a concert, which is figured by Robinson in this way:

> Then some other transcriber had gone in the opposite direction, arranging the *Hammerklavier* sonata for string quartet. Here, even though four instruments were now playing a piece written for one, it was still a challenge to cover the *Hammerklavier*'s intensity. Broken out among two violins, viola, and cello it all unpacked beautifully: the magnificent anger of the first movement; the aching beauty of the slow movement, one of Beethoven's finest; and then the finale, another big fugue. It all sounded very like the late quartets to Wahram's ear—*thus a new late quartet, by God!* It was tremendous to hear. Wahram glanced around at the audience and saw the wind players and the pianists were standing on their feet behind the chairs, bouncing, swaying in place, faces uplifted and eyes closed, as if in prayer. (129–30)

In his most recent novel, *Red Moon* (2018), Robinson develops another wonderful figuration of practices of art to come in a collective low gravity lunar performance of Philip Glass's 1979 opera, *Satyagraha*.[30]

Each of the places visited in *The Best of All Possible Worlds* similarly serves as the afterimage of events in the condition of science. Let this description of a long-abandoned underground city, rediscovered late in the expedition's journey, serve as the placeholder for the reader's own encounters with these diverse figures:

> We turned away from the lights onto a less even path, scrambled through a few narrow places, and then we were there. It was worth it! I'd missed seeing Piedra in real life, so I had no comparison, but as far as cities carved out of sheer rock go, this was damned impressive. I hurt my neck swiveling around trying to get my headlight to capture the full scope of an arch that was two stories high and bracketed by windows that hinted at more rooms within the rock. The arch itself led into a cathedral of a passageway with more windows high in the walls and arched doorways a little above path level, their steps crumbling as if eroded by running water. I could imagine the subterranean street lit by cool, pale lamps during the night and warm, bright lamps in the day. . . . A glitter caught my eye, and I went closer to see the muted sheen of crystal in the rock, not excavated but incorporated into the carvings of the door lintel. It was a rich place, an unexpected Eden. (*BA*, 238)

At the same time, new practices of theater and opera are presented throughout the novel:

> Our seats were midhouse near the central aisle—decent enough for what we were seeing and hearing. It was of a style referred to as neo-opera. It combined an absence of technological enhancement with a blend of contemporary styles of music, which meant that the performers had to be both vocally powerful and versatile. I wish I had the time to tell you about the whole neo-opera movement and how it relates to the *rustica* backlash against audio smoothing and augmentation in musical performance and *realissimo* effects in holovidding. I will say that there is a

> simplicity in the staging. Not minimalist—that's another style—but a simplicity that pretends at amateurism but most definitely isn't. (142)

The regret Grace expresses in this passage is akin to that of Bellamy's Julian West and should be understood as Lord's way of underscoring both Bloch's insight into the unrepresentability of the evental work of art and Badiou's more general axiom that an event—"what arises from a truth-process"—"cannot be communicated."[31]

All of this leaves unaccounted for the last of the four conditions and its corresponding evental genre—those of politics and universal history. As I have already suggested in Bellamy's case, in older utopias the proliferation of events in the other three conditions is presented as possible only because the singular political event, the revolutionary break with the status quo, is located in the distant past. This then creates an often-derided appearance in utopian fictions of static, post-historical worlds. The first practice to recognize and exploit this appearance was the dialectical other, the negation of the negation, of both naturalism and the late nineteenth-century utopian fiction, and that would become one of the most popular and successful literary genres of the twentieth century, the dystopia.[32]

This genealogy offers a way of further specifying the differences between the kin practices, identified by Lyman Tower Sargent in his taxonomy of the dystopia, critical dystopia, and antiutopia.[33] If the world-changing political or universal historical event figured in a text aims for the restoration of a nostalgically longed-for lost order (the good old days), then we are in the domain of the classic dystopia, or what I describe in my first book, following the lead of Karl Mannheim, as the *conservative utopia*.[34] If, however, this event horizon opens up onto a transformed, radically other future, we are dealing with an example of what Tom Moylan names the "critical dystopia," a practice of which Robinson's earlier *The Gold Coast* (1988), the second novel of his Three Californias trilogy, stands as one of Moylan's first examples.[35] Finally, it is only with the antiutopia that history can be said to be shown as coming to an end—and this is often intended as an object lesson for its readers in what will occur if they have the hubris to mess with the reigning natural order or at least the "least bad" of all possible worlds.

However, this is not end of the story. Elliott's deeply dialectical formulation of the relationships between utopia, dystopia, and the anti-utopia blocks out the space for the development of a new practice, what Elliott calls the "anti-anti-utopia" and the first glimmers of which he locates in Aldous Huxley's *Island* (1962). It is precisely this new practice that will shortly be named by Moylan and Peter Fitting as the *critical utopia*.[36] The critical utopias—*The Female Man, The Dispossessed,* Delany's *Triton* (1976), Marge Piercy's *Woman on the Edge of Time* (1976), and other pioneering works—learn the lesson of both its negative kin, the dystopia and the antiutopia, and reinscribe the political event of universal historical change back within the horizons of the utopian narrative itself.

This is precisely what Robinson does in *2312*: the universal event of the founding of Mars is now unveiled as less an end of history than its long-deferred inauguration. Although the lives of the spacers have given expression to radically new forms of human being and doing in the world, the life lived on earth remains sadly very near our own:

> That was life on Earth. Split, fractionated, divided into castes or classes. The wealthiest lived as if they were spacers on sabbatical, mobile and curious, actualizing themselves in all the ways possible, augmenting themselves—genderizing—speciating—dodging death, extending life. Whole countries seemed like that, in fact, but they were small countries—Norway, Finland, Chile, Australia, Scotland, California, Switzerland; on it went for a few score more. Then there were struggling countries; then the patchwork post-nations, the cobbled-together struggles against failure, or the completely failed. (*2312*, 315)

Shortly after this recognition, Swan proclaims to Wahram, "There are people down there living in cardboard shacks. You know how it is. It's always that way, and it looks like it'll go on forever. So they'll always hate us, and some will attack us. And we pop like soap bubbles. There's no solution but justice for everyone. It's the only thing that will make us safe." Wahram replies, "So . . . to protect ourselves, you're saying, we have to orchestrate a global revolution on Earth" (356). Swan then *names* this universal historical event: "The revolution of full employment. The place is trashed, they're cooked, they need to do it. In effect Earth needs terraforming as much as Venus or Titan!" (357). While the spacers' surprise intervention on the planet kick-starts such a process—"'Charity is always aggressive,' Swan said. 'Don't you know that?'" (375)—the novel shows that this too represents only another beginning in an infinite series of rebeginnings without guarantee. The consequences of these further revolutions are only hinted at in the text's margins, in a series of fragmentary notes written by a historian looking backward from some indeterminate future. The historian often breaks off in midsentence, thereby designating a redeemed future that cannot yet be described: "After the reanimation, problems on Earth became ecological and logistical, and focused on transport, dispersion, mitigation, compensation, and legal and physical defense. The reanimation itself was not the end of the story; indeed many decades were to pass before it was understood to have been a key moment in the eventual" (410).

Similarly, in *The Best of All Possible Worlds* it is not the Sadiri goal of founding a new community that is the utopia offered to us in the text but rather the inauguration of the process itself. The Sadiri eventually come to realize the impossibility of restoring their lost world in all its purity; nor can they ever, as we learn in a subplot that draws upon the resources of the science fiction alternate history and contemporary multiverse theory, change what has occurred in their past:

> The amount of complex multivariate calculus in that report *was* somewhat off-putting. However, the gist of it was that there are already stable parallel time lines in existence. Naraldi was not able to change our fate, because he had no way of navigating to our past. He was able to reach many other pasts of different time lines and see other presents and futures as well. But his own line he could not touch. (*BA*, 224)[37]

Thus, to survive, and to thrive, means becoming hybrids, creoles—a name pointing toward some things or, more properly, some persons that have not yet existed in the world. At one point, Grace teases Dllenahkh (and such joyful teasing exchanges lie, as Cavell reminds us, at the very center of the utopian discourse of the comedy of remarriage) with the claim, "'Just admit it—we've turned you into a Cygnian.'" Dllenahkh responds in a way that reanimates the commonplace phrase, which Lord draws on for her novel's title: "'And would that be such a terrible thing to admit?' he said in a tone of cheerful surrender. 'This is my universe, my time, my world. There is no going back to what was. There is only the future'" (230). The novel then concludes with Dllenahkh and Grace reencountering again for the first time the mindship pilot Naraldi, who first brought to Dllenahkh the terrible news of the murder of their world and who aids the couple later in a moment of crisis:

> Dllenahkh felt a sensation of overwhelming, devastating déjà vu—another time, another beach, Naraldi rising out of the ocean to destroy the universe with a few words. His mind had been punctured in that instant, leaving behind a fragmented, perilous memory that could spin him into endless orbit around nothingness. For his own sake, he had learned to forget that day. Now his mind fractured again to take in the reality that he was standing by the sea and hearing Naraldi's voice, not merely without desolation but with actual gladness. Memory and moment combined violently, and he struggled to shield Delarua from the sudden maelstrom.
>
> She did not look at him. She did not have to. She took firm hold of his hand and silently gave him her storm of joy to navigate instead.
>
> "Welcome, Naraldi!" she cried. "Welcome home!" (302–3)

This ending both recalls the title of Le Guin's great utopia *Always Coming Home* (1985) and Bloch's own stirring closing line in *The Principle of Hope*: "Once he has grasped himself and established what is his, without expropriation and alienation, in real democracy, there arises in the world something which shines into the childhood of all and in which no one has yet been: homeland."[38]

Here, then, we come to the most significant lesson of both novels, one that we might now be better placed to understand has been not only central to the pedagogical labors of the four-decades-long tradition of the critical utopia—hinted at by Huxley and launched in earnest by Russ, Le Guin, Delany, and others—but also throughout the five centuries of thought, which Thomas More's extraordinary invention made possible: utopia was never the end of history, but rather only its beginning. In the face of the posthistorical malaise of postmodern, late, or global neoliberal capitalism, or the eras of the Global Minotaur or Trumpism and whatever can be said to follow it—in short, our great Dithering—it is only in utopia that the possibility of an authentic event, of the truly new, can make its tiger's leap into our world.

Conclusion

Optimism and Pessimism in Cloud Atlas

> Good. He was getting mawkish. "You're my Verlaine."
>
> "Am I, young Rimbaud? Then where is your *Saison en Enfer*?"
>
> "In sketches, in my skull, in my gut, Ayrs. In my future."
>
> —David Mitchell, *Cloud Atlas: A Novel*

> People to whom despair is not a technical term may ask whether it would be better for nothing at all to be than something.
>
> —Theodor Adorno, *Negative Dialectics*

> Optimism disappoints, but hope does not.
>
> —Pope Francis, *On Hope*

OURS IS A TIME of proliferating pessimisms. Not only is there an increasingly global sense that the conditions in the future will be worse than those in the present, there has been a surge of major intellectual schools—Afro-pessimism, the antisocial turn in queer theory, and climate pessimism, to name a few prominent examples—whose point of departure is a deep and rigorous questioning of the possibility of positive change.[1] Moreover, in January 2018, the Bulletin of the Atomic Scientists moved their Doomsday Clock for only the second time since its founding in 1947 to two minutes to midnight: this is because during the first year of the Trump regime, "world leaders failed to respond effectively to the looming threats of nuclear war and climate change, making the world security situation more dangerous than it was a year ago—and as dangerous as it has been since World War II."[2] Alain Badiou observes, "The commonplace pessimism, again dominant in these times, is that human nature dooms us to inequality."[3] All of these dire turns reflect the fact that, as Fredric Jameson puts it in an often-repeated observation from the early 1990s, "it seems to be easier for us today to imagine the thoroughgoing deterioration of the earth and of nature than the breakdown of late capitalism."[4] The question in confronting such pessimism, especially given the substantive and legitimate grounds upon which it is based, is an old one: What is to be done? How do we live and act in the face of such terrible knowledge of the past, present, and likely futures? These questions are at the very center of one of the first great works of fiction, "a profoundly serious investigation into the human case," to appear in our millennium, David Mitchell's *Cloud Atlas* (2004).

In order most effectively to bring into focus *Cloud Atlas*'s engagement with these concerns, it would be useful to compare the novel with its 2012 film adaptation, directed by the great left popular auteurs Lana and Lilly Wachowski and Tom Tykwer. Both the novel and the film are composed of six interwoven stories, set in a variety of locales and in different historical periods: mid-nineteenth-century Pacific islands, 1930s Belgium (moved to Edinburgh in the film), 1970s California, contemporary Great Britain, a dystopian near-future Korea, and a postapocalyptic Hawai'i. Moreover, and what is even more readily apparent in the novel, each narrative takes the form of a virtuoso pastiche of a popular subgenre while also invoking what Jameson describes as "a multiplicity of informational and communicational technologies."[5] These are, respectively, the travel narrative and handwritten journal; Künstlerroman and epistolary novel; conspiracy thriller and print journalism; the British comic novel and the contemporary culture industry (print, film, and television); dystopia and digital recording; and postapocalypse and oral tale. There is also an internal tripartite division of the stories such that the first two are understood to be set in the past—mapping a long wave of colonial modernity that comes to its conclusion with the Second World War—and the next two in our contemporary situation: the mid-1970s of *Cloud Atlas* being, much as in Jameson's own theorization, the moment of the consolidation of the "infrastructure and superstructures—the economic system and the cultural 'structure of feeling'" of a postmodernity that in the novel's periodizing imagination continues on into the opening decade of the new millennium (and which, only now, might we be in a position to understand as coming to an end in 2008 with what has been variously referred to as the global "great contraction," the end of the reign of the global Minotaur, and the beginnings of a new phase of "punitive neoliberalism").[6] Finally, the novel gives us a science fictional future, its twinned forms representing, in Jameson's words, "the farthest points our own thought can reach, namely dystopia and regression, world dictatorship and the reversion to savagery, civilization and barbarism. . . . These alternatives are today for the moment the only ways in which we can imagine our future, the future of late capitalism; and it is only by shattering their twin dominion that we might conceivably be able again to think politically and productively, to envisage a condition of genuine revolutionary difference, to begin once again to think Utopia."[7] The same set of oppositions—dystopia and regression—are similarly the settings of Margaret Atwood's great contemporary science fiction novel *Oryx and Crake* (2003), and the imagining of something beyond them is the task Atwood also undertakes in the trilogy's subsequent and originally unplanned sequels, *The Year of the Flood* (2009) and *MaddAddam* (2013).

At the same time, there are a number of significant changes that take place in the film adaptation of *Cloud Atlas.* Most immediately evident is the restructuring of Mitchell's unique narrative presentation (*syuzhet*). In the first half of the novel, beginning with "The Pacific Journal of Adam Ewing" and moving forward in historical order, Mitchell presents a portion of the first five narratives, breaking off in the middle of the action; the future postapocalypse tale, "Sloosha's Crossin' an' Ev'rythin' After," is presented in its entirety; and then, in the novel's second half, the sequence is reversed, concluding with the final portion of Ewing's narrative. These six stories are connected in two ways. First, they are linked through the devices of the found text, be it that of print or visual recording: the composer, Robert Frobisher, in the second story finds a copy of the first half of Adam Ewing's travel journal; the contemporary London publisher, Timothy Cavendish, receives in the mail half of the manuscript of the conspiracy thriller; the future rebel Sonmi-451 views a film adaptation of Cavendish's story; and the Hawaiian tribesman Zachry sees a holographic recording of Sonmi-451's testimony, of which in the novel he points out, "For ev'ry word I und'standed 'bout five—six followed what I din't."[8] (I will return in a moment to the linking device used in the 1970s thriller.) Secondly, the novel provides clues to suggest that the protagonist is a reincarnation of her or his predecessors, something indicated by a "comet-shaped birthmark" they share (120, 198, 303).

The film maintains both connecting devices but expands the reincarnation trope in a manner akin to Kim Stanley Robinson's great alternate history *The Years of Rice and Salt* (2002), such that an entire collective moves together through time—a fact underscored by the ensemble cast.[9] Of the adaptation, Jameson notes that it "may not be a great film, even though one cannot say that it is inferior to the book, but it is a magnificent collection of performances."[10] Even more significantly, however, the film abandons Mitchell's ascending-descending structure in favor of an intercutting between stories, a voice-over from one narrative often continuing across the visuals of another. A similar interweaving structure has been deployed again to great effect by the Wachowskis in their equally extraordinary and even more global-spanning Netflix series *Sense8* (2015–2018), whose triumphant and joyful final episode Mitchell helped script.

Lost in this change are the science fiction roots of the formal structure of Mitchell's novel. Although only the final two episodes are explicit science fiction subgenres, the novel's formal structure ingeniously mirrors the plot of one of the founding texts of modern science fiction, H. G. Wells's *The Time Machine* (1895). (Wells is invoked at one point in the text when Frobisher alludes to "an abortive opera based on *The Island of Dr. Moreau,* whose Viennese production was cancelled by the war" [84].) Both Wells's and Mitchell's narratives trace a journey from the nineteenth century to a far-future postapocalyptic world and back again. In both cases too, the story concludes with a nineteenth-century narrator directly addressing the reader. Moreover, the far-future worlds at which both works arrive are uncannily similar, with a humanity divided into two groups, Wells's Eloi and Morlocks and Mitchell's valley folk and Kona. In each case too, the latter group predates on the former. The film further reinforces this link by suggesting that the Kona literally feed on the valley folk, while in the novel they "merely" enslave them: "busted in sprit by the killin' we'd seem a' the slaved future we seen b'fore us. No fam'ly, no freeness, no nothin' but work an' pain' an' work an' pain till we died" (291). (Another consequence of this shift is that the novel's theme of imprisonment and enslavement, at the heart of every story, is made secondary in the film.) Mitchell's far-future world even has its own version of a time traveler, in the figure of the visiting Meronym, a member of the Prescients, the last people on earth who still possess the advanced technologies developed by the "Old 'Uns" in the days before the catastrophic events known as the Fall. While both the novel and the film thus undertake what we have seen throughout this book to be a central labor of the utopian narrative from Thomas More onward—what E. P. Thompson, following the lead of Miguel Abensour, refers to as an "'education of desire . . . to open a way to aspiration' for a radically other future"—they do so in quite different ways.[11]

A seemingly more minor change occurs in the 1930s Künstlerroman section, "Letters from Zedelghem," with the fictional work of art that provides the novel's title. The young and ambitious English composer Robert Frobisher describes his masterpiece in a way that also applies to the novel's formal structure:

> A "sextet for overlapping soloists": piano, clarinet, 'cello, flute, oboe, and violin, each in its own language of key, scale, and color. In the first set, each solo is interrupted by its successor: in the second, each interruption is recontinued, in order. Revolutionary or gimmicky? Shan't know until it's finished. (445)

Jameson reads this practice as an example of "an aesthetic of singularity in which what is constructed is not meant to be the elaboration of a style or the practice of a genre (even a newly minted one), but rather the experimental projection of a single one-time conceit, unimitable and without a legacy or any intention of founding a tradition formal or otherwise: not a new style, but the assemblage of various styles."[12] A similar assemblage of various styles and different standpoints on our contemporary global reality are at work in the formal structure of Jameson's own earlier study *The Geopolitical Aesthetic: Cinema and Space in the World System* (1992), making the latter a prefiguration of the operation of global cognitive mapping so effectively realized in Mitchell's novel.[13]

It is Frobisher's singular avant-garde work that the 1970s conspiracy thriller's protagonist, Luisa Rey, later encounters firsthand:

> The music in the Lost Chord Music Store subsumes all thoughts of *Spyglass*, Sixsmith, Sachs, and Grimaldi. The sound is pristine,

> river-like, spectral, hypnotic . . . *intimately familiar.* Luisa stands, entranced, as if living in a stream of time. "I *know* this music," she tells the store clerk, who eventually asks if she's okay. "What the hell is it?" (408)

When this scene is repeated in the adaptation, we, the viewers, along with Luisa (Halle Berry) hear the actual music. Moreover, it is used throughout the film as part of the score. In presenting the "Cloud Atlas Sextet" in this way, the film, as in the adaptation of "Babette's Feast" I discussed in chapter 5, violates Ernst Bloch's proscription on providing a fully realized representation of the imagined work of art.

All of this points toward the nature of the more consequential changes that occur in the adaptation. These are most readily apparent in the film's radically different concluding scene. Both narratives come to their climax with Ewing's confrontation with his father-in-law concerning his newfound resolution to pledge himself to "the Abolitionist cause, because I owe my life to a self-freed slave & because I must begin somewhere" (508). Even here though, the presentation differs significantly: whereas in the novel, Ewing imagines a future confrontation, in the end leaving undetermined for the reader whether it ever takes place, in the film it takes place in a San Francisco parlor, Ewing's dedicated wife, Tilda (Doona Bae), by his side. At this confrontation, Ewing's father-in-law, Haskell Moore (played in the film by Hugo Weaving of the Wachowskis' *Matrix* fame), warns of the dangers of this undertaking, presented in the novel in this way:

> Oh, you'll grow hoarse, poor & gray in causes! You'll be spat on, shot at, lynched, pacified with medals, spurned by backwoodsmen! Crucified! Naïve, dreaming Adam. He who would do battle with the many-headed hydra of human nature must pay a world of pain & his family must pay it along with him! (508–9)

In both narratives, the closing line of his speech is the same—"Only as you gasp your dying breath shall you understand, your life amounted to no more than one drop in a limitless ocean!"—as is Ewing's (Jim Sturgess) response, "Yet what is any ocean but a multitude of drops?" (509). The novel concludes with these words; however, the film adds a coda in which we see Zachry (Tom Hanks), as well as his family, inhabiting a utopian community located on another world, the Earth but a bright blue star in the sky. (This desire for an escape to the stars—also underwriting Christopher Nolan's epic film *Interstellar* [2014]—is confronted head-on in Kim Stanley Robinson's starship novel *Aurora* [2015].) This direct figuration of a utopian future gives the lie to Ewing's father-in-law's words and redeems the sacrifices the young man plans to undertake.

In fact, every narrative in the film similarly concludes with a glimpse of an achieved utopia of sorts. For example, the present-day story, "The Ghastly Ordeal of Timothy Cavendish," comes to its climax with the reunion of the long-ago lovers, Cavendish (Jim Broadbent) and Ursula (Susan Sarandon). Both narratives end with Cavendish declaring, "Like Solzhenitsyn laboring in Vermont, I shall beaver away in exile, far from the city that knitted my bones" (387). However, in the film, Cavendish then adds, "Unlike Solzhenitsyn I shan't be alone," the camera panning out to reveal Ursula walking up to join him as he concludes on his typewriter the manuscript we have just read or viewed. This has the effect of transforming Mitchell's farcical tale into the evental genre of the comedy of remarriage I discussed in the previous two chapters. Indeed, in another departure from the novel, all the narratives in the film present us with lovers separated from one another and seeking, and achieving, reunion. The one exception to this rule is the Luisa Rey story—although even here, through the characters played in the film by Berry (Rey) and Hanks (the scientist, Isaac Sachs), as well as Sachs's realization immediately before his death in a plane bombing that he is "in love" with Rey, the narrative looks forward to the climactic "green world" reunion of the couple that takes place in the postapocalypse story. In this way, the film both fills in the absent place—in a novel that already contains the universal history, Künstlerroman, and science fiction—of the fourth and most explicitly filmic of the evental genres and transforms the resolution of the composite narrative as a whole into a comedic one.

Indeed, the film goes out of its way to assure its viewers that following the conclusion of the dystopian plot, the revolution begun by the clone corporate slave, Sonmi-451 (Doona Bae), and her comrades has been a success: this is indicated by the heroic statues built to honor Sonmi-451 that Zachry encounters during his journey through the mountaintop ruins of the "old 'uns." This conclusion departs utterly from Mitchell's original, which comes to a climax with the unsettling revelation that the entire plot has been staged by the corporate Unanimity in order "to generate the show trial of the decade. To make every last pureblood in Nea So Copros mistrustful of every last fabricant. To manufacture downstrata consent for the Juche's new Fabricant Xpiry Act. To discredit Abolitionism. You can see, the whole conspiracy has been a resounding success" (348–49). (It should be evident how this statement echoes the then recent 9/11 Truth movement's conspiracy theories.) Similarly, no rescue occurs at the end of Zachry's story, and all indications are that human civilization has permanently collapsed or will, at best—and along the lines first plotted by Walter M. Miller Jr.'s classic Cold War postapocalyptic novel, *A Canticle for Leibowitz* (1959)—begin again its long arduous climb only to fall once more in some even more distant future. All of this suggests that in the novel, unlike in the film, Ewing's father-in-law's misanthropic views are the true ones. The vision of history underlying such an outlook is ruthlessly summarized by the malevolent physician treating Ewing, Dr. Henry Goose, whose first rule is "The weak are meat the strong do eat" (489).

It would be far too easy to conclude from this that the film counters the novel's tragic pessimism with a more properly comedic optimism. But to view the matter in this binary fashion would be to miss the richly dialectical nature of Mitchell's narrative. By eschewing the guarantees of success offered in the film, Mitchell relocates utopia elsewhere, into our actions in the present. In the novel's penultimate paragraph, Ewing declares, "A life spent shaping a world I *want* Jackson [his son] to inherit, not one I *fear* Jackson shall inherit, this strikes me as a life worth the living" (508). We should hear in these words echoes of the conclusion of Wells's *The Time Machine,* in which the narrator similarly recalls that the now vanished Time Traveler "thought but cheerlessly of the Advancement of Mankind" and, like Walter Benjamin's equally pessimistic angel of history, "saw in the growing pile of civilization only a foolish heaping that must inevitably fall back upon and destroy its makers in the end."[14] The Traveler's experiences, which have just been narrated to us, seem to verify his earlier views. However, the narrator then immediately adds, "If that is so, it remains for us to live as though it were not so."[15] In both Mitchell's and Wells's narratives, what is being unveiled here is the fictional nature of all such imaginings of the future. Such fictions serve as mirrors reflecting back to us in a distorted form our deepest held beliefs, the fundamental fantasies that underpin reality itself. Thus, as Ewing puts it, underscoring the pedagogical labor of all storytelling, "Belief is both prize & battlefield, within the mind & in the mind's mirror, the world" (508).

In this regard, both narratives resonate with the outlook of one of the twentieth century's greatest dialectical thinkers, Antonio Gramsci. Gramsci lived in a moment not unlike our own, when a rising tide of unreason and authoritarian populism seemed poised to swamp the world. Gramsci paid for his efforts to swim against this flood with more than a decade of imprisonment and deteriorating health, ultimately resulting in his death. In one of his most celebrated and moving letters from prison, Gramsci writes:

> It seems to me that under such conditions prolonged for years, and with such psychological experiences, a man should have reached the loftiest stage of stoic serenity and should have acquired such a profound conviction that man [*sic*] bears within himself the sources of his own moral strength, that everything depends on him, on his energy, on his will, on the iron coherence of the aims that he sets for himself and the means he adopts to realize them, that he will never again despair and lapse into those vulgar, banal states of mind that are called pessimism and optimism. My state of mind synthesizes these two emotions and overcomes them: I'm a pessimist because of intelligence but an optimist because of will. In all circumstances I think first of the worst possibility in order to set in motion all the reserves of my will and be in a position to knock down the obstacle. I have never entertained any illusions and I have never suffered disappointments.[16]

It is precisely such a thinking first of the worst possibilities that is undertaken by both Wells and Mitchell in their respective fictions.

The film, however, offers a thrilling example of utopian romanticism, an optimism of the intellect that aims to encourage an optimism of the will to act to realize such a world.[17] While this may well indicate the limits of radical pedagogy currently available in Hollywood blockbuster cinema—and for this, let me be clear, I applaud the efforts to push to these limits by the Wachowskis, Tykwer, Joss Whedon, and others working in a similar vein, and hope they continue—Gramsci warns that the dangers in such a stance are twofold. On the one hand, an optimism of the intellect can give way to the passivity, or pessimism of the will, found in various strands of progressivist ideologies: If the future is guaranteed, why do we need to take the risk of acting in our own lives to bring it about? In his *Prison Notebooks,* Gramsci describes such a position as that of "mechanical determinism" or "finalism," and, ever the dialectical thinker, he stresses its great value in moments such as his (and our) own:

> When you don't have the initiative in the struggle and the struggle itself comes eventually to be identified with a series of defeats, mechanical determinism becomes a tremendous force of moral resistance, of cohesion and of patient and obstinate perseverance. "I have been defeated for the moment, but the tide of history is working for me in the long term." Real will takes on the garments of an act of faith in a certain rationality of history and in a primitive and empirical form of impassioned finalism which appears in the role of a substitute for Predestination or Providence of confessional religions.[18]

Gramsci then continues:

> Indeed one should emphasize how fatalism is nothing other than the clothing worn by real and active will when in a weak position. This is why it is essential at all times to demonstrate the futility of mechanical determinism: for, although it is explicable as a naïve philosophy of the mass and as such, but only as such, can be an intrinsic element of strength, nevertheless when it is adopted as a thought-out and coherent philosophy on the part of the intellectuals, it becomes a cause of passivity, of idiotic self-sufficiency. This happens when they don't even expect that the subaltern will become directive and responsible.[19]

The ultimate end of such a disappointed progressivism would be its collapse into cynicism, the fatal combination, in Gramsci's terms, of pessimism of both the intellect and the will. (To offer one final Greimasian square, the relationship between the four positions implicit in Gramsci's argument would appear as in Figure 14.)

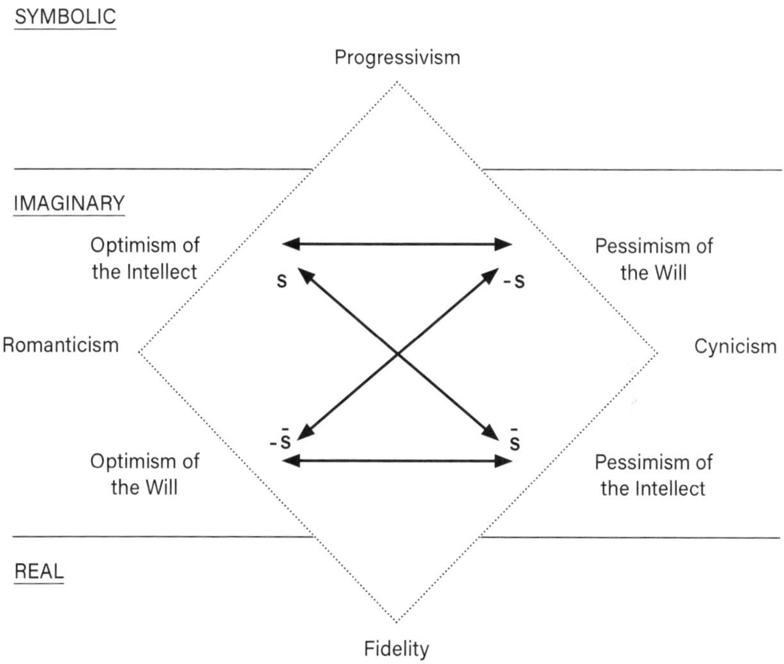

FIGURE 14

It is just such a cynicism that Slavoj Žižek characterizes as the quintessential contemporary form of ideology:

> The cynical subject is quite aware of the distance between the ideological mask and the social reality, but he none the less still insists upon the mask. The formula, as proposed by Sloterdijk, would then be: "they know very well what they are doing, but still they are doing it." Cynical reason is no longer naïve, but is a paradox of an enlightened false consciousness: one knows the falsehood very well, one is well aware of a particular interest hidden behind an ideological universality, but still one does not renounce it.[20]

More recently, Žižek notes, "Something is obviously very wrong here—it is not that people 'do not know what they want,' but rather that cynical resignation prevents them from acting upon it, with the result that a weird gap opens up between what people think and how they act (or vote). Such frustration can foment dangerous extra-parliamentary explosions."[21]

In the end, the novel's Ewing remains clear-eyed about his prospects for success: "I am not deceived. It is the hardest of worlds to make real. Tortuous advances won over generations can be lost by a single stroke of a myopic president's pen or a vainglorious general's sword" (508). And yet even in the face of such disastrous outcomes—realized in our history in the events following 9/11, to which this passage obliquely refers, and now unfolding every day under the current myopic and vainglorious U.S. presidential administration—Ewing's fidelity, like that of Du Bois's John Brown, Dinesen's Babette Hersant, and Adam Sandler's Henry Roth, as well as so many of the other figures I have touched on in this book, to the universal historical truth he has encountered in his journey remains firm. This is even more so the case for the doomed Sonmi-451—who opens her testimony expressing the deeply Badiouian sentiment, "Truth is singular. Its 'versions' are mistruths"—when she reminds her interrogator, "As Seneca warned Nero: No matter how many of us you kill, you will never kill your successor" (185, 349). Sonmi-451's point here is that hope is ineradicable and, as long as there are subjects committed to truth, the future remains open. The lesson in these two narratives—as in all the others examined in this book—is that utopia is never no-where, an imagined perfected future, but in fact always already potentially exists in the concrete now-here, in our collective fidelity to the project of making a world we so desire rather than a world we fear. It is in its encouragement of us to occupy the former where lies the true brilliance of *Cloud Atlas.*

Acknowledgments

In *The Politics of Friendship*, Jacques Derrida observes, "For to love friendship, it is not enough to know how to bear the other in mourning; one must love the future." Whatever hope I invoke for the future in these pages arises from the many undeserved friends whose generosity, love, and deep listening have contributed so much to my life. This is a book that is about dialogue and each chapter was composed in dialogue with a number of others, whom I have decided to thank individually in the opening note of each chapter. This project also benefitted immensely from other readings and conversations with, among so many others, Alain Badiou, Antonis Balasopoulos, Kelly Beck, Jill Belli, Pietro Bianchi, Nick Brown, Susan Buck-Morss, Sid Dobrin, Peter Fitting, Pamela Gilbert, Sean Grattan, Brian Greenspan, Christian Haines, Terry Harpold, Rafael Hernandez, Peter Hitchcock, Sarah Hogan, Caren Irr, Naomi Jacobs, Fredric Jameson, Thomas Johnson, Jin-Ho Kang, Kenneth Kidd, Sam Kimball, Ethan Knapp, Burçu Kuheylan, Dragan Kujundzic, Tim Lanzendörfer, Rob Lehman, Carolyn Lesjak, Roger Maioli, Kel Martin, Mike Mayne, Carl Miller, Mathias Nilges, Oded Nir, Chris Pavsek, Aron Pease, Arun Pokhrel, Gib Prettyman, Romy Rajan, Craig Rinne, Bruce Robbins, Kim Stanley Robinson, Ken Roemer, Kristen Ross, Michael Rothberg, Raúl Sanchéz, Pete Sands, Malini Schueller, Dina Smith, Yannis Stavrakakis, Darko Suvin, Mark Tabone, Maureen Turim, Patricia Ventura, Jennifer Wagner-Lawlor, Audrey Wasser, Vince Wing, and Jane Winston. I want to extend a special debt of gratitude to Avi Alpert, Susan Hegeman, John Hartzog, Derrick King, Tom Moylan, Mitch Murray, Eric Smith, and Rob Seguin—and especially Chris Breu, John Leavey, and Rob Tally—for reading, and in some cases offering detailed commentaries on, the entire manuscript. This book, and many others like it, might never have come into being if not for the support and patience of Danielle Kasprzak at the University of Minnesota Press. My sincere gratitude as well to Pieter Martin, Anne Carter, and so many other wonderful people at the Press for helping bring the project to completion.

I would also like to express my gratitude to the many students from my now just completed first quarter century of teaching at the University of Florida: most especially, the undergraduates in my fall 2016 literary theory course, where, as my Introduction and first chapter make clear, the major ideas for this book began to crystallize; my spring 2017 and spring 2019 graduate seminars for all their input on the early stages and final draft of the project; and, finally, the wonderfully diverse students in my spring 2019 pilot general education course on reading and the examined life, where so many of the claims I make here had the opportunity to be put into practice—its momentary reality proves other ways of doing and being are possible. You have all taught me so much and given me so much hope for the trials ahead.

The period of the writing of this book saw the passing of four longtime colleagues at the University of Florida—Don Ault, Andrew Gordon, Mildred Hill-Lubin, and David Leverenz. Each was in their own unique way a pioneer, and together they helped make UF such a special place to be during my early years here. In fall 2018, my family also lost our stepfather for very nearly one-half of my life, Edward Hanson. Ed helped my family recover from what otherwise would have been the unthinkable disaster of the early unanticipated death of my own father, Kenneth Wegner, and for this as well as so much more I will always remain in his debt. They all will be borne in mourning.

In these times, I can never be thankful enough for both the love and the challenges offered by my extended families—Wegner, Toms, Hanson, and Hegeman. A true source of joy in the recent dark years has been having my brother Paul, the second of our seven siblings, and his extraordinary life partner and brilliant legal mind, Monica, join us here in the Deep South. (It was at their wedding many years ago where I first read the passage from Ernst Bloch that is at the heart of chapter 6.) I have had the special privilege of living in the best of all possible worlds with our now teenage twins, Nadia and Owen. As always, my most profound gratitude goes to Susan Hegeman, who has unceasingly and without condition offered me, for more than three decades now, "something else, some kind of . . . pairing, like Pluto and Charon, with the center of gravity between the two." Finally, I would like to acknowledge the person to whom this book is dedicated, our former colleague, a brilliant translator and scholar, dedicated and visionary department leader, and unwavering friend and confidant, John Leavey, for whom it will never be too dark to stop invoking hope.

Notes

Introduction

1. Bertolt Brecht, "An Die Nachgeborenen," in *Selected Poems* (New York: Grove Press, 1947), 172–73; translation modified. The poem was first introduced to me by my dear friend Chris Pavsek, who has also created a superb short film entitled *To Those Born After* (2005).

2. See Rita Felski, *The Limits of Critique* (Chicago: University of Chicago Press, 2015). Also see the discussion of Felski's intervention in *PMLA* 132, no. 2 (2017). I would note here that the case is very different for what has been theorized by Franco Moretti as "distant reading," which in fact still engages in the practices of deep, close, critical reading but does so on a very difference scale of text. See Franco Moretti, *Distant Reading* (New York: Verso, 2013).

3. Crystal Bartolovich, "Humanities of Scale: Marxism, Surface Reading—and Milton," *PMLA* 127, no. 1 (2012): 116.

4. Carolyn Lesjak, "Reading Dialectically," *Criticism* 55, no. 2 (2013): 237.

5. Lesjak, "Reading Dialectically," 244.

6. Fredric Jameson, *Valences of the Dialectic* (New York: Verso, 2009), 490.

7. Nico Baumbach, "All That Heaven Allows: What Is, or Was, Cinephilia (Part One)," *Film Comment,* March 12, 2012, www.filmcomment.com/entry/all-that-heaven-allows-what-is-or-was-cinephilia-part-one.

8. Hoon Song, "James Clifford and the Ethical Turn in Anthropology," *Cultural Critique* 97 (2017): 178.

9. Fredric Jameson, *The Political Unconscious: Narrative as a Socially Symbolic Act* (Ithaca, N.Y.: Cornell University Press, 1981), 59, 115. For a recent discussion on the ways such an ethical binary manifests itself in current debates concerning "peak television," see Thomas Johnson, "The Bicameral (Hive) Mind: *Westworld* and the Forensic/Thematic Binary," (forthcoming).

10. George Ciccariello-Maher, *Decolonizing Dialectics* (Durham, N.C.: Duke University Press, 2017), 61. In her recent study *Generous Thinking: A Radical Approach to Saving the University* (Baltimore: Johns Hopkins University Press, 2019), Kathleen Fitzpatrick similarly points out that "the critique of critique *is still critique*" (31). This opens up onto one of her book's key insights: "Rather than critical thinking, the dark opposite of generous thinking, that

which has in fact created an imbalance in scholarly work—and not just in the humanities, but across the curriculum—is *competitive* thinking, thinking that is compelled by what sociologist and economist Thorstein Veblen called 'invidious comparison,' or what [Winfried] Fluck refers to as the 'race for professional distinction.' It is the competitive that has undermined the capacity for community-building, both within our campuses and between our campuses and the broader public" (33). While I did not encounter Fitzpatrick's study until my own book was well into production, the argument it advances for generosity of mind and openness to possibility complements the claims I advance in the pages that follow.

11. Clint Burnham, *The Jamesonian Unconscious: The Aesthetics of Marxist Theory* (Durham, N.C.: Duke University Press, 1995), 88.

12. Joseph North, *Literary Criticism: A Concise Political History* (Cambridge, Mass.: Harvard University Press, 2017), 3.

13. North, *Literary Criticism,* 60.

14. North, 105.

15. Georg Wilhelm Friedrich Hegel, *Hegel's Preface to the "Phenomenology of the Spirit,"* trans. Yirmiyahu Yovel (Princeton, N.J.: Princeton University Press, 2005), 102. For more on the relationship between Cartesian and dialectical practices of reading, also see Theodor Adorno, *An Introduction to Dialectics,* trans. Nicholas Walker (Cambridge: Polity Press, 2017).

16. Bruce Robbins, "Discipline and Parse: The Politics of Close Reading," review of *Literary Criticism: A Concise Political History,* by Joseph North, *Los Angeles Review of Books,* May 8, 2017, https://www.lareviewofbooks.org/article/discipline-and-parse-the-politics-of-close-reading#; and Francis Mulhern, "Critical Revolutions," *New Left Review* 110 (2018): 39–54. It should be pointed out that Mulhern was also one of the Harvard University Press readers of the manuscript of North's book.

17. See, for example, my chapter "Theoretical Modernisms (1970s)," in *Periodizing Jameson: Dialectics, the University, and the Desire for Narrative* (Chicago: Northwestern University Press, 2014), 43–59; Robert T. Tally Jr., *Fredric Jameson: The Project of Dialectical Criticism* (London: Pluto Press, 2014), 64–69; and Andrew Cole, *The Birth of Theory* (Chicago: University of Chicago Press, 2014), 126–32, 149–50.

18. Holberg Prize, "The Holberg Lecture 2008: Fredric Jameson: 'Foreign Relations in World Literature,'" June 4, 2012, YouTube video, 26:26, https://www.youtube.com/watch?v=Key1dnyAyYU, cited in North, *Literary Criticism,* 101.

19. North, *Literary Criticism,* 101.

20. Fredric Jameson, *Marxism and Form: Twentieth-Century Dialectical Theories of Literature* (Princeton, N.J.: Princeton University Press, 1971), 306.

21. North, *Literary Criticism,* 104.

22. Fredric Jameson, "Science versus Ideology," *Humanities in Society* 6 (1983): 283.

23. Jameson, *Valences of the Dialectic,* 372.

24. Thomas More, *Utopia,* ed. Edward Surtz and J. H. Hexter, vol. 4 of *The Yale Edition of the Complete Works of St. Thomas More* (New Haven, Conn.: Yale University Press, 1965), 245. I will return to this important passage in chapter 3.

25. For only the most cursory of samplings, see the final chapter, "The Dialectic of Utopia and Ideology," in *The Political Unconscious,* 281–99; *Late Marxism: Adorno, or the Persistence of the Dialectic* (New York: Verso, 1990); *The Cultural Turn: Selected Writings on the Postmodern, 1983–1998* (New York: Verso, 1998); *A Singular Modernity: Essay on the Ontology of the Present* (New York: Verso, 2002); *Valences of the Dialectic*; and "Third World Literature in the Era of Multinational Capitalism," now reprinted with an extended new commentary in *Allegory and Ideology* (New York: Verso, 2019), 159–215.

26. Fredric Jameson, introduction to *The Historical Novel,* by Georg Lukács, trans. Hannah Mitchell and Stanley Mitchell (Lincoln: University of Nebraska Press, 1983), 1.

27. Jameson quoted in Sianne Ngai, *Our Aesthetic Categories: Zany, Cute, Interesting* (Cambridge, Mass.: Harvard University Press, 2012), back cover.

28. North, *Literary Criticism,* 104.

29. See Christopher Breu, *Insistence of the Material: Literature in the Age of Biopolitics* (Minneapolis: University of Minnesota Press, 2014).

30. For a superb recent discussion of the assaults on academic intellectual freedom, see Susan Hegeman, "Oppenheimer's House; or, the Contradictions of Academic Life from the Cold War to Neoliberalism," *JAF: AAUP Journal of Academic Freedom* 8 (2017): https://www.aaup.org/sites/default/files/Hegeman.pdf. For an invaluable reading that uses institutional transformations at the University of Florida as a template for understanding changes in the U.S. university system as a whole, see Kim Emery, "'Crisis Management' in Higher Education: RCM and the Politics of Crisis at the University of Florida," *Cultural Logic* 17 (2010): https://doi.org/10.14288/clogic.v17i0.191541.

For a sampling of some of the recent literature responding to these transformations in higher education, see Christopher Newfield, *Unmaking the Public University: The Forty-Year Assault on the Middle Class* (Cambridge, Mass.: Harvard University Press, 2008); Henry A. Giroux, *Neoliberalism's War on Higher Education* (Chicago: Haymarket, 2014); Wendy Brown, *Undoing the Demos: Neoliberalism's Stealth Revolution* (Cambridge, Mass.: MIT Press, 2015); Christopher Schaberg, *The Work of Literature in an Age of Post-Truth* (New York: Bloomsbury, 2018); Henry Reichman, *The Future of Academic Freedom* (Baltimore: Johns Hopkins University Press, 2019); Herb Childress,

The Adjunct Underclass: How America's Colleges Betrayed Their Faculty, Their Students, and Their Mission (Chicago: University of Chicago Press, 2019); and Fitzpatrick, *Generous Thinking.* Finally, I take up these institutional changes and the various responses to them in a number of other places. See Phillip E. Wegner, "Lacan avec Greimas: Formalization, Theory, and the 'Other Side' of the Study of Culture," *Minnesota Review* 77 (2011): 62–86; "The Beat Cops of History: Or, The Paranoid Style in American Intellectual Politics," in *Shockwaves of Possibility: Essays on Science Fiction, Globalization, and Utopia* (Oxford: Peter Lang, 2014), 131–48; and "Unfinished Business: On the Dialectic of the University in Late Capitalism," in *Periodizing Jameson: Dialectics, the University, and the Desire for Narrative* (Chicago: Northwestern University Press, 2014), 153–82.

31. Bill Readings, *The University in Ruins* (Cambridge, Mass.: Harvard University Press, 1996), 153.

32. Sara Ahmed, *Living a Feminist Life* (Durham, N.C.: Duke University Press, 2017), 9–10.

33. North, *Literary Criticism,* 61.

34. See Cole, *Birth of Theory.*

35. A case in point is Mark Bauerlein. For an example of his recent defenses of Trump, see Mark Bauerlein, "Trump's in His Glory, and It's Driving Liberals Nuts," CNN, May 11, 2018, https://www.cnn.com/2018/05/10/opinions/trump-is-having-a-great-foreign-policy-week-bauerlein/index.html. Also see Isaac Chotiner, "'He's Learning on the Job': A Lonely Trump Defender in the Academy Attempts to Continue Defending Trump," *Slate,* April 24, 2017, http://www.slate.com/articles/news_and_politics/interrogation/2017/04/mark_bauerlein_of_emory_university_still_defends_donald_trump.html. In the latter interview, Bauerlein makes explicit the class ressentiment motivating his damning moralizing judgments of humanities intellectuals: "I had a very unprivileged childhood. I won't even go into the things that happened to me. But I also ate dirt for many years as a college student and after, living in squalor. I *can't listen* to tenured professors at distinguished institutions who have had charmed lives who are white or black talk about white privilege" (emphasis added). I hope to return to this issue in a future essay.

36. Christopher Newfield, "Yes to the New Education, but What Kind?" *PMLA* 133, no. 3 (2018): 690. Also see Newfield's *The Great Mistake: How We Wrecked the Public Universities and How We Can Fix Them* (Baltimore: Johns Hopkins University Press, 2016).

37. Raymond Williams, *Problems in Materialism and Culture* (London: Verso, 1980), 38–40; Hazard Adams, *Critical Theory Since Plato* (San Diego: Harcourt Brace Jovanovich, 1971), 847; North, *Literary Criticism,* 104; and Virginia Woolf, *A Room of One's Own* (New York: Harcourt Brace, 1929), 18.

38. Jameson, *Late Marxism,* 134.

39. See Phillip E. Wegner, "Are You Now or Have You Ever Been a Suvinian?: Beyond the Moralizing Temptation; or, How Not to Read," *Utopian Studies* 30, no. 2 (2019): 300–44.

40. Richard Gawthrop and Gerald Strauss, "Protestantism and Literacy in Early Modern Germany," *Past & Present* 104 (1984): 34.

41. "The Twelve Articles of the Swabian Peasants (February 27–March 1, 1525)," *German History in Documents and Images,* http://germanhistorydocs.ghi-dc.org/pdf/eng/Doc.52-ENG-12%20Articles_en.pdf.

42. Gawthrop and Strauss, "Protestantism and Literacy," 35.

43. Gawthrop and Strauss, 39.

44. John R. Searle, "Reiterating the Differences: A Reply to Derrida," *Glyph* 1 (1977): 198, 204.

45. Searle, "Reiterating the Differences," 203, 206.

46. The relevant documents are collected together in the volume *Limited Inc,* trans. Samuel Weber (Evanston, Ill.: Northwestern University Press, 1988).

47. I touch on the changing valences of Huxley's utopianism in my introduction to *The Shape of Utopia: Studies in a Literary Genre,* by Robert C. Elliott (Oxford: Peter Lang, 2013), xxiii–xxvi.

48. Aldous Huxley, *Tomorrow and Tomorrow and Tomorrow and Other Essays* (New York: Signet, 1964), 76.

49. Huxley, *Tomorrow and Tomorrow,* 69–70.

50. Paul Greenstein, Nigley Lennon, and Lionel Rolfe, *Bread & Hyacinths: The Rise and Fall of Utopian Los Angeles* (Los Angeles: California Classics Books, 1992), 116.

51. Mike Davis, *City of Quartz: Excavating the Future in Los Angeles* (New York: Verso, 1991), 11. For two further nuanced critical readings of the events leading to the Llano's establishment and its eventual collapse, see Dolores Hayden, *Seven American Utopias: The Architecture of Communitarian Socialism, 1790–1975* (Cambridge, Mass.: MIT Press, 1976); and Greenstein, Lennon, and Rolfe, *Bread & Hyacinths.*

52. This passage from the September 1847 issue of *Kommunistische Zeitschrift* is cited in Louis Marin, *Utopiques: jeux d'espaces* (Paris: Les Éditions de Minuet, 1973), 350; my translation. Also see Louis Marin, *Utopics: The Semiological Play of Textual Spaces,* trans. Robert A. Vollrath (Highlands Park, N.Y.: Humanities Press, 1984), 278. I touch on the debate over Cabet's decision to migrate to the United States and found his Icarian colony in *Life between Two Deaths, 1989–2001: U.S. Culture in the Long Nineties* (Durham, N.C.: Duke University Press, 2009), 210–11.

53. An especially pernicious tactic of moralizing ethical criticism is to offer as evidence of certain sins statements made in "private and unverifiable"

conversations, during conferences or other informal presentations, or, worst of all, on the part of one's students. Jacques Derrida documents such practices in *Limited Inc,* 158–59n12.

54. Robert S. Lehman, *Impossible Modernism: T. S. Eliot, Walter Benjamin, and the Critique of Historical Reason* (Stanford, Calif.: Stanford University Press, 2016), xiii; and George Ciccariello-Maher, "A Critique of Du Boisian Reason: Kanye West and the Fruitfulness of Double-Consciousness," *Journal of Black Studies* 39, no. 3 (2009): 372.

55. Fredric Jameson, *Postmodernism, or the Cultural Logic of Late Capitalism* (Durham, N.C.: Duke University Press, 1991), 298. Also see the superb reading of this passage in Ngai, *Our Aesthetic Categories,* 48–51.

56. Jameson, *Postmodernism,* 183.

57. Gilles Deleuze and Félix Guattari, *What Is Philosophy?,* trans. Hugh Tomlinson and Graham Burchell (New York: Columbia University Press, 1994), 28–29.

58. Friedrich Nietzsche, *The Portable Nietzsche,* trans. Walter Kaufman (New York: Viking Press, 1954), 139.

59. On the important distinction between negative and infinite judgments or negating a predicate (not to engage) and affirming a nonpredicate (to *not*-engage), see Slavoj Žižek, *The Parallax View* (Cambridge, Mass.: MIT Press, 2006), 381–83.

60. William Blake, *The Early Illuminated Books,* ed. Morris Eaves, Robert N. Essic, and Joseph Viscomi (London: Tate Gallery and William Blake Trust, 1993), 154; and Martin Luther King Jr., "Martin Luther King Jr.'s 'Letter from Birmingham Jail,'" *Atlantic* (February 2018): https://www.theatlantic.com/magazine/archive/2018/02/letter-from-birmingham-jail/552461/.

61. North, *Literary Criticism,* 204; Muriel Spark, *The Prime of Miss Jean Brodie* (New York: HarperPerennial, 1999), 7–8; and Franz Kafka, *Letters to Friends, Family, and Editors,* trans. Richard and Clara Watson (New York: Schocken Books, 1977), 16.

62. Ahmed, *Living a Feminist Life,* 252.

63. Pierre Bayard, *How to Talk about Books You Haven't Read,* trans. Jeffrey Mehlman (New York: Bloomsbury, 2007), 12; and James Joyce, *Ulysses,* ed. Hans Walter Gabler (New York: Vintage, 1986), 23. Fredric Jameson also uses the phrase "creative reading" in his introduction to *Representing Capital: A Reading of Volume One* (New York: Verso, 2011): "Any creative reading of *Capital* today is a translation process, whereby a language and conceptuality invented for the first industrial age of Victorian society is transcoded by remaining faithful to its 'original' construction, and secures its contemporary representationality by a virtue of a grasp of the ambitious dimensions and the structural intricacy of its initial representation" (9). For further discussion of

Jameson's deployment of the notion of transcoding see Wegner, *Periodizing Jameson,* 6 and 218n12.

64. On the Žižekian logic of "repeating" and its difference from "return," see Wegner, *Periodizing Jameson,* 3–4 and 195. For another call for new forms of reparative reading, see Sean Austin Grattan, *Hope Isn't Stupid: Utopian Affects in Contemporary American Literature* (Iowa City: University of Iowa Press, 2017).

65. See Phillip E. Wegner, *Imaginary Communities: Utopia, the Nation, and the Spatial Histories of Modernity* (Berkeley: University of California Press, 2002).

66. Fredric Jameson, *The Ideologies of Theory* (New York: Verso, 2008), 222; and "The Aesthetics of Singularity," *New Left Review* 92 (2015): 110.

67. Nicola Gess, "Gaining Sovereignty: On the Figure of the Child in Walter Benjamin's Writing," *MLN* 125, no. 3 (2010): 707–8. Also see the useful discussion of Benjamin's practices in Lehman, *Impossible Modernism.*

68. Walter Benjamin, *The Origin of German Tragic Drama,* trans. John Osborne (London: New Left Books, 1977), 235.

69. See Ward Pafford, "Coleridge's Wedding-Guest," *Studies in Philology* 60, no. 4 (1963): 618–26.

70. In the introduction to her superb exploration of the rich and diverse utopian imaginaries flourishing in medieval Europe, *Nowhere in the Middle Ages* (Philadelphia: University of Pennsylvania Press, 2016), Karma Lochrie cites a passage from *Imaginary Communities,* which reads in full: "Although its roots extend much further back into older traditions of 'utopian' thought and representation, the modern narrative utopia has a distinct moment of birth in the 1516 work by the English Christian humanist Thomas More, which at once introduces a new word, literary institution, and conceptual problematic into the European cultural imagination" (xxi). (Lochrie begins her citation after the first comma.) Lochrie then maintains, "These remarks by Phillip Wegner, whose work on utopianism and modernity is otherwise historically and theoretically astute, assimilate the 'modern narrative utopia' with its 'birth' to the date of *Utopia*'s first printing, in 1516. Although More is the birthing parent of the triplet that utopia is—word, literary genre, and concept—modernity is also generally regarded as utopia's precondition" (2). Although I cannot speak for the general regard, I will say that in no way do I consider utopia in the sense that Lochrie seems to be using it here—as utopian impulse—as having its precondition in European modernity. A few pages further on, Lochrie argues, "Using More to define utopianism unnecessarily restricts all utopianism to a back formation of his 1516 work, at the expense of other utopian possibilities afoot in the Middle Ages and beyond" (4). In this I completely concur, both in *Imaginary Communities* and today. More's book, rather than More himself,

gives "birth" to two things: a name and a new literary technology or genre, which More, or rather those reader-writers who follow him, *name* utopia. A name is not, as I will later argue, a stand-in for a set of characteristics but rather what Saul Kripke names a "rigid designator," fixing the referent. The name created by More is then extended to encompass the impulse Lochrie refers to as utopianism, which Bloch maintains, in an axiom that is as fundamental to my own work as I believe it is for Lochrie, exists in *all* human societies, past and present, *and* a strategy of reading backward and forward, which Lochrie so effectively deploys throughout her superb book. That such a double achievement, the production of a new literary technology and a name, comes about in response to concrete and specific historical conditions—in this case, the nascence of the long cultural revolution that has been named modernity (or, as I, following the lead of Louis Marin, more specifically refer to as an "in-between" moment [*Imaginary Communities,* 34])—is indeed an absolute presupposition of the historical materialism to which I here also reconfirm my fidelity.

71. Fredric Jameson, "Introduction/Prospectus: To Reconsider the Relationship of Marxism to Utopian Thought," *Minnesota Review* 6 (1976): 58.

72. Jameson, *Valences of the Dialectic,* 415.

73. Jameson, *Allegory and Ideology,* xvi.

74. Ruth Levitas, *The Concept of Utopia* (Syracuse, N.Y.: Syracuse University Press, 1990), 88.

75. Jameson, *Valences of the Dialectic,* 17. For a valuable discussion of the fortunes of structuralism in France, see François Dosse's two-volume *History of Structuralism,* trans. Deborah Glassman (Minneapolis: University of Minnesota Press, 1997).

76. Claude Lévi-Strauss, *Structural Anthropology,* trans. Claire Jacobson and Brooke Grundfest Schoepf (New York: Basic Books, 1963), 230.

77. Jameson, *Singular Modernity,* 176.

78. Louis Althusser, *Reading Capital: The Complete Edition,* trans. Ben Brewster and David Fernbach (New York: Verso, 2015), 13.

79. Althusser, *Reading Capital,* 27.

80. For a contemporary and also valuable exploration of Jameson's project, see Tally, *Fredric Jameson.*

81. Wegner, *Periodizing Jameson,* 168.

82. Jonathan Culler, *Literary Theory: A Very Short Introduction* (Oxford: Oxford University Press, 2011), 15.

83. Jacques Derrida, *Of Grammatology,* trans. Gayatri Chakravorty Spivak (Baltimore: Johns Hopkins University Press, 2016), 172.

84. Adorno, *Introduction to Dialectics,* 131.

85. Jameson, *Valences of the Dialectic,* 83.

86. Bertolt Brecht, *Life of Galileo,* trans. Wolfgang Sauerlander and Ralph

Manheim, in *Collected Plays,* vol. 5, ed. Ralph Manheim and John Willett (New York: Vintage Books, 1972), 18.

87. Brecht, "An Die Nachgeborenen," 172; Roland Barthes, *Mythologies,* trans. Richard Howard and Annette Lavers (New York: Hill and Wang, 2012), 162–63.

88. Walter Benjamin, "Conversations with Brecht," trans. Anya Bostock, in *Aesthetics and Politics,* ed. Ronald Taylor (London: Verso, 1980), 99.

89. Bruce Robbins, *The Beneficiary* (Durham, N.C.: Duke University Press, 2017), 3.

90. Robbins, *Beneficiary,* 5.

91. Ciccariello-Maher, *Decolonizing Dialectics,* 159–60. Also see Michael Rothberg, *The Implicated Subject: Beyond Victims and Perpetrators* (Stanford, Calif.: Stanford University Press, 2019).

92. Michel Foucault, preface to *Anti-Oedipus: Capitalism and Schizophrenia,* by Gilles Deleuze and Félix Guattari, trans. Robert Hurley, Mark Seem, and Helen R. Lane (Minneapolis: University of Minnesota Press, 1983), xiii. Also now see Natasha Lennard, *Being Numerous: Essays on Non-Fascist Life* (New York: Verso, 2019).

93. See Fredric Jameson, *Late Marxism: Adorno, or the Persistence of the Dialectic* (New York: Verso, 1990), 151–54. I discuss Jameson's reading of *Dialectic of Enlightenment* in more detail in *Periodizing Jameson,* 157–65.

94. Max Horkheimer and Theodor W. Adorno, *Dialectic of Enlightenment,* trans. John Cumming (New York: Continuum, 1972), 172. The book has been retranslated by Edmund Jephcott as *Dialectic of Enlightenment: Philosophical Fragments* (Stanford, Calif.: Stanford University Press, 2002), 141. The German passages are taken from Max Horkheimer und Theodor W. Adorno, *Dialektik der Aufklärung: Philosophische Fragmente* (Frankfurt: Fischer Taschenbuch Verlag, 2000), 210. For an important related discussion of such ressentiment in the context of Reagan-era efforts to defund the arts and humanities, see Eve Kosofsky Sedgwick, "Queer and Now," in *Tendencies* (Durham, N.C.: Duke University Press, 1993), 1–20. I discuss both essays further in *Periodizing Jameson,* 162–64. Also now see the discussion of contemporary white male ressentiment in Wendy Brown, *In the Ruins of Neoliberalism: The Rise of Antidemocratic Politics in the West* (New York: Columbia University Press, 2019), 172–82.

95. Horkheimer and Adorno, *Dialectic of Enlightenment* (1972), 257–58; *Dialectic of Enlightenment* (2002), 214; and *Dialektik der Aufklärung,* 322–23.

96. Roland Barthes, *Mythologies,* trans. Annette Lavers (New York: Hill and Wang, 1972), 5.

97. Richard Howard, translator's note to *Mythologies* (2012), vii.

98. Howard, viii.

99. Barthes, *Mythologies* (2012), 218.

100. See Romain Souillac, *Le mouvement Poujade: De la défense professionnelle au populisme nationaliste (1953–1962)* (Paris: Presses de Sciences Po, 2007).

101. Kristen Ross, *Fast Cars, Clean Bodies: Decolonization and the Reordering of French Culture* (Cambridge, Mass.: MIT Press, 1995), 138.

102. Barthes, *Mythologies* (2012), 214.

103. Steven Levitsky and Daniel Ziblatt, *How Democracies Die* (New York: Crown, 2018), 2.

104. V-Dem Institute, *Democracy for All?: V-Dem Annual Democracy Report 2018* (Gothenburg, Sweden: University of Gothenburg Press, 2018), 7, 27. Also see the V-Dem Institute website at https://www.v-dem.net/en/.

105. Such moralizing claims have now been given a "respectable" instantiation in the longtime *New York Times* book critic Michiko Kakutani's *The Death of Truth: Notes on Falsehood in the Age of Trump* (New York: Tim Duggan Books, 2018). However, for a useful rejoinder see Aaron Hanlon, "Postmodernism Didn't Cause Trump: It Explains Him," *Washington Post*, August 31, 2018, https://www.washingtonpost.com/outlook/postmodernism-didnt-cause-trump-it-explains-him/2018/08/30/0939f7c4-9b12-11e8-843b-36e177f3081c_story.html?noredirect=on&utm_term=.c8cac483e9a2.

106. William Davies, "The New Neoliberalism," *New Left Review* 101 (2016): 121–34. Among the most valuable studies of these changes, also see David Harvey, *The New Imperialism* (Oxford: Oxford University Press, 2005); David Harvey, *A Brief History of Neoliberalism* (Oxford: Oxford University Press, 2005); Wendy Brown, "American Nightmare: Neoliberalism, Neoconservatism, and De-democratization," *Political Theory* 34, no. 6 (2006): 690–714; Naomi Klein, *The Shock Doctrine: The Rise of Disaster Capitalism* (New York: Henry Holt, 2007); Gérard Duménil and Dominque Lévy, *The Crisis of Neoliberalism* (Cambridge, Mass.: Harvard University Press, 2011); Yanis Varoufakis, *The Global Minotaur: America, Europe, and the Future of the Global Economy* (London: Zed Books, 2015); Brown, *Undoing the Demos*; Tariq Ali, *The Extreme Centre: A Second Warning* (New York: Verso, 2018); Jason Stanley, *How Fascism Works: The Politics of Us and Them* (New York: Random House, 2018); Levitsky and Ziblatt, *How Democracies Die*; William Davies, *Nervous States: Democracy and the Decline of Reason* (New York: Norton, 2019); Brown, *In the Ruins of Neoliberalism*; Nancy Fraser, *The Old is Dying and the New Cannot Be Born: From Progressive Neoliberalism to Trump and Beyond* (New York: Verso, 2019); and Michael Hardt and Antonio Negri, "Empire, Twenty Years On," *New Left Review* 120 (2019): 67–92.

107. Bertolt Brecht, *The Resistible Rise of Arturo Ui*, trans. Susan Hingley, adapted by Bruce Norris (London: Bloomsbury, 2017), 7.

108. Gilles Deleuze and Félix Guattari, *Anti-Oedipus: Capitalism and Schizophrenia* (Minneapolis: University of Minnesota Press, 1983), 260.

109. Deleuze and Guattari, *Anti-Oedipus,* 260.
110. Brecht, "An Die Nachgeborenen," 174.
111. Jameson, *Political Unconscious,* 106.
112. I posit the notion of the heuristic genre in *Shockwaves of Possibility,* 72.

1. Reading the Event of the New Criticism and the Fate of the *Republic*

The first version of this chapter was originally presented on November 16, 2016, at a symposium on the thought of Badiou sponsored by the Humanities Center at the University of Alabama, Huntsville. I want to offer my deepest thanks to the center's director, and my former doctoral student and now extraordinary scholar and teacher in his own right, Eric Smith, for the invitation to present at this event and for the opportunity to meet and engage with for the first time, among so many others, Alain Badiou, Kenneth Reinhard, and Susan Spitzer.

1. Alain Badiou, *Theoretical Writings,* ed. and trans. Ray Brassier and Alberto Toscano (London: Continuum, 2004), xiv.

2. Fredric Jameson, *The Ideologies of Theory, Essays 1971–1986,* vol. 1, *Situations of Theory* (Minneapolis: University of Minnesota Press, 1988), 114.

3. Jameson, *Ideologies of Theory,* 1:115; and Clint Burnham, *The Jamesonian Unconscious: The Aesthetics of Marxist Theory* (Durham, N.C.: Duke University Press, 1995), 23.

4. For an extraordinary reconsideration of the significance of the Parthenon and its pedagogical role in the classical Athenian polis more generally, see Joan Breton Connelly, *The Parthenon Enigma* (New York: Vintage, 2014).

5. For more on the Greek response to the crisis, see Yanis Varoufakis, *And the Weak Must Suffer What They Must?: Europe's Crisis and America's Economic Future* (New York: Nation Books, 2016); Yanis Varoufakis, *Adults in the Room: My Battle with the European and American Deep Establishment* (New York: Farrar, Straus, and Giroux, 2017); Alain Badiou, *Greece and the Reinvention of Politics,* trans. David Broder (New York: Verso, 2018); and Stathis Kouvelakis, "Borderland: Greece and the EU's Southern Question," *New Left Review* 110 (2018): 5–34. For a sampling of literary responses, see Karen Van Dyke, ed., *Austerity Measures: The New Greek Poetry* (New York: New York Review of Books, 2017); and Christos Ikonomou, *Something Will Happen, You'll See,* trans. Karen Emmerich (Brooklyn: Archipelago Books, 2016).

6. Alain Badiou, *Plato's "Republic": A Dialogue in 16 Chapters,* trans. Susan Spitzer (New York: Columbia University Press, 2012), xxx.

7. Phillip E. Wegner, *Periodizing Jameson: Dialectics, the University, and the Desire for Narrative* (Evanston, Ill.: Northwestern University Press, 2014), 81–117. The subsequent paragraphs draw upon my earlier book.

8. See A. J. Greimas, *On Meaning: Selected Writings in Semiotic Theory,* trans. Paul J. Perron and Frank H. Collins (Minneapolis: University of Minnesota Press, 1987), 48–62; and Ronald Schleifer, introduction to *Structural Semantics: An Attempt at Method,* by A. J. Greimas, trans. Danielle McDowell, Ronald Schleifer, and Alan Velie, xi–lvi (Lincoln: University of Nebraska Press, 1983).

9. Aristotle, *On Interpretation,* trans. H. P. Cooke (Cambridge, Mass.: Harvard University Press, 1938), 144–45.

10. Gilles Deleuze and Félix Guattari, *What Is Philosophy?,* trans. Hugh Tomlinson and Graham Burchell (New York: Columbia University Press, 1994), 5.

11. The first three examples are to be found in Lévi-Strauss's founding texts of structuralism, the 1955 essay "The Structural Study of Myth," in *Structural Anthropology,* trans. Claire Jacobson and Brooke Grundfest Schoepf, 206–31 (New York: Basic Books, 1963); and *Tristes Tropiques,* trans. John Weightman and Doreen Weightman (1955; New York: Penguin, 1992).

12. See Phillip E. Wegner, *Life between Two Deaths, 1989–2001: U.S. Culture in the Long Nineties* (Durham, N.C.: Duke University Press, 2009), 94.

13. For a landmark discussion of the function of "interesting" as an aesthetic judgment, see Sianne Ngai, *Our Aesthetic Categories: Zany, Cute, Interesting* (Cambridge, Mass.: Harvard University Press, 2012).

14. Burhanuddin Baki, *Badiou's "Being and Event" and the Mathematics of Set Theory* (London: Bloomsbury, 2014), loc. 2015, ebook.

15. Fredric Jameson, *Signatures of the Visible* (New York: Routledge, 1990), 34.

16. Deleuze and Guattari, *What Is Philosophy?,* 16.

17. Karl Marx and Friedrich Engels, *Manifest Der Kommunistischen Partei* (Berlin: Dietz Verlag, 1989), 10.

18. Alain Badiou, *In Praise of Mathematics,* trans. Susan Spitzer (Cambridge: Polity, 2016), 111. Also see Badiou's sympathetic new appraisal of Derrida's project in *Pocket Pantheon: Figures of Postwar Philosophy,* trans. David Macey (New York: Verso, 2009), 125–44.

19. Jacques Derrida, *Limited Inc,* trans. Samuel Weber (Evanston, Ill.: Northwestern University Press, 1988), 116–17.

20. Ngai, *Our Aesthetic Categories,* 40.

21. Ngai, 98.

22. Derrida, *Limited Inc,* 35. Because Searle "declined" to allow his essay to be republished in the volume, a short summary is offered in its place (Derrida, 25–27). The original can be consulted in *Glyph* 1 (1977): 198–208.

23. I develop this claim further in my essay "Are You Now or Have You Ever Been a Suvinian?: Beyond the Moralizing Temptation; or, How Not to Read," *Utopian Studies* 30, no. 2 (2019): 300–44.

24. R. G. Collingwood, *An Essay on Metaphysics* (Read Books, 2011), loc. 435, ebook.

25. Kenneth Reinhard, introduction to *Plato's "Republic": A Dialogue in 16 Chapters,* by Alain Badiou, trans. Susan Spitzer (New York: Columbia University Press, 2012), xx.

26. Fredric Jameson, "Science versus Ideology," *Humanities in Society* 6 (1983): 288; Louis O. Mink, *Mind, History, and Dialectic: The Philosophy of R. G. Collingwood* (Middletown, Conn.: Wesleyan University Press, 1987), 143; and Ian Stewart, *The Great Mathematical Problems: Marvels and Mysteries of Mathematics* (London: Profile Books, 2013), 10–11. I discuss axioms further in *Periodizing Jameson,* especially 8–11 and 133–34.

27. Fredric Jameson, foreword to *On Meaning: Selected Writings in Semiotic Theory,* by A. J. Greimas, trans. Paul J. Perron and Frank H. Collins (Minneapolis: University of Minnesota Press, 1987), xv.

28. Fredric Jameson, *The Political Unconscious: Narrative as a Socially Symbolic Act* (Ithaca, N.Y.: Cornell University Press, 1981), 166.

29. See Fredric Jameson, "Of Islands and Trenches: Neutralization and the Production of Utopian Discourse," in *Ideologies of Theory,* vol. 2, *Syntax of History* (Minneapolis: University of Minnesota Press, 1988), 75–102. Reprinted in the single volume *The Ideologies of Theory* (New York: Verso, 2008), 386–414.

30. Fredric Jameson, *Archaeologies of the Future: The Desire Called Utopia and Other Science Fictions* (New York: Verso, 2005), 212.

31. Alain Badiou, *Theory of the Subject,* trans. Bruno Bosteels (New York: Continuum, 2009), 54.

32. Slavoj Žižek, *The Parallax View* (Cambridge, Mass.: MIT Press, 2006), 121.

33. Fredric Jameson, "Lacan and the Dialectic: A Fragment," in *Lacan: The Silent Partners,* ed. Slavoj Žižek (New York: Verso, 2006), 376.

34. Jacques Lacan, *Le séminaire Livre I, Le écrits techniques de Freud, 1953–1954,* ed. Jacques-Alain Miller (Paris: Éditions du Seuil, 1975), 80; Jacques Lacan, *The Seminar of Jacques Lacan, Book I: Freud's Papers on Technique, 1953–1954,* trans. John Forrester (New York: Norton, 1991), 66; and Jameson, *Ideologies of Theory,* 1:104.

35. Lorenzo Chiesa, *Subjectivity and Otherness: A Philosophical Reading of Lacan* (Cambridge, Mass.: MIT Press, 2007), 105.

36. Slavoj Žižek, *Absolute Recoil: Towards a New Foundation of Dialectical Materialism* (New York: Verso, 2014), 321.

37. Alain Badiou, *Ethics: Toward an Understanding of Radical Evil,* trans. Peter Hallward (New York: Verso, 2001), 41.

38. Badiou, *Ethics,* 68.

39. Peter Hallward, *Badiou: A Subject to Truth* (Minneapolis: University of Minnesota Press, 2003), xxv, 114.

40. Baki, *Badiou's "Being and Event,"* loc. 1020.

41. Gilles Deleuze and Félix Guattari, *A Thousand Plateaus: Capitalism and Schizophrenia,* trans. Brian Massumi (Minneapolis: University of Minnesota Press, 1987), 454; and Christopher Breu, *Insistence of the Material: Literature in the Age of Biopolitics* (Minneapolis: University of Minnesota Press, 2014), 9–10.

42. W. K. Wimsatt, *The Verbal Icon: Studies in the Meaning of Poetry* (Lexington: University of Kentucky Press, 1954), 21. Hereafter cited in the text as *VI.*

43. For the now canonical discussion of the power of the voice, see Mladen Dolar, *A Voice and Nothing More* (Cambridge, Mass.: MIT Press, 2006).

44. For a superb recent short history of close reading, see Barbara Herrnstein Smith, "'What Was Close Reading'?: A Century of Method in Literary Studies," *Minnesota Review* 87 (2016): 57–85.

45. For an discussion of the scene and whether McLuhan "intended" to say what he did, see W. J. T. Mitchell, "Addressing Media," *MediaTropes* 1 (2008): 1–18; and Anthony Breznican, "The Movie Theater Blowhard from *Annie Hall* Finally Gets His Say," *Entertainment Weekly,* April 5, 2017, http://ew.com/movies/2017/04/05/annie-hall-ticket-line-untold-story/.

46. Cleanth Brooks, *The Well Wrought Urn: Studies in the Structure of Poetry* (New York: Harcourt, Brace, and Co., 1947), 207.

47. Rebecca Comay and Frank Ruda, *The Dash—The Other Side of Absolute Knowing* (Cambridge, Mass.: MIT Press, 2018), 5.

48. See Derrida, *Limited Inc*; and Paul de Man, *The Resistance to Theory* (Minneapolis: University of Minnesota Press, 1986).

49. Brooks, *Well Wrought Urn,* 206.

50. Joseph Conrad, *Typhoon and Other Tales* (New York: Signet, 1962), 21.

51. Badiou, *Ethics,* 51.

52. A more extensive close reading of *The Verbal Icon* would require that we account for all of the book's chapters, situating each in relationship to the larger narrative whole that makes up the text. I experiment with such an approach in the opening three chapters of *Periodizing Jameson,* offering close readings of Jameson's *Marxism and Form* (1971), *The Political Unconscious* (1981), and *Postmodernism; or, The Cultural Logic of Late Capitalism* (1991) as, respectively, realist, modernist, and postmodernist narratives.

53. For two valuable engagements with the reading practices of the Chicago School Neo-Aristotelians, see Vincent Leitch, "The Chicago School," in *American Literary Criticism from the 30s to the 80s* (New York: Columbia University Press, 1988), 60–80; and Donald Ault, "Blake's De-formation of Neo-Aristotelianism," in *Critical Paths: Blake and the Argument of Method,* ed. Dan Miller, Mark Bracher, and Donald Ault, 111–38 (Durham, N.C.: Duke University Press, 1987).

54. Badiou, *Ethics,* 83, 85.

55. I would also suggest a productive correspondence between the three New Critical fallacies and what Bill Readings, in his classic study *The University in Ruins* (Cambridge, Mass.: Harvard University Press, 1996), terms the three "misplaced pedagogical commitments": the authoritative, demagogic, and technocratic modes of education (156–57).

56. Jameson, foreword to Greimas, *On Meaning,* xxii.

57. See Herrnstein Smith, "'What Was Close Reading'?," 59–63; Vincent Leitch, "The 'New Criticism,'" in *American Literary Criticism from the 30s to the 80s* (New York: Columbia University Press, 1988), 24–59; Bruce Robbins, *Secular Vocations: Intellectuals, Professionalism, Culture* (London: Verso, 1993), 64–79; and Robert H. Brinkmeyer Jr., *The Fourth Ghost: White Southern Writers and European Fascism, 1930–1950* (Baton Rouge: Louisiana State University Press, 2009).

58. For the place of New Criticism in late modernism, see Fredric Jameson, *A Singular Modernity: Essay on the Ontology of the Present* (New York: Verso, 2002), 168–79. I take up the issue of late modernism again in chapters 4 and 6.

59. Leitch, *American Literary Criticism,* 28.

60. Terry Eagleton, *Literary Theory: An Introduction* (Minneapolis: University of Minnesota Press, 1983), 47.

61. Cleanth Brooks, "Irony as a Principle of Structure," in *Literary Opinion in America,* 3rd ed., ed. Morton Dauwen Zabel (Gloucester, Mass.: Peter Smith, 1968), 738.

62. Brooks, "Irony as a Principle of Structure," 740; emphasis added.

63. Geoffrey Galt Harpham, *What Do You Think, Mr. Ramirez?: The American Revolution in Education* (Chicago: University of Chicago Press, 2017), 155. I became aware of Harpham's study late in the revisions of this manuscript and will only briefly touch on it here. As will be evident to any careful reader, there is great deal of resonance with my claims in this chapter and his reading of what he terms the "radical democratic event" of the development of new reading practices in the postwar American university (ix). Moreover, while Harpham also has valuable things to say about I. A. Richards's significant influence on these developments, he takes very different lessons from Richards's project than does Joseph North, whose claims I discussed in the previous chapter: "And last, interpretation is 'general' in that it is a comprehensively good thing when done right, especially when done right by all. Unlike, for example, aesthetic appreciation, which can be enjoyed, in an often-used example, by the concentration camp commandant relaxing to the strains of a symphony after a trying day in the slaughterhouse, disciplined textual interpretation has an all but moral value as a focused and intensified form of the ordinary activities of observation and reflection, and then of conversation and persuasion, in which we 'read' and are read by our fellow citizens" (169). Harpham's subsequent short concluding chapter is entitled "In Praise of Depth,"

intended by the author, I assume, as an implicit distancing of his argument from that of the surface readers. However, for all that I find valuable and persuasive in his study, his narrative slips into moralizing ethical criticism at the point when he locates in the moment of theory (which he periodizes, 1968–1990), a practice at once too narrowly and too broadly defined, a "fall" from an imagined national ideal: "Behind the debates dominating the theory wars was a thinly veiled struggle between American and foreign modes of thinking" (159). I have no idea, then, how one can conclude that the author of *The Political Unconscious* "attacks the primacy of interpretation" (162), unless one understands the goal of interpretation, meaning, to be an unmediated expression of a narrow, deeply gendered, fully conscious, and liberal individualist notion of "authorial intention." Harpham does go on to champion "the Americanism" of Steven Knapp and Walter Benn Michaels's 1980s polemical essay "Against Theory:" "With the details of the theoretical arguments no longer commanding fascinated attention, we can see that the real issue is political and national" (165). See Jameson's deep and careful reading of the "Against Theory" essay and its role in enabling Michaels in his later New Historicist writings to productively "rediscover and reinvent" the problems taken up by continental theory in *Postmodernism; or, The Cultural Logic of Late Capitalism* (Durham, N.C.: Duke University Press, 1991), 181–217. For Harpham's own insightful earlier engagements with both moralizing hagiographic narratives and the "asceticism" of the New Criticism, see *The Ascetic Imperative in Culture and Criticism* (Chicago: University of Chicago Press, 1987), esp. 220 and 250–54. Also see Harpham's earlier comments on Jameson's project, reprinted in *Shadows of Ethics: Criticism and the Just Society* (Durham, N.C.: Duke University Press, 1999), 162–79.

64. Alan Taylor, "The Virtue of an Educated Voter," *American Scholar*, September 6, 2016, https://theamericanscholar.org/the-virtue-of-an-educated-voter/#.

65. Taylor, "Virtue of an Educated Voter."

66. Taylor, "Virtue of an Educated Voter."

67. Wendy Brown, *Undoing the Demos: Neoliberalism's Stealth Revolution* (Cambridge, Mass.: MIT Press, 2015), 185.

68. Brown, *Undoing the Demos,* 186.

69. Taylor, "Virtue of an Educated Voter."

70. Patrick J. Deneen, *Why Liberalism Failed* (New Haven, Conn.: Yale University Press, 2018), 12. Also see his chapter "Liberalism against the Liberal Arts," 110–30. I hope it is clear in what follows that while I find value in Deneen's diagnosis of the crisis of liberalism, in both its right "classical" and left "progressive" forms, I diverge from both his reductive characterization of the contemporary humanities and, even more significantly, his proposal for a return to late nineteenth-century forms of local community. Just as Deneen persuasively articulates left and right forms of liberalism, we need to

maintain the possibility and importance of ideological struggle between right (communitarian) and left (communist) visions of collective life to come. For an insightful review, see Gerardo Muñoz, "The Triumph of Res Idiotica and Communitarianism: On Patrick Deneen's *Why Liberalism Failed*," *Infrapolitical Deconstruction*, December 26, 2017, https://infrapolitica.com/2017/12/26/the-triumph-of-res-idiotica-and-communitarianism-on-patrick-deneens-why-liberalism-failed-by-gerardo-munoz/. And for a brief dialectical discussion of both the potential and limits of communitarianism more generally, see Fredric Jameson, "Morality versus Ethical Substance; or, Aristotelian Marxism in Alasdair MacIntyre," in *Ideologies of Theory*, 1:181–85, and in *Ideologies of Theory* (2008), 189–93.

71. See Jean-François Lyotard, *The Postmodern Condition: A Report of Knowledge*, trans. Geoff Bennington and Brian Massumi (Minneapolis: University of Minnesota Press, 1984), 44–51. Also see Readings's extension of Lyotard's insights in *University in Ruins*.

72. Brinkmeyer, *Fourth Ghost*, 52.

73. Taylor, "Virtue of an Educated Voter."

74. Christopher Newfield, *Unmaking the Public University: The Forty-Year Assault on the Middle Class* (Cambridge, Mass.: Harvard University Press, 2008).

75. Badiou, *Plato's "Republic,"* 229. Hereafter cited in the text as *PR*. For Badiou's reflections on mathematical education, see *In Praise of Mathematics*.

76. Deneen, *Why Liberalism Failed*, 39.

77. Jacques Derrida, *Of Grammatology*, trans. Gayatri Chakravorty Spivak (Baltimore: Johns Hopkins University Press, 2016), 172–73. Also see Derrida's illuminating commentary on this passage in *Limited Inc*, 143–50.

78. Giorgio Agamben, "Introductory Note on the Concept of Democracy," in *Democracy in What State?*, trans. William McCuaig (New York: Columbia University Press, 2011), 2.

79. Gilbert Chinard, "Polybius and the American Constitution," *Journal of the History of Ideas* 1, no. 1 (1940): 38–58.

80. Bettany Hughes, *The Hemlock Cup: Socrates, Athens, and the Search for the Good Life* (New York: Vintage, 2010), 46.

81. Hughes, *Hemlock Cup*, 303, 309.

82. Connelly, *Parthenon Enigma*, 290–91.

83. Anne Carson, introduction to *Orestes*, in *An Oresteia*, trans. Anne Carson (New York: Faber and Faber, 2009), 177–78.

84. Peter Burian, introduction to *Trojan Women*, in *The Complete Euripides*, vol. 1, *"Trojan Women" and Other Plays*, ed. Peter Burian and Alan Shapiro (Oxford: Oxford University Press, 2010), 153.

85. Reinhard, introduction, xi.

86. Reinhard, xxii.

87. Reinhard, xiii.

88. Jo Walton, *Necessity* (New York: Tor, 2016), 174.

89. Alain Badiou, *Second Manifesto for Philosophy,* trans. Louise Burchill (Cambridge: Polity, 2011), 19. Also see Alain Badiou, "A Speculative Disquisition on the Concept of Democracy," in *Metapolitics,* trans. Jason Barker, 78–95 (New York: Verso, 2005); and Alain Badiou, "The Democratic Emblem," in *Democracy in What State?* trans. William McCuaig (New York: Columbia University Press, 2011), 6–15.

90. De Man, *Resistance to Theory,* 16.

91. Badiou, "Democratic Emblem," 6.

92. Alain Badiou, *Being and Event,* trans. Oliver Faltham (New York: Continuum, 2005), 433.

93. Badiou, "Democratic Emblem," 15. For a related discussion, see Miguel Abensour, *Democracy against the State: Marx and the Machiavellian Moment,* trans. Max Blechman and Martin Breaugh (Cambridge: Polity, 2011).

94. Alain Badiou, *In Praise of Love,* trans. Peter Bush (New York: New Press, 2012), 90. I return to this book in chapter 6.

95. Jo Walton, *The Just City* (London: Corsair, 2015), 269.

96. Kojin Karatani, *Isonomia and the Origins of Philosophy,* trans. Joseph A. Murphy (Durham, N.C.: Duke University Press, 2017), 130.

97. Karatani, *Isonomia and the Origins of Philosophy,* 75.

98. Karatani, 131–32.

99. Karatani, 133.

100. Karatani, 153.

101. Bertram Gross, *Friendly Fascism: The New Face of Power in America* (New York: Open Road, 2016).

102. Reinhard, introduction, xiii–xiv.

2. Toward Non-reading *Utopia*

The first version of this essay was presented October 21, 2016, at University of Florida's English Graduate Organization's (EGO) conference "Futures Near and Far: Utopia, Dystopia, and Futurity." I would like to thank the conference organizers, Norma Aceves and Jaquelin Elliott, and all of the extraordinary graduate students in our program, past, present, and future, for so much insight and inspiration over the last quarter century.

1. Jay McInerney, "Faking It," *New York Times,* November 11, 2007, http://www.nytimes.com/2007/11/11/books/review/McInerney-t.html. Hereafter cited in the text.

2. Jacques Derrida, *Of Grammatology,* trans. Gayatri Chakravorty Spivak (Baltimore: Johns Hopkins University Press, 2016), 65.

3. Pierre Bayard, *How to Talk about Books You Haven't Read,* trans. Jeffrey Mehlman (New York: Bloomsbury, 2007), 6; and Pierre Bayard, *Comment parler des livres que l'on n'a pas lus?* (Paris: Éditions de minuit, 2007), 23. Hereafter the English translation is cited in the text as *HT.*

4. Fredric Jameson, *The Political Unconscious: Narrative as a Socially Symbolic Act* (Ithaca, N.Y.: Cornell University Press, 1981), 9.

5. Jameson, *Political Unconscious,* 9–10.

6. Charles Yu, *How to Live Safely in a Science Fictional Universe* (New York: Vintage, 2010), 104.

7. Jacques Derrida, *Limited Inc,* trans. Samuel Weber (Evanston, Ill.: Northwestern University Press, 1988), 146.

8. Stanley Fish, *Is There a Text in This Class? The Authority of Interpretive Communities* (Cambridge, Mass.: Harvard University Press, 1980), 168–69.

9. Fish, *Is There a Text?,* 171.

10. Catherine Malabou, *The Future of Hegel: Plasticity, Temporality and Dialectic,* trans. Lisabeth During (London: Routledge, 2005), 181–82.

11. Roland Barthes, *S/Z: An Essay,* trans. Richard Miller (New York: Hill and Wang, 1974), 4.

12. For further discussion of the modernism of Barthes's notion of the writerly text, see Fredric Jameson, "The Ideology of the Text," in *The Ideologies of Theory: Essays 1971–1986,* vol. 1, *Situations of Theory* (Minneapolis: University of Minnesota Press, 1988), esp. 55–67.

13. Roland Barthes, *Mythologies,* trans. Richard Howard and Annette Lavers (New York: Hill and Wang, 2012), 163–64.

14. See Mark McGurl, *The Program Era: Postwar Fiction and the Rise of Creative Writing* (Cambridge, Mass.: Harvard University Press, 2009). I will return to McGurl's book in the next chapter.

15. Warren Motte, review of *How to Talk about Books You Haven't Read,* by Pierre Bayard, *World Literature Today,* March 2008, https://www.worldliteraturetoday.org/how-talk-about-books-you-havent-read-pierre-bayard.

16. Toby Lichtig, "Never Read Ulysses? Me Neither," *Guardian,* January 6, 2008, https://www.theguardian.com/books/2008/jan/06/fiction.society.

17. Derrida, *Limited Inc,* 44.

18. Derrida, 44.

19. N. G. Wilson, "The Name Hythlodaeus," *Moreana* 29, no. 110 (1992): 33.

20. Louis Marin, *Utopics: The Semiological Play of Textual Spaces,* trans. Robert A. Vollrath (Highlands Park, N.Y.: Humanities Press, 1984), 163. I discuss Marin's work in some detail in *Imaginary Communities: Utopia, the Nation, and the Spatial Histories of Modernity* (Berkeley: University of California Press, 2002), 34–49.

21. Robert C. Elliott, *The Shape of Utopia: Studies in a Literary Genre*

(Oxford: Peter Lang, 2013), 24. Also see my introduction to this reprint edition of Elliott's book. For a further discussion of the dialectic of carnival and commonwealth in More's text, see Christopher Kendrick, *Utopia, Carnival, and Commonwealth in Renaissance England* (Toronto: University of Toronto Press, 2004). Finally, for a dialectical reading of the practice of utopia, see Tom Moylan, *Becoming Utopian: The Culture and Politics of Radical Transformation* (New York: Bloomsbury, 2020).

22. Elliott, *Shape of Utopia,* 23.

23. Joseph Conrad, *Lord Jim* (New York: Penguin, 1986), 292–93.

24. Thomas More, *Utopia,* ed. Edward Surtz and J. H. Hexter, *The Yale Edition of the Complete Works of St. Thomas More,* vol. 4 (New Haven, Conn.: Yale University Press, 1965), 23. Hereafter cited in the text as *U.*

25. I touch on some of these locations of Utopia in *Imaginary Communities,* 35.

26. Pierre Bayard, *How to Talk about Places You've Never Been: On the Importance of Armchair Travel,* trans. Michele Hutchison (New York: Bloomsbury, 2016), xii.

27. See Karl Marx, *Capital: A Critique of Political Economy,* vol. 1, trans. Ben Fowkes (New York: Penguin, 1990), 880, 898.

28. Stephen Greenblatt, *Renaissance Self-Fashioning: From More to Shakespeare* (Chicago: University of Chicago Press, 1980), 36. On the *genera mixta,* see Rosalie Colie, *The Resources of Kind: Genre-Theory in the Renaissance* (Berkeley: University of California Press, 1973); and Marina Leslie, *Renaissance Utopias and the Problem of History* (New York: Cornell University Press, 1998). Also see Kendrick's discussion of Greenblatt's reading in *Utopia, Carnival, and Commonwealth,* 56–60. Finally, see Greenblatt's useful reading of the lessons in Shakespeare for confronting our contemporary situation in *Tyrant: Shakespeare on Politics* (New York: Norton, 2018).

29. For another effective discussion of this passage and its importance in More's text, see Jennifer Wagner-Lawlor, "Anticipating Utopia: Utopian Narrative and an Ontology of Representation," in *Handbook of Anticipation,* ed. Roberto Poli, 1–21 (Springer, 2017), https://doi.org/10.1007/978-3-319-31737-3_63-1.

30. Also now see the superb discussion of the role of *Utopia* in the development of a global imperial imaginary in Sarah Hogan, *Other Englands: Utopia, Capital, and Empire in an Age of Transition* (Stanford, Calif.: Stanford University Press, 2018).

31. Kendrick, *Utopia, Carnival, and Commonwealth,* 34.

32. *Plato's Phaedrus,* trans. R. Hackforth (Cambridge: Cambridge University Press, 1952), 158.

33. E. P. Thompson, *William Morris: Romantic to Revolutionary,* rev. ed. (New York: Pantheon, 1977), 791. Also see Raymond Williams, "Utopia and

Science Fiction," in *Problems in Materialism and Culture* (London: Verso, 1980), 196–212.

34. Fredric Jameson, *An American Utopia: Dual Power and the Universal Army* (New York: Verso, 2016), 54–55.

35. Ruth Levitas, *The Concept of Utopia* (Syracuse, N.Y.: Syracuse University Press, 1990), 124. For another effective discussion of the role of utopia in the education of desire, see Sean Austin Grattan, *Hope Isn't Stupid: Utopian Affects in Contemporary American Literature* (Iowa City: University of Iowa Press, 2017).

36. Slavoj Žižek, *Absolute Recoil: Towards a New Foundation of Dialectical Materialism* (New York: Verso, 2014), 237.

37. Žižek, *Absolute Recoil,* 125.

38. Miguel Abensour, *Utopia from Thomas More to Walter Benjamin,* trans. Raymond N. MacKenzie (Minneapolis: Univocal, 2017), 48. See my forthcoming review of Abensour's book in *Cultural Critique.*

39. Bayard, *How to Talk about Places,* 141.

40. Bayard, 143.

41. Jo Walton, *The Just City* (London: Corsair, 2015), 270.

42. I non-read *Fight Club* as a dystopia in *Life between Two Deaths, 1989–2001: U.S. Culture in the Long Nineties* (Durham, N.C.: Duke University Press, 2009), chap. 5. Also see Anna Kornbluh, *Marxist Film Theory and Fight Club* (New York: Bloomsbury, 2019).

43. Alain Badiou, *In Praise of Love,* trans. Peter Bush (New York: New Press, 2012), 90.

44. Derrida, *Limited Inc,* 19.

45. Derrida, 157.

46. Patrocinio P. Schweickart, "Toward a Feminist Theory of Reading," in *Gender and Reading: Essays on Readers, Texts, and Contexts,* ed. Elizabeth A. Flynn and Patrocinio P. Schweickart (Baltimore: Johns Hopkins University Press, 1986), 53.

47. Byung-Chul Han, *The Expulsion of the Other: Society, Perception and Communication Today,* trans. Weiland Hoban (Cambridge: Polity, 2018), 70, ebook.

48. Paul Goldberger, *Building Art: The Life and Work of Frank Gehry* (New York: Vintage, 2017), 100.

49. Goldberger, *Building Art,* 138.

50. Abensour, *Utopia,* 48.

51. Kendrick, *Utopia, Carnival, and Commonwealth,* 73.

52. Theodor Reik, *Listening with the Third Ear: The Inner Experience of a Psychoanalyst* (New York: Farrar, Strauss, and Giroux, 1948), 147.

53. Reik, *Listening with the Third Ear,* 150.

54. Reik, 156.

55. Jacques Lacan, *Écrits: The First Complete Edition in English,* trans. Bruce Fink (New York: Norton, 2006), 294.

56. Jacques Lacan, *The Seminar of Jacques Lacan,* book 11, *The Four Fundamental Concepts of Psychoanalysis,* trans. Alan Sheridan (New York: Norton, 1981), 258–59.

57. Fredric Jameson, "Imaginary and Symbolic in Lacan," in *The Ideologies of Theory, Essays 1971–1986,* vol. 1 (Minneapolis: University of Minnesota Press, 1988), 115.

58. Han, *Expulsion of the Other,* 72.

59. Slavoj Žižek, "Introduction: Remembering, Repeating and Working Through," in V. I. Lenin, *Lenin 2017: Remembering, Repeating and Working Through* (New York: Verso, 2017), xxv.

60. Jacques Lacan, *Talking to Brick Walls: A Series of Presentations in the Chapel at Sainte-Anne Hospital,* trans. A. R. Price (Cambridge: Polity Press, 2017), 74.

61. The phrase "engaged spirituality" comes from Robert H. King, *Thomas Merton and Thich Nhat Hanh: Engaged Spirituality in an Age of Globalization* (New York: Continuum, 2001). For a significant reconsideration of the relationship between Buddhism and critical theory, see Marcus Boon, Eric Cazdyn, and Timothy Morton, *Nothing: Three Inquiries in Buddhism* (Chicago: University of Chicago Press, 2015).

62. Thich Nhat Hanh, *Silence: The Power of Quiet in a World of Noise* (New York: HarperCollins, 2015), 95–96.

63. Nhat Hanh, *Silence,* 98.

64. Nhat Hanh, 99.

65. Nhat Hanh, 100. Also now see the discussion of listening in Kathleen Fitzpatrick, *Generous Thinking: A Radical Approach to Saving the University* (Baltimore: Johns Hopkins University Press, 2019), 72–81.

66. I discuss the film as a comedy of remarriage in *Life between Two Deaths,* 31–32.

67. I discuss in some detail Lacan's theorization of the four discourses and their applicability to the pedagogical scene in "Lacan avec Greimas: Formalization, Theory, and the 'Other Side' of the Study of Culture," *Minnesota Review* 77 (2011): 62–86. While critical of Lacan's earlier structuralist model of analysis (223), Bill Readings posits a pedagogical practice of deep listening not unlike that formulated by Lacan in his later work. See *The University in Ruins* (Cambridge, Mass.: Harvard University Press, 1996), 158–63.

68. Alain Badiou, *Ethics: Toward an Understanding of Radical Evil,* trans. Peter Hallward (New York: Verso, 2001), 85.

69. Junot Díaz, *The Brief Wondrous Life of Oscar Wao* (New York: Riverhead Books, 2007), 335.

3. Beyond Ethical Reading; or, Reading Again the James–Wells Debate

An earlier version of this chapter appeared in *The Henry James Review.* I sincerely thank the editor Susan M. Griffin for her invitation to participate in this outstanding forum.

1. James Wood, "David Mitchell's *The Bone Clocks,*" *New Yorker,* September 8, 2014, https://www.newyorker.com/magazine/2014/09/08/soul-cycle. Hereafter cited in the text.

2. For a valuable recent discussion of storytelling in *The Bone Clocks,* along with its prequel/sequel, *Slade House* (2015), see Mitch R. Murray, "David Mitchell's Storytelling and the Metalife of Utopia," *ASAP/Journal* 5, no. 1 (2020). And for further discussion of the relationship between *The Bone Clocks* and *Cloud Atlas,* see Caroline Edwards, *Utopian and the Contemporary British Novel* (Cambridge: Cambridge University Press, 2019), 131–42.

3. Fredric Jameson, *Marxism and Form: Twentieth-Century Dialectical Theories of Literature* (Princeton, N.J.: Princeton University Press, 1971), 358.

4. See Mark McGurl, *The Program Era: Postwar Fiction and the Rise of Creative Writing* (Cambridge, Mass.: Harvard University Press, 2009). Jameson's discussion of McGurl's book has been reprinted in *The Ancients and the Postmoderns: On the Historicity of Forms* (New York: Verso, 2015), 279–92.

5. Sianne Ngai, *Our Aesthetic Categories: Zany, Cute, Interesting* (Cambridge, Mass.: Harvard University Press, 2012), 136.

6. Joseph Conrad, *Lord Jim* (New York: Penguin, 1986), 43.

7. Ngai, *Our Aesthetic Categories,* 11–12. Also see Susan Hegeman's fascinating discussion of the category of the interesting in terms of twentieth-century popular social sciences, "American Popular Social Science: The Boasian Legacy," *Amerikastudien / American Studies* (2019): 441–56.

8. Jameson, *Marxism and Form,* 356.

9. Fredric Jameson, *The Political Unconscious: Narrative as a Socially Symbolic Act* (Ithaca, N.Y.: Cornell University Press, 1981), 222.

10. Jameson, *Political Unconscious,* 121.

11. Fredric Jameson, *Postmodernism, or the Cultural Logic of Late Capitalism* (Durham, N.C.: Duke University Press, 1991), 183.

12. Fredric Jameson, *Valences of the Dialectic* (New York: Verso, 2009), 408.

13. Jameson, *Political Unconscious,* 117.

14. For a useful survey of the varieties of moralizing "anti-" criticisms directed at literature—as a threat to authority, truth, morality, and society—see William Marx, *The Hatred of Literature,* trans. Nicholas Elliott (Cambridge, Mass.: Harvard University Press, 2018).

15. Gilles Deleuze and Félix Guattari, *Anti-Oedipus: Capitalism and*

Schizophrenia, trans. Robert Hurley, Mark Seem, and Helen R. Lane (Minneapolis: University of Minnesota Press, 1983), 311.

16. William Lloyd Garrison, preface to *Narrative of the Life of Frederick Douglass, an American Slave: Written by Himself,* by Frederick Douglass (New York: Dell, 1997), xxxiii.

17. Ernesto Laclau and Chantal Mouffe, *Hegemony and Socialist Strategy: Towards a Radical Democratic Politics* (New York: Verso, 1985), 128.

18. Friedrich Nietzsche, *Beyond Good and Evil/On the Genealogy of Morals,* trans. Adrian Del Caro (Stanford, Calif.: Stanford University Press, 2014), 229.

19. Raymond Williams, *Problems in Materialism and Culture* (London: Verso, 1980), 42.

20. Fredric Jameson, *Allegory and Ideology* (New York: Verso, 2019), 73.

21. Nietzsche, *Beyond Good and Evil,* 231.

22. Sara Ahmed, *Living a Feminist Life* (Durham, N.C.: Duke University Press, 2017), 5.

23. The significance of James's theatrical failure for the development of the modern novel is superbly treated, in ways that deeply resonate with my claims in this chapter, in David Kurnick, *Empty Houses: Theatrical Failure and the Novel* (Princeton, N.J.: Princeton University Press, 2011).

24. Henry James, *The Future of the Novel: Essays on the Art of Fiction,* ed. Leon Edel (New York: Vintage, 1956), 30–42.

25. James, *Future of the Novel,* xv.

26. Leon Edel and Gordon N. Ray, eds., *Henry James and H. G. Wells: A Record of Their Friendship, Their Debate on the Art of Fiction, and Their Quarrel* (Westport, Conn.: Greenwood, 1979), 267. Hereafter cited in the text as *HJHG.*

27. T. S. Eliot, "*Ulysses,* Order, and Myth," in *Modernism: An Anthology,* ed. Lawrence Rainey (Malden, Mass.: Blackwell, 2005), 167.

28. Fredric Jameson, *The Antinomies of Realism* (New York: Verso, 2013), 26. Hereafter cited in the text as *AR.*

29. For Jolas's essay, see Rainey, *Modernism,* 1011. For a detailed discussion of the origins and development of Pound's slogan, see Michael North, *Novelty: A History of the New* (Chicago: University of Chicago Press, 2013), 162–70.

30. Virginia Woolf, "Mr. Bennett and Mrs. Brown," in *Essentials of the Theory of Fiction,* ed. Michael Hoffman and Patrick Murphy (Durham, N.C.: Duke University Press, 1988), 31.

31. Woolf, "Mr. Bennett and Mrs. Brown," 33.

32. See Virginia Woolf, *To the Lighthouse* (New York: Harcourt, 1989), 191, 201.

33. See Bruce Robbins, *The Beneficiary* (Durham, N.C.: Duke University Press, 2017). Also see Williams's still indispensable essay, "The Bloomsbury Fraction," in *Problems in Materialism and Culture,* 148–69.

34. James, *Future of the Novel,* xv.

35. David Bleich, *Utopia: The Psychology of a Cultural Fantasy* (Ann Arbor, Mich.: UMI, 1984), 100.

36. A similar set of conclusions are drawn in Joseph Wiesenfarth, "The Art of Fiction and the Art of War: Henry James, H. G. Wells, and Ford Madox Ford," *Connotations* 1, no.1 (1991): 55–73.

37. Fredric Jameson, *A Singular Modernity: Essay on the Ontology of the Present* (New York: Verso, 2002), 165–66. I discuss late modernism further in "The Ends of Culture; or, Late Modernism, Redux," in *Literary Materialisms,* ed. Mathias Nilges and Emilio Sauri (New York: Palgrave Macmillan), 241–57.

38. McGurl, *Program Era,* 99. McGurl explicitly touches on the rejection of Wells by midcentury champions of the Jamesian aesthetic, such as Mark Schorer, in his first book, *The Novel Art: Elevations of American Fiction after Henry James* (Princeton, N.J.: Princeton University Press, 2001), 179–80.

39. Jameson, *Singular Modernity,* 176–77.

40. McGurl, *Program Era,* 103.

41. See Ronald Taylor, ed., *Aesthetics and Politics* (London: Verso, 1980).

42. Fredric Jameson, "Third World Literature in the Era of Multinational Capitalism," *Social Text* 15 (1986): 65. This essay has been reprinted with an extended new commentary in *Allegory and Ideology* (New York: Verso, 2019), 159–215.

43. Richard Chase, *The American Novel and Its Tradition* (New York: Doubleday, 1957), 12.

44. Chase, *American Novel and Its Tradition,* 13.

45. Chase, 5.

46. I further discuss the spatial turn in literary and cultural studies, and deploy it in a reading of Conrad's *Lord Jim,* in "Space and Place in Critical Reading," in *Criticism at the 21st Century,* 2nd ed., ed. Julian Wolfreys (Edinburgh: Edinburgh University Press, 2015), 233–58. For important discussions of spatial theory more generally, see Robert Tally Jr., *Spatiality* (New York: Routledge, 2013); and *Topophrenia: Place, Narrative, and the Spatial Imagination* (Bloomington: Indiana University Press, 2019).

47. Jameson, *Political Unconscious,* 112.

48. Jameson, 112.

49. Fredric Jameson, *Archaeologies of the Future: The Desire Called Utopia and Other Science Fictions* (New York: Verso, 2005), 306.

50. Jameson, *Archaeologies of the Future,* 313.

51. Mikhail M. Bakhtin, *The Dialogic Imagination: Four Essays,* trans. Caryl Emerson and Michael Holquist (Austin: University of Texas Press, 1981), 400–15.

52. H. G. Wells, *Tono-Bungay* (Lincoln: University of Nebraska Press, 1978), 54.

53. For a superb discussion of *Tono-Bungay* emphasizing its spatial mapping dimensions, see Regina Martin, "Finance Capitalism and the Creeping London of *Howards End* and *Tono-Bungay*," *Criticism* 55, no. 3 (2013): 447–59. Also see Jed Esty, *Unseasonable Youth: Modernism, Colonialism, and the Fiction of Development* (Oxford: Oxford University Press, 2012), 115–26.

54. Wood, "David Mitchell's *The Bone Clocks*."

55. Jameson, *Archaeologies of the Future,* 313.

56. Jameson, *Ancients and the Postmoderns,* 312–13.

57. Jameson, *Valences of the Dialectic,* 279.

58. Rebecca Comay and Frank Ruda, *The Dash—The Other Side of Absolute Knowing* (Cambridge, Mass.: MIT Press, 2018), 28.

59. Jacques Derrida, *Of Grammatology,* trans. Gayatri Chakravorty Spivak (Baltimore: Johns Hopkins University Press, 2016), 5.

60. See Comay and Ruda, *Dash,* 69–75.

4. John Brown, W. E. B. Du Bois, and Universal History

The first version of this chapter was presented in April 2012 at the University of Illinois's Unit for Criticism and Interpretive Theory conference, "Beyond Utopia? Art, Theory, and the Coming of 'Spring.'" I would like to thank so many of those associated with the unit, and especially Lauren M. E. Goodlad and Michael Rothberg, for making for so many years Urbana-Champaign such an inspiring place to visit.

1. W. E. Burghardt Du Bois, *John Brown* (New York: International Publishers, 1962), 4. I would also like to point out that 2018 was the 150th anniversary of Du Bois's birth.

2. Du Bois, *John Brown,* 5. For a profound meditation on the question of Brown's political violence, see Ted A. Smith, *Weird John Brown: Divine Violence and the Limits of Ethics* (Stanford, Calif.: Stanford University Press, 2015).

3. Du Bois, *John Brown,* 144

4. Du Bois, 399.

5. Du Bois, 399–400.

6. W. E. B. Du Bois, *John Brown,* ed. David Roediger (New York: Modern Library, 2001), 127 (hereafter cited in the text as *JB*).

7. Susan Buck-Morss, *Hegel, Haiti, and Universal History* (Pittsburgh: University of Pittsburgh Press, 2009), 16.

8. Buck-Morss, *Hegel, Haiti, and Universal History,* 42.

9. Buck-Morss, 59–60.

10. Buck-Morss, 55–56. For a major alternative reading of the origins of this passage, see Andrew Cole, *The Birth of Theory* (Chicago: University of Chicago Press, 2014), 65–85. I should make it clear here that I am less interested in the

facticity of Buck-Morss's reading than the way it forces a theorization of universal history.

11. Buck-Morss, *Hegel, Haiti, and Universal History,* 74–75.

12. I discuss this period in great detail in *Life between Two Deaths, 1989–2001: U.S. Culture in the Long Nineties* (Durham, N.C.: Duke University Press, 2009). Also now see Michael Hardt and Antonio Negri, "Empire, Twenty Years On," *New Left Review* 120 (2019): 67–92.

13. Buck-Morss, *Hegel, Haiti, and Universal History,* 110.

14. Buck-Morss, 133.

15. See Avram Alpert, *Global Origins of the Modern Self, from Montaigne to Suzuki* (Albany: SUNY Press, 2019).

16. Buck-Morss, *Hegel, Haiti, and Universal History,* 148.

17. Slavoj Žižek, *The Parallax View* (Cambridge, Mass.: MIT Press, 2006), 406.

18. I thank Christopher Breu for reminding me of Fink's useful distinction between "*Real* 1, or *R* 1" and "*Real* 2, or *R* 2." See Breu, *Insistence of the Material: Literature in the Age of Biopolitics* (Minneapolis: University of Minnesota Press, 2014), 9.

19. Žižek, *Parallax View,* 406.

20. Bruno Bosteels, *Badiou and Politics* (Durham, N.C.: Duke University Press, 2011), 34.

21. Burhanuddin Baki, *Badiou's "Being and Event" and the Mathematics of Set Theory* (London: Bloomsbury, 2014), loc. 461, ebook.

22. Louis Althusser, *On the Reproduction of Capitalism: Ideology and Ideological State Apparatuses,* trans. G. M. Goshgarian (New York: Verso, 2014), 188. For further discussion, see Phillip E. Wegner, "On Althusser's Not Un-usefulness (Notes Toward an Investigation)," *Mediations* 30, no. 2 (2017): http://www.mediationsjournal.org/articles/Not_Un-usefulness.

23. Alain Badiou, *Plato's "Republic": A Dialogue in 16 Chapters,* trans. Susan Spitzer (New York: Columbia University Press, 2012), 290.

24. Fredric Jameson, *Marxism and Form: Twentieth-Century Dialectical Theories of Literature* (Princeton, N.J.: Princeton University Press, 1971), 135. I discuss Zamyatin's work in *Imaginary Communities: Utopia, the Nation, and the Spatial Histories of Modernity* (Berkeley: University of California Press, 2002), chap. 5.

25. Jo Walton, *Lent* (New York: Tor, 2019), 275.

26. See Phillip E. Wegner, "Lacan avec Greimas: Formalization, Theory, and the 'Other Side' of the Study of Culture," *Minnesota Review* 77 (2011): 62–86.

27. Phillip E. Wegner, *Shockwaves of Possibility: Essays on Science Fiction, Globalization, and Utopia* (Oxford: Peter Lang, 2014), 70–73.

28. Phillip E. Wegner, "The Event of 1907; or, James Joyce, Artist," *Modernist Cultures* 13, no. 2 (2018): 141–64.

29. Stephanie J. Shaw, *W. E. B. Du Bois and "The Souls of Black Folk"* (Chapel Hill: University of North Carolina Press, 2013), 12. Cole also discusses the Hegelian literary historicism that emerged in this moment in Great Britain and the United States in *The Birth of Theory,* 136–47.

30. Shaw, *W. E. B. Du Bois,* 111.

31. Shaw, 104.

32. Shaw, 102.

33. George Ciccariello-Maher, *Decolonizing Dialectics* (Durham, N.C.: Duke University Press, 2017), 156.

34. George Ciccariello-Maher, "A Critique of Du Boisian Reason: Kanye West and the Fruitfulness of Double-Consciousness," *Journal of Black Studies* 39, no. 3 (2009): 384, 373.

35. Ciccariello-Maher, *Decolonizing Dialectics,* 156.

36. David Roediger, introduction to *John Brown,* by W. E. B. Du Bois, ed. David Roediger (New York: Modern Library, 2001), xi.

37. Roediger, introduction, xi.

38. Shaw, *W. E. B. Du Bois,* 3.

39. Roediger, introduction, xiii, xix.

40. Bill V. Mullen, *Un-American: W. E. B. Du Bois and the Century of World Revolution* (Philadelphia: Temple University Press, 2015), 22.

41. Mullen, *Un-American,* 24.

42. Robert Saunders Jr., review of *The Dunning School: Historians, Race, and the Meaning of Reconstruction,* edited by John David Smith and J. Vincent Lowery, *Alabama Review* 68, no. 2 (2015): 196.

43. Martin Luther King Jr., "Martin Luther King Jr.'s 'Letter from Birmingham Jail,'" *Atlantic* (February 2018): https://www.theatlantic.com/magazine/archive/2018/02/letter-from-birmingham-jail/552461/; and Ibram X. Kendi, "More Devoted to Order Than to Justice," *Atlantic* (June 28, 2018): https://www.theatlantic.com/politics/archive/2018/06/incivility/563963/.

44. David S. Reynolds, *John Brown, Abolitionist: The Man Who Killed Slavery, Sparked the Civil War, and Seeded Civil Rights* (New York: Alfred A. Knopf, 2005), 496.

45. Cited in Reynolds, *John Brown,* 250.

46. Roediger, introduction, xx–xxi.

47. Georg Lukács, *A Defense of "History and Class Consciousness": Tailism and the Dialectic,* trans. Esther Leslie (New York: Verso, 2000), 55.

48. Russell Banks, *Cloudsplitter: A Novel* (New York: Harper Perennial, 1999), 606–7.

49. Banks, *Cloudsplitter,* 607–8.

50. Terry Bisson, *Fire on the Mountain* (New York: Avon Books, 1988), 97. I discuss Bisson's novel in more detail in "The Last Bomb: Historicizing History in Terry Bisson's *Fire on the Mountain* and Gibson and Sterling's *The*

Difference Engine," Comparatist 23 (1991): 141–51. I discuss the science fiction subgenre of the alternate history in *Shockwaves of Possibility,* chaps. 9–11.

51. Bisson, *Fire on the Mountain,* 123.

52. See Bisson, 128, 155.

53. Bisson, 70–71.

54. Alberto Toscano, *Fanaticism: On the Uses of an Idea* (New York: Verso, 2010), xiii, xxiii. Toscano's insightful study briefly touches on Du Bois's book on pages 11–12.

55. On the distinction between exploitation and domination, see Fredric Jameson, *Representing "Capital": A Reading of Volume One* (New York: Verso, 2011), 149–51; as well as my discussion in *Periodizing Jameson: Dialectics, the University, and the Desire for Narrative* (Chicago: Northwestern University Press, 2014), 209.

56. Bisson, *Fire on the Mountain,* 137.

57. Smith, *Weird John Brown,* 174.

58. Shaw, *W. E. B. Du Bois,* 112.

59. Buck-Morss, *Hegel, Haiti, and Universal History,* 133.

60. Michelle Cliff, *Free Enterprise: A Novel of Mary Ellen Pleasant* (San Francisco: City Lights, 2004), 137, 141.

61. Fredric Jameson, *Postmodernism; or, The Cultural Logic of Late Capitalism* (Durham, N.C.: Duke University Press, 1991), 209.

62. Smith, *Weird John Brown,* 175.

63. Buck-Morss, *Hegel, Haiti, and Universal History,* 148.

64. Georg Lukács, *The Historical Novel,* trans. Hannah and Stanley Mitchell (Lincoln: University of Nebraska Press, 1983), 265.

65. Bhaskar Sunkara, "What's Your Solution to Fighting Sexism and Racism? Mine Is: Unions," *Guardian,* September 1, 2018, https://www.theguardian.com/commentisfree/2018/sep/01/unions-fight-sexism-racism-equality-pay-gap.

66. Buck-Morss, *Hegel, Haiti, and Universal History,* 148.

5. Politics, Art, and Utopia in "Babette's Feast"

An earlier version of this chapter was presented April 2, 2016, at the Ohio State University's Germanic Graduate Student Association conference "Between Utopia and Dystopia: Visions of Germany." I would like to thank the graduate student organizers—Sarah Larson, Bill Baker, Carly Martin, and Obenewaa Oduro-Opuni—faculty, and other presenters for our engaging dialogue throughout the weekend.

1. Alain Badiou, *The Communist Hypothesis,* trans. Bruno Bosteels (New York: Verso, 2010), 205–6. Also see the related discussion in Miguel Abensour, *Democracy against the State: Marx and the Machiavellian Moment,* trans. Max Blechman and Martin Breaugh (Cambridge: Polity, 2011), 84–88.

2. Judith Thurman, *Isak Dinesen: The Life of a Storyteller* (New York: St. Martin's, 1982), 329.

3. Isak Dinesen, "Babette's Feast," in *Babette's Feast and Other Anecdotes of Destiny* (New York: Vintage, 1988), 12, 4; hereafter cited in the text as *BF.*

4. See "Parisians Lament the Café Anglais," *New York Times,* March 9, 1913, http://query.nytimes.com/mem/archive-free/pdf?res=FA0B1FFE345E13738DDDA00894DB405B838DF1D3.

5. "Pommes de terre 'Anna,'" Cuisine Collection, http://ja6.free.fr/fichiers/f2571.htm.

6. Ernst Bloch, *The Utopian Function of Art and Literature,* trans. Jack Zipes and Frank Mecklenberg (Cambridge, Mass.: MIT Press, 1988), 267.

7. Bloch, *Utopian Function of Art and Literature,* 276.

8. Bloch, 277.

9. Bloch, 275.

10. Ernst Bloch, *The Principle of Hope,* trans. Neville Plaice, Stephen Plaice, and Paul Knight (Cambridge, Mass.: MIT Press, 1995), 146.

11. Charles Yu, *How to Live Safely in a Science Fictional Universe* (New York: Vintage, 2010), 125.

12. Ruth Levitas, *The Concept of Utopia* (Syracuse, N.Y.: Syracuse University Press, 1990), 89.

13. Fredric Jameson, *Marxism and Form: Twentieth-Century Dialectical Theories of Literature* (Princeton, N.J.: Princeton University Press, 1971), 131–32.

14. Alain Badiou, *Being and Event,* trans. Oliver Faltham (New York: Continuum, 2005), 329.

15. Alain Badiou, *Ethics: Toward an Understanding of Radical Evil,* trans. Peter Hallward (New York: Verso, 2001), 51.

16. Badiou, *Ethics,* 40.

17. Badiou, 43.

18. Badiou, 43.

19. Badiou, *Being and Event,* 193.

20. Badiou, 202–3.

21. Badiou, *Ethics,* 41–42. For a further deepening of Badiou's notion of the subject, see Slavoj Žižek, *Absolute Recoil: Towards a New Foundation of Dialectical Materialism* (New York: Verso, 2014), 72–81.

22. Fredric Jameson, *The Antinomies of Realism* (New York: Verso, 2013), 146–47, 149.

23. E. T. A. Hoffmann, *The Life and Opinions of the Tomcat Murr,* trans. Anthea Bell (New York: Penguin, 1999), 60, 103.

24. Maurice Beebe, *Ivory Towers and Sacred Founts: The Artist as Hero in Fiction from Goethe to Joyce* (New York: New York University Press, 1964).

25. Thurman, *Isak Dinesen,* 381.

26. Fredric Jameson, *Postmodernism; or, The Cultural Logic of Late Capitalism* (Durham, N.C.: Duke University Press, 1991), 19.

27. Fredric Jameson, "Adaptation as a Philosophical Problem," in *True to the Spirit: Film Adaptation and the Question of Fidelity,* ed. Colin MacCabe, Kathleen Murray, and Rick Warner (Oxford: Oxford University Press, 2011), 217–18.

28. "One should bring this paradox to its conclusion: it is not only that one can remain really faithful to an author by way of betraying him (the actual letter of his thought); at a more radical level, the inverse statement holds even more—one can only truly betray an author by way of repeating him, by remaining faithful to the core of his thought." Slavoj Žižek, *In Defense of Lost Causes* (New York: Verso, 2008), 140.

29. Saul A. Kripke, *Naming and Necessity* (Cambridge, Mass.: Harvard University Press, 1980), 57. Burhanuddin Baki touches on some of the parallels between Kripke's and Badiou's thought in *Badiou's "Being and Event" and the Mathematics of Set Theory* (London: Bloomsbury, 2014).

30. For further discussion of the dialectical of universal, particular, and individual, see C. L. R. James, *Notes on Dialectics: Hegel, Marx, Lenin* (Westport, Conn.: Lawrence Hill, 1980), 120–31.

31. Wikipedia, s.v. "Aurélian Scholl," April 7, 2019, https://fr.wikipedia.org/wiki/Aurélien_Scholl; translation mine.

32. Richard B. Vowles, "Boganis, Father of Osceola; or Wilhelm Dinesen in America 1872–1874," *Scandinavian Studies* 48, no. 4 (1976): 369–83.

33. Wilhelm Dinesen, *Paris Sous la Commune,* trans. Denise Bernard-Folliot (Paris: Michel de Maule, 2003), 396. All translations are mine.

34. Dinesen, *Paris Sous la Commune,* 15.

35. Dinesen, 392.

36. Dinesen, 393.

37. Mary Elizabeth Podles, "Babette's Feast: Feasting with Lutherans," *Antioch Review* 50, no. 3 (1992): 551.

38. Slavoj Žižek, *The Sublime Object of Ideology* (New York: Verso, 1989), 61.

39. Edith Thomas, *The Women Incendiaries,* trans. James Atkinson and Starr Atkinson (Chicago: Haymarket Books, 2007), 166–67.

40. Thomas, *Women Incendiaries,* xiv. Also see Gay L. Gullickson, *Unruly Women of Paris: Images of the Commune* (Ithaca, N.Y.: Cornell University Press, 1996).

41. Badiou, *Communist Hypothesis,* 183.

42. Kristin Ross, *Communal Luxury: The Political Imaginary of the Paris Commune* (New York: Verso, 2015), 50.

43. Ross, *Communal Luxury,* 57.

44. Ross, 6.

45. Ross, 29.

46. Badiou, *Ethics,* 70.

47. Bloch, *Principle of Hope,* 1005.

48. I discuss this character in Joyce's "The Dead" in "The Event of 1907; or, James Joyce, Artist," *Modernist Cultures* 13, no. 2 (2018): 141–64.

49. Sara Stambaugh, *The Witch and the Goddess in the Stories of Isak Dinesen: A Feminist Reading* (Ann Arbor, Mich.: UMI Research Press, 1988), 80.

50. Esther Rashkin, *Unspeakable Secrets and the Psychoanalysis of Culture* (Albany: SUNY Press, 2008), 32.

51. Rashkin's analysis draws upon the Abraham-Torok model of mourning that has been often revived in the years after 9/11. Rashkin, *Unspeakable Secrets,* 30–31. For a discussion of the limits of such a model, see Jacques Derrida, "Forword: *Fors:* The Anglish Words of Nicolas Abraham and Maria Torok," trans. Barbara Johnson, in *The Wolf Man's Magic Word: A Cryptonymy,* by Nicolas Abraham and Maria Torok, trans. Nicholas Rand (Minneapolis: University of Minnesota Press, 1986), xi–xlviii.

52. Rashkin, *Unspeakable Secrets,* 37–38.

53. Jacques Lacan, *Écrits,* trans. Bruce Fink (New York: Norton, 2006), 684–85.

54. See Jacques Lacan, *The Seminar of Jacques Lacan,* book 7, *The Ethics of Psychoanalysis 1959–1960,* trans. Dennis Porter (New York: Norton, 1992).

55. Walter Benjamin, *Selected Writings,* vol. 4, *1939–1940,* trans. Edmund Jephcott et al. (Cambridge, Mass.: Harvard University Press, 2003), 391.

56. Fredric Jameson, *Late Marxism: Adorno, or the Persistence of the Dialectic* (New York: Verso, 1990), 147.

57. Also see Stambaugh's discussion of the imagery of witchcraft in the story *The Witch and the Goddess,* 81.

58. Max Horkheimer and Theodor W. Adorno, *Dialectic of Enlightenment: Philosophical Fragments,* trans. Edmund Jephcott (Stanford, Calif.: Stanford University Press, 2002), 26–27. I discuss this passage in more detail in *Periodizing Jameson: Dialectics, the University, and the Desire for Narrative* (Chicago: Northwestern University Press, 2014), 163–64.

59. Jameson, *Late Marxism,* 130. This passage is also cited by Sianne Ngai in her brilliant meditation on Adorno's aesthetics in *Our Aesthetic Categories: Zany, Cute, Interesting* (Cambridge, Mass.: Harvard University Press, 2012), 103.

60. I discuss Orwell's major place in the context of late modernism in *Imaginary Communities: Utopia, the Nation, and the Spatial Histories of Modernity* (Berkeley: University of California Press, 2002), chap. 6.

61. Susan Hardy Aiken, *Isak Dinesen and the Engendering of Narrative* (Chicago: University of Chicago Press, 1990), 185, 254.

62. Aiken, 254–55.

63. Isak Dinesen, "The Diver," in *Babette's Feast and Other Anecdotes of Destiny* (New York: Vintage, 1988), 68.

64. Badiou, *Ethics,* 52.

6. Repetition, Love, and Concrete Utopia in *50 First Dates*

An earlier version of this chapter appeared in *The Minnesota Review.* Allow me to thank my fellow contributors, Tom Moylan and Eric Smith, and the journal's extraordinary editor, Janell Watson, for their support and encouragement in this project and so much else besides. As I was working on the revisions of this essay in early spring 2018, word came of Ursula K. Le Guin's passing. This chapter is dedicated in memory of her sustaining vision.

1. Slavoj Žižek, *Looking Awry: An Introduction to Jacques Lacan through Popular Culture* (Cambridge, Mass.: MIT Press, 1991), viii.

2. Phillip E. Wegner, "The Pretty Woman Goes Global: Or, Learning to Love 'Americanization' in *Notting Hill,*" *Genre* 38, no. 3 (2006): 309–26; *Life between Two Deaths, 1989–2001: U.S. Culture in the Long Nineties* (Durham, N.C.: Duke University Press, 2009), 31–32; and "If Everything Means Something Else: Technology, Allegory, and Events in *Roadside Picnic* and *Stalker,*" in *Shockwaves of Possibility: Essays on Science Fiction, Globalization, and Utopia* (Oxford: Peter Lang, 2014), 67–87.

3. Northrop Frye, *Anatomy of Criticism: Four Essays* (Princeton, N.J.: Princeton University Press, 1971), 163.

4. Fredric Jameson, *Valences of the Dialectic* (New York: Verso, 2011), 509.

5. Stanley Cavell, *Pursuits of Happiness: The Hollywood Comedy of Remarriage* (Cambridge, Mass.: Harvard University Press, 1981), 1.

6. For a superb discussion of such a turn in film studies, see Nico Baumbach, "All That Heaven Allows: What Is, or Was, Cinephilia (Part One)," *Film Comment,* March 12, 2012, www.filmcomment.com/entry/all-that-heaven-allows-what-is-or-was-cinephilia-part-one.

7. Cavell, *Pursuits of Happiness,* 272.

8. Žižek, *Looking Awry,* viii.

9. Theodor Adorno, *An Introduction to Dialectics,* trans. Nicholas Walker (Cambridge: Polity Press, 2017), 149.

10. Cavell, *Pursuits of Happiness,* 265.

11. Ernst Bloch, *The Principle of Hope,* trans. Neville Plaice, Stephen Plaice, and Paul Knight (Cambridge, Mass.: MIT Press, 1995), 327.

12. Cavell, *Pursuits of Happiness,* 17–18.

13. Cavell, 126–27.

14. Alain Badiou, *In Praise of Love,* trans. Peter Bush (New York: New Press, 2012), 16–17.

15. Badiou, *In Praise of Love,* 27–28.

16. Badiou, 22.

17. George Ciccariello-Maher, *Decolonizing Dialectics* (Durham, N.C.: Duke University Press, 2017), 111.

18. Badiou, *In Praise of Love,* 38–39.

19. Badiou, 35–36.

20. For a landmark interrogation of the philosophical treatment of friendship, see Jacques Derrida, *Politics of Friendship,* trans. George Collins (New York: Verso, 1997). In this study, Derrida traces the emergence of a radically other notion of friendship, one near to Nietzsche's stance of "love of one's enemies" I discussed in chapter 3, and hence with a kinship to Badiou's condition of love.

21. Badiou, *In Praise of Love,* 75.

22. Badiou, 80.

23. Ursula K. Le Guin, *The Dispossessed: An Ambiguous Utopia* (New York: HarperPrism, 1994), 334. On the Odonian philosophy of marriage, see *The Dispossessed,* 244–47. I discuss Le Guin's novel in more detail in *Imaginary Communities: Utopia, the Nation, and the Spatial Histories of Modernity* (Berkeley: University of California Press, 2002), 172–82.

24. Ruth Levitas, *The Concept of Utopia* (Syracuse, N.Y.: Syracuse University Press, 1990), 88.

25. Chinua Achebe, "An Image of Africa," *Massachusetts Review* 18, no. 4 (1977): 788.

26. Walter Benjamin, *Selected Writings,* vol. 4, *1938–1940,* ed. Howard Eiland and Michael W. Jennings, trans. Edmund Jephcott et al. (Cambridge, Mass.: Harvard University Press, 2003), 392.

27. David R. Shumway, *Modern Love: Romance, Intimacy, and the Marriage Crisis* (New York: NYU Press, 2003), 87.

28. Shumway, *Modern Love,* 82.

29. Cavell, *Pursuits of Happiness,* 146.

30. Alain Badiou, *Ethics: Toward an Understanding of Radical Evil,* trans. Peter Hallward (New York: Verso, 2001), 42.

31. Badiou, *Ethics,* 52.

32. Badiou, 51.

33. Benjamin, *Selected Writings,* 395.

34. Le Guin, *The Dispossessed,* 244–45.

35. Badiou, *Ethics,* 79.

36. Frye, *Anatomy of Criticism,* 183.

37. Bloch, *Principle of Hope,* 146.

38. Fredric Jameson, "Reification and Utopia in Mass Culture," in *Signatures of the Visible* (New York: Routledge, 1990), 25.

39. See Lee Edelman, *No Future: Queer Theory and the Death Drive* (Durham,

N.C.: Duke University Press, 2004). I discuss Edelman's concept in more detail in *Life between Two Deaths,* 153–54.

40. Cavell, *Pursuits of Happiness,* 1–2.

41. Alain Badiou, *Conditions,* trans. Steven Corcoran (London: Continuum, 2008), 193.

42. Badiou, *Conditions,* 196–97.

43. Cavell, *Pursuits of Happiness,* 59.

44. Judith Butler, *Antigone's Claim: Kinship between Life and Death* (New York: Columbia University Press, 2000), 74; and Armistead Maupin, *Logical Family: A Memoir* (New York: Harper, 2017), 2. Also see my discussion of the resignification of family in *Life between Two Deaths,* chap. 8.

45. Cavell, *Pursuits of Happiness,* 231.

46. Quoted in Fredric Jameson, *Archaeologies of the Future* (New York: Verso, 2005), 18.

7. Conditions of Utopia in *2312* and *The Best of All Possible Worlds*

The first version of this chapter was presented March 2, 2016, at the Wake Forest University conference "Utopia: Dreaming the Social" and again in May 2016 at the Onassis Cultural Centre's symposium "Utopia 500" held in Delphi and Athens, Greece. Let me thank the organizers of these events, Sarah Hogan and Herman Rapaport, and Pasqua Vorgia, Christos Carras, and Yannis Stavrakakis for their warmth, hospitality, and generosity on what turned out to be truly inspiring occasions.

1. Edward Bellamy, *Looking Backward, 2000–1887* (New York: New American Library, 1960), 121–22. I discuss Bellamy's novel in more detail in *Imaginary Communities: Utopia, the Nation, and the Spatial Histories of Modernity* (Berkeley: University of California Press, 2002), chap. 3.

2. Bellamy, *Looking Backward,* 122.

3. Elliott, *Shape of Utopia,* 91.

4. Joanna Russ, "Untitled Review (1971)," in *The Shape of Utopia: Studies in a Literary Genre,* by Robert C. Elliott (Oxford: Peter Lang, 2013), 117.

5. Russ, "Untitled Review," 117–18. I discuss Russ's review and its relationship to her then ongoing project in my introduction to the new edition of Elliott's *Shape of Utopia,* xiii–xxx.

6. Nalo Hopkinson, "Beautiful Shape-Shifter: Karen Lord's 'The Best of All Possible Worlds,'" *Los Angeles Review of Books,* April 22, 2013, https://lareviewofbooks.org/article/beautiful-shape-shifter-karen-lords-the-best-of-all-possible-worlds/#!.

7. For some of the significant scholarship on the Mars trilogy, see the essays collected together in William J. Burling, ed., *Kim Stanley Robinson Maps*

the Unimaginable: Critical Essays (Jefferson, N.C.: MacFarland, 2009); Fredric Jameson, *Archaeologies of the Future: The Desire Called Utopia and Other Science Fictions* (New York: Verso, 2005); and Reinhold Martin, *The Urban Apparatus: Mediapolitics and the City* (Minneapolis: University of Minnesota Press, 2016). Robinson has further let me know that while *2312* is not set in the same universe as the Mars trilogy, there is enough kinship between the two to enable a reading of the former as an engagement with and response to this critical dialogue surrounding the trilogy.

8. Kim Stanley Robinson, *2312* (New York: Orbit, 2012), 244–45, ebook; hereafter cited in the text as *2312*. For an outstanding treatment of *2312* in the context of Robinson's larger and happily ongoing project, see Tom Moylan, "'N-H-N': Kim Stanley Robinson's Dialectics of Ecology," in *Becoming Utopian: The Culture and Politics of Radical Transformation* (New York: Bloomsbury, 2020).

9. I discuss the original Terminator trilogy (1984, 1991, 2003) in *Life between Two Deaths, 1989–2001: U.S. Culture in the Long Nineties* (Durham, N.C.: Duke University Press, 2009), chap. 2; the fourth entry, *Terminator Salvation* (2009), in *Shockwaves of Possibility: Essays on Science Fiction, Globalization, and Utopia* (Oxford: Peter Lang, 2014), 166–69; and the failed reboot, *Terminator Genisys* (2015), in "The Economics of *Terminator Genisys*," *Science Fiction Film and Television* 10, no. 1 (2017): 115–24.

10. Karen Lord, *The Best of All Possible Worlds* (New York: Del Rey, 2013), 16; hereafter cited in the text as *BA*.

11. A linguist is also the central character and narrator in the most profound and moving "first contact" narrative to appear in recent decades, Ted Chiang's "Story of Your Life" (1998), the basis for the successful, if quite different, film *Arrival* (2016). Indeed, the relationship between "Story of Your Life" and *Arrival* parallels that between the two works I will discuss in my final chapter, David Mitchell's *Cloud Atlas* (2004) and its 2012 film adaptation.

12. Slavoj Žižek, *Absolute Recoil: Towards a New Foundation of Dialectical Materialism* (New York: Verso, 2014), 274–75.

13. Jameson, *Archaeologies of the Future*, 221.

14. Also now see the superb discussion of the utopianism of *The Faerie Queene* in Sarah Hogan, *Other Englands: Utopia, Capital, and Empire in an Age of Transition* (Stanford, Calif.: Stanford University Press, 2018).

15. Alain Badiou, *In Praise of Love*, trans. Peter Bush (New York: New Press, 2012), 22.

16. I discuss Butler's notions further in *Life between Two Deaths*, 203–6. For another discussion of the reimagining of forms of community in contemporary literature, see Jennifer A. Wagner-Lawlor, *Postmodern Utopias and Feminist Fictions* (Cambridge: Cambridge University Press, 2013).

17. Darko Suvin, *Positions and Presuppositions in Science Fiction* (Kent, Ohio: Kent State University Press, 1988), 38.

18. Ernst Bloch, *The Principle of Hope,* trans. Neville Plaice, Stephen Plaice, and Paul Knight (Cambridge, Mass.: MIT Press, 1995), 202–3.

19. Bellamy, *Looking Backward,* 80.

20. Bellamy, 49. I offer a different reading of these two scenes in *Imaginary Communities.*

21. Stanley Cavell, *Pursuits of Happiness: The Hollywood Comedy of Remarriage* (Cambridge, Mass.: Harvard University Press, 1981), 49.

22. Bellamy, *Looking Backward,* 219.

23. James Joyce, *Ulysses,* ed. Hans Walter Gabler (New York: Vintage, 1986), 4, 23, 41, 90. I outline the possibility of such a reading in my essay "The Event of 1907; or, James Joyce, Artist," *Modernist Cultures* 13, no. 2 (2018): 141–64.

24. Joyce, *Ulysses,* 601. For a discussion of Joyce's use with Cantor, see Ray Mines and Reed Way Dasenbrock, "'Nought Nowhere Was Never Reached': Mathematics in *Ulysses,*" *James Joyce Quarterly* 35, no. 1 (1997): 25–26. For a useful interrogation of the limits of Joyce's actual grasp of advanced mathematics, see Michael Livingston, "'Dividends and Divisors Ever Diminishing': Joyce's Use of Mathematics in 'Ithaca,'" *James Joyce Quarterly* 41, no. 3 (2004): 441–45.

25. See Raymond Williams, *The Country and the City* (Oxford: Oxford University Press, 1973), 12; and *Marxism and Literature* (Oxford: Oxford University Press, 1977), 128–35.

26. Robinson, *2312,* 125; see Williams, *Marxism and Literature,* 121–27.

27. See Robinson, *2312,* 84, 172.

28. Kim Stanley Robinson, *Red Mars* (New York: Bantam, 1993), 217–20; and *The Years of Rice and Salt* (New York: Bantam, 2002), 635–37. I discuss the latter novel in *Shockwaves of Possibility,* chap. 10.

29. Fredric Jameson, *Valences of the Dialectic* (New York: Verso, 2011), 279.

30. Kim Stanley Robinson, *Red Moon* (New York: Orbit, 2018), 253–56.

31. Alain Badiou, *Ethics: Toward an Understanding of Radical Evil,* trans. Peter Hallward (New York: Verso, 2001), 51–52.

32. I discuss the rise of the dystopia in *Life between Two Deaths, 1989–2001,* chap. 5; and "The British Dystopian Novel from Wells to Ishiguro," in *A Companion to British Literature,* vol. 4, *Victorian and Twentieth-Century Literature, 1837–2000,* ed. Bob DeMaria, Heesok Chang, and Samantha Zache, 454–70 (Malden, Mass.: Wiley-Blackwell, 2014).

33. See Lyman Tower Sargent, "The Three Faces of Utopianism Revisited," *Utopian Studies* 5, no. 1 (1994): 1–37.

34. Wegner, *Imaginary Communities,* 194–97.

35. See Tom Moylan, *Scraps of the Untainted Sky: Science Fiction, Utopia, Dystopia* (Boulder, Colo.: Westview Press, 2001). I discuss the first novel of

the trilogy, *The Wild Shore* (1984), in "Science Fiction and Postmodernism (1980s–1990s)," in *The Cambridge History of Science Fiction,* ed. Gerry Canavan and Eric Carl Link (Cambridge: Cambridge University Press, 2018), 502–18.

36. See the new and expanded edition of Tom Moylan's landmark 1986 study, *Demand the Impossible: Science Fiction and the Utopian Imagination* (Oxford: Peter Lang, 2014), and Peter Fitting's groundbreaking essay "The Modern Anglo-American SF Novel: Utopian Longing and Capitalist Cooptation," *Science Fiction Studies* 6, no. 1 (1979): 59–76.

37. I treat the alternate history in some detail in *Shockwaves of Possibility,* chaps. 9–11.

38. Bloch, *Principle of Hope,* 1376.

Conclusion

A shorter version of this chapter first appeared in *Science Fiction Film and Television* 9, no. 1 (2016): 114–18. Allow me to thank the journal editors, Mark Bould, Sherryl Vint, and Gerry Canavan, for their tireless efforts to make possible exciting and innovative scholarship.

1. See Jared Sexton, "Afro-Pessimism: The Unclear Word," *Rhizomes: Cultural Studies in Emerging Knowledge* 29 (2016): http://www.rhizomes.net/issue29/sexton.html; Asad Haider, *Mistaken Identity: Race and Class in the Age of Trump* (New York: Verso, 2018); the essays collected together in the special section "The Antisocial Thesis in Queer Theory," *PMLA* 121, no. 3 (2006): 819–28; Ezra Klein, "7 Reasons America Will Fail on Climate Change," *Vox,* June 5, 2014, https://www.vox.com/2014/6/5/5779040/7-reasons-America-fail-global-warming; and David Wallace-Wells, "The Uninhabitable Earth," *New York Magazine,* July 9, 2017, http://nymag.com/daily/intelligencer/2017/07/climate-change-earth-too-hot-for-humans.html.

2. "It Is Now Two Minutes to Midnight: 2018 Doomsday Clock Statement," *Bulletin of the Atomic Scientists,* https://thebulletin.org/2018-doomsday-clock-statement.

3. Alain Badiou, *Greece and the Reinvention of Politics,* trans. David Broder (New York: Verso, 2018), 3.

4. Fredric Jameson, *The Seeds of Time* (New York: Columbia University Press, 1994), xii.

5. Fredric Jameson, *The Antinomies of Realism* (New York: Verso, 2013), 309. Jameson returns to Mitchell's novel in his most recent book, *Allegory and Ideology* (New York: Verso, 2019), 336–42.

6. Fredric Jameson, *Postmodernism; or, The Cultural Logic of Late Capitalism* (Durham, N.C.: Duke University Press, 1991), xx. For the continued importance of the notion of postmodernity, also see Fredric Jameson, "The

Aesthetics of Singularity," *New Left Review* 92 (2015): 101–32. For discussions of the significance of 2008, see Gérard Duménil and Dominque Lévy, *The Crisis of Neoliberalism* (Cambridge, Mass.: Harvard University Press, 2011); Yanis Varoufakis, *The Global Minotaur: America, Europe and the Future of the Global Economy* (London: Zed Books, 2015); and William Davies, "The New Neoliberalism," *New Left Review* 101 (2016): 121–34. Finally, for another approach to these questions, see Phillip E. Wegner, "The Economics of *Terminator Genisys*," *Science Fiction Film and Television* 10, no. 1 (2017): 115–24.

7. Jameson, *Antinomies of Realism*, 308–9.

8. David Mitchell, *Cloud Atlas: A Novel* (New York: Random House, 2004), 264; hereafter cited in the text.

9. I discuss Robinson's novel in *Shockwaves of Possibility: Essays on Science Fiction, Globalization, and Utopia* (Oxford: Peter Lang, 2014), chap. 10.

10. Jameson, *Antinomies of Realism*, 310.

11. E. P. Thompson, *William Morris: Romantic to Revolutionary*, rev. ed. (New York: Pantheon, 1977), 791.

12. Jameson, *Antinomies of Realism*, 304.

13. Also see my discussion of *The Geopolitical Aesthetic* in *Periodizing Jameson: Dialectics, the University, and the Desire for Narrative* (Chicago: Northwestern University Press, 2014), 75–77.

14. H. G. Wells, *The Time Machine* (New York: Dover, 1995), 91.

15. Wells, *Time Machine*, 91.

16. Antonio Gramsci, *Letters from Prison*, vol. 1, trans. Raymond Rosenthal (New York: Columbia University Press, 1994), 299.

17. For a brilliant examination of the varieties of radical and utopian romanticisms, see Michael Löwy and Robert Sayre, *Romanticism against the Tide of Modernity*, trans. Catherine Porter (Durham, N.C.: Duke University Press, 2001).

18. Antonio Gramsci, *Selections from the Prison Notebooks*, ed. and trans. Quintin Hoare and Geoffrey Nowell Smith (New York: International Publishers, 1971), 336.

19. Gramsci, *Selections from the Prison Notebooks*, 337.

20. Slavoj Žižek, *The Sublime Object of Ideology* (New York: Verso, 1989), 29. There is also a relationship here to what Žižek critiques as "principled pessimism" and whose "negation of the negation" is "self-negated pessimism." See Slavoj Žižek, *Absolute Recoil: Towards a New Foundation of Dialectical Materialism* (New York: Verso, 2014), 338–39.

21. Slavoj Žižek, *Living in the End Times* (New York: Verso, 2010), 390.

Index

Page numbers in italics refer to illustrations.

Phillip E. Wegner is Marston-Milbauer Eminent Scholar and professor of English at the University of Florida. He is the author of *Imaginary Communities: Utopia, the Nation, and the Spatial Histories of Modernity*; *Life between Two Deaths, 1989–2001: U.S. Culture in the Long Nineties*; *Periodizing Jameson: Dialectics, the University, and the Desire for Narrative*; and *Shockwaves of Possibility: Essays on Science Fiction, Globalization, and Utopia,* as well as the editor of a new edition of Robert C. Elliott's *The Shape of Utopia: Studies in a Literary Genre.*